CITIZEN HOLLYWOOD

ALSO BY TIMOTHY STANLEY

The Crusader

Kennedy vs. Carter

CITIZEN HOLLYWOOD

How the Collaboration Between
LA and DC Revolutionized
American Politics

TIMOTHY STANLEY

Thomas Dunne Books
St. Martin's Press ♒ New York

THOMAS DUNNE BOOKS.
An imprint of St. Martin's Press.

CITIZEN HOLLYWOOD. Copyright © 2014 by Timothy Stanley.
All rights reserved. Printed in the United States of America. For information,
address St. Martin's Press, 175 Fifth Avenue, New York, N.Y. 10010.

www.thomasdunnebooks.com
www.stmartins.com

Designed by Anna Gorovoy

The Library of Congress Cataloging-in-Publication Data is available upon request.

ISBN 978-1-250-03249-2 (hardcover)
ISBN 978-1-250-03250-8 (e-book)

St. Martin's Press books may be purchased for educational, business, or
promotional use. For information on bulk purchases, please contact Macmillan
Corporate and Premium Sales Department at 1-800-221-7945, extension 5442,
or write specialmarkets@macmillan.com.

First Edition: May 2014

10 9 8 7 6 5 4 3 2 1

To Luke
I'm dedicating this book to you in the hope that
you might actually read it.

CONTENTS

CONTENTS

CONTENTS

NOTES

INDEX

DIRTY HARRY VS. HAROLD AND KUMAR

This is a book about the relationship between Hollywood and American politics. Reading that sentence, conservatives will probably think of airhead celebrities doing benefits to save the piranha and ban Christmas. Liberals may well think of Charlton Heston defending his inalienable right to shoot quail with a bazooka.

Yes, there's some truth to those stereotypes—and you'll meet a lot of people who resemble them in this book. Close personal friends of Fidel Castro, wannabe cowboys, soap actors who think they've got the answer to global warming, and the ever ubiquitous Barbra Streisand. But it's my mission to convince you that Hollywood's impact on U.S. politics has been considerably deeper, more complex, and even more disturbing than those clichés suggest. The decades-long collaboration between the moviemakers and the politicians has changed both of their institutions for both good and bad, shaping their characters, their etiquettes, and even their core beliefs. The effect upon U.S. democracy has not been good. Hollywood has fed Washington's addiction to campaign money, helped redefine politicians as celebrities, and reduced important, difficult issues to simplistic fights between good and evil—all adding to the partisanship and paralysis of contemporary government. Hollywood almost writes the script for modern politics: Statesmen are actors, elections are plot, and you and I have become spectators in a theater of the absurd. This was never more obvious than during the 2012 presidential election.

The most memorable moment of the 2012 Republican convention was the appearance of the eighty-two-year-old actor Clint Eastwood. His prime-time speech, which came just before Mitt Romney's, was billed as a surprise—although the press had been tipped off twenty-four hours in advance—and when he walked onstage the red state audience went wild. Clint went on to deliver a rambling, overlong speech that some people called a "senior moment." He pointed to an empty chair and said it was Obama, and that the president had joined him to discuss policy. The idea of debating an empty chair probably started as a joke, but Clint seemed to take it more and more seriously as the evening wore on. "Mr. President, how have you handled promises that you made when you were running for election?" he asked the furniture. "How do you handle them, I mean, what do you say to people?" He questioned the empty chair about Afghanistan, Oprah Winfrey, Obama's promise to close the prison at Guantánamo, the war in Iraq, and if there were too many lawyers in politics (by the way, Mitt Romney was trained in law). The five-minute speech dragged on for twelve minutes and only ended when someone shouted, "Say 'make my day!'"—Eastwood's catchphrase from the Dirty Harry movies. With obvious reluctance, Clint said, "Oh, alright then. 'Go ahead,

Mr. President—make my day.'" The audience applauded, and mercifully, it was over.[1]

Clint Eastwood's performance was a debacle for Team Romney. Polls showed that most people thought it was the highlight of the convention, but mostly because it was so funny. In *The New Yorker*, comedian Andy Borowitz wrote:

> When asked the question, "Who cares more about people like me?" thirty-seven percent of voters responded, "Mitt Romney," while fifty-two percent said, "Chair." The poll numbers for the chair represent the largest post-convention bounce for an inanimate object since the nomination of Michael Dukakis, in 1988.[2]

How was this embarrassment allowed to happen? The answer tells us a lot about the power of celebrity: The Mitt Romney campaign was so starstruck by the very idea of Eastwood speaking that they didn't bother to set any parameters for what he should say. It all began, Romney's senior strategist Stuart Stevens told me, weeks before, when Clint gave an enthusiastic endorsement of Mitt at a fund-raiser in Idaho. Coming offstage, Romney said, "Clint just made my day! What a guy!" Convinced that Eastwood's appearance at the Republican convention would be a game changer for the flagging campaign, a giddy Team Romney invited him to speak without any discussion about what he might talk about.[3]

Eastwood later admitted that he appeared onstage without a script or a plan. "I told [the Romney people] 'You can't do that with me, because I don't know what I'm going to say.'" The idea of speaking to an empty chair only came to Eastwood fifteen minutes before he went live. He explained, "There was a stool there, and some fella kept asking me if I wanted to sit down. When I saw the stool sitting there, it gave me the idea. I'll just put the stool out there, and

I'll talk to Mr. Obama and ask him why he didn't keep all of the promises he made to everybody."[4] Stuart Stevens admits that Clint was given a degree of freedom by the Romney campaign—including not using a teleprompter—that would never have been given to a politician. They couldn't bring themselves to tell the Man with No Name what to do.[5]

This wasn't an isolated example of Hollywood stealing the show at the 2012 conventions. Not by a long shot. The Democrats gave a prime-time slot to an Indian American actor called Kal Penn. Penn is best known as the costar of the raunchy Harold and Kumar movies, which are about two foulmouthed college-age stoners who always end up in trouble. In real life he has a serious political pedigree: Penn campaigned for Obama in 2008, and in 2009 he quit acting to work as an associate director in the White House Office of Public Engagement. To take up that job he had to be written out of a medical drama he was featured in, *House*. Kal's character committed suicide in a dramatic example of Hollywood sacrificing itself in the service of its country.[6]

Kal Penn was front and center in the promotional material for the 2012 Democratic convention. He starred in a video in which Obama telephones someone unseen to ask them if they could come outdoors and canvas for him. The camera pulls back to reveal that he's actually talking to Harold and Kumar, who are chilling out on a sofa, eating a big pile of junk food. So when he spoke at the convention, like Clint Eastwood, Kal Penn was exhibiting two identities. On the one hand, he was playing himself—making an impassioned plea for Obama and his policies. On the other hand, he was playing his stoner character, Kumar—laughing along with the fans watching at home. The mix of styles was evident in the jokey, satirical way that he referenced Clint's own speech from the Republican show just a week before. Kal said, "I've worked on a lot of fun movies, but my favorite job was having a boss who gave the order to kill Osama bin Laden and who is cool with getting gay married. So, thank you, invisible man in the chair."[7]

The prominence of Clint Eastwood and Kal Penn at their respective conventions tells us something important about 2012. It wasn't an election about reaching out to the middle; it was an election about motivating ideological bases—identifying the key Republican or Democrat demographics and bringing them to the polls in as large numbers as possible. Kal Penn was used to appeal to young people and ethnic minorities—or rather, his character was. In reality, Penn was thirty-five and has said that he's never touched marijuana in his life. But Team Obama hoped that grassroots Democrats would identify him with his twenty-something stoner alter ego and so make the president look cool by association.[8] Likewise, Clint Eastwood at the Republican convention was both playing himself—an ordinary concerned citizen—and his character, Dirty Harry, a no-nonsense, tough-minded conservative type who shoots first and asks questions later. Again, never mind that in private Clint is quite different—he's liberal enough to support abortion rights and gay marriage, and in his convention speech he even criticized George W. Bush's war in Afghanistan.[9] What mattered was that the character Dirty Harry plays well among the Republican base of middle-class white men. After all, if only white men voted, then no Democrat would've won the White House after 1964.

Different people watched these conventions and responded to Kal Penn and Clint Eastwood in different ways. Liberals might've watched Penn and thought, "Cool, it's Kumar!" Conservatives might've thought, "Who is this hippie?" Vice versa, liberals might've watched Eastwood and thought, "This guy needs to retire." Conservatives might've thought, "We could do with a man like that in the

White House!" What all this tells us is that there is a worrying fusion between entertainment and politics going on. Worrying because it elevates celebrities beyond their skill set, bestowing upon them an authority that they do not deserve. It is true that Clint Eastwood has served as the mayor of Carmel, California— but he was elected partly on the issue of legalizing the sale of ice cream cones. It is hard to understand why he was given the second most important speaking slot over, say, John McCain or Chris Christie.[10]

What is worse is that this fusion between Washington and Hollywood reduces serious issues to a competition between movie archetypes. At a time when America ought to be engaging in serious debates about very tricky matters—the size of government; the proper role of society in regulating the sex life of individuals; how far the United States can afford to sustain involvements overseas; or the desirability/affordability of government-mandated health care insurance coverage—the 2012 conventions preferred instead to set the election up as a conflict between Clint's vigilantes and Kal's stoners. The stars contributed toward turning the election into a highly polarized affair, with much of the voting preferences easily categorized by race, gender, age, and class. The fruits of that divide are a Balkanized and paralyzed government that—in 2013— shut down over the fate of health care reform. There is something very wrong with the republic, and Hollywood sure isn't helping.

How did America get to the point that Clint Eastwood and Kal Penn could become figureheads for conservatism and liberalism? As you'll see in the pages that follow, it's my contention that 2012 was one of the, if not the, most Hollywood-influenced elections in history, and—given how much the contest inflated the movie industry's status—we should expect more in 2016. I'll argue that Hollywood has achieved this status by methods that are both overt and subtle. Its obvious forays into politics include fund-raising, promoting fashionable causes, and networking—all of which reached a dizzy height in the Clinton era and continue to influence politics today. But it has also shaped the way that Americans subconsciously think about politics, through the creation of cinematic or televisual images and archetypes. Television shows like *The West Wing* have helped define the ideal of a liberal president, while silver-screen tough men such as Chuck Norris have become synonymous with red-meat conservatism. Crucially, the Hollywoodization of the political process hasn't happened by accident. Politicians have gone out of their way to appropriate cinematic imagery, and moviemakers have gone out of their way to use their art to redefine politics. Aaron Sorkin, the creator of *The West Wing*, wanted his show to tell the Democrats a thing or two about principle and sticking to your guns; Chuck Norris, a cheerleader for the National Rifle Association (NRA), has used his celebrity to encourage folks to stick to their guns in a rather more literal manner. As we shall also discover, John Kennedy based some of his style on Gary Cooper, Richard Nixon courted John Wayne as a friend and political symbol, Ronald Reagan's love of the "American way" was ingrained in him by the studio system, and even Barack Obama—a man who otherwise has a complicated, prickly relationship with Hollywood—has allowed himself to be cast as Batman, Abraham Lincoln, and Atticus Finch.

I'll show that this fluid exchange of ideas has its limits; Hollywood has had less success changing American attitudes toward faith and abortion than either conservatives believe or liberals hope. But it's impossible to deny that moviemakers have had a huge impact on the American political imagination, both good and bad. With an emphasis upon the bad. Hollywood has not only dumbed-down politics but simultaneously encouraged the impression that the presidency is far more powerful than it either is or constitutionally should be. Also, as I shall document, Washington has had almost as big an impact upon Hollywood as Hollywood has had upon Washington. There has been a mutual exchange of ideas and working methods that has altered the culture of both spheres of influence.

What I detail in this book is an evolving relationship between two centers of power—a relationship rooted in large part in personality. Moviemakers and politicians are very similar types of people: Vain, ambitious, egotistical performers who love crowds, they're drawn to one another's charisma. Their alliances have often tipped over into interdependence; they are hooked on each other's power and money. The dynamic can be creative, but it can also be self-destructive.

The back-and-forth was on show at the 2004 Democratic National Convention, when actor Ben Affleck was first introduced to then representative Anthony Weiner. Affleck had spent the day signing autographs, creating buzz for a bid for Congress. He told Weiner that he was thinking of a run. "Where?" asked Weiner. "For the seat of Mike Capuano in Massachusetts," Affleck replied. To everyone's horror, Weiner shouted, "Don't fucking do that! Who told you to do that? You'll get killed!" Affleck was shocked. But later he reflected, "Nine out of ten other guys would politely lie, or go away without telling the poor feckless celebrity that you're going to get killed." But Weiner had the guts to say no. Affleck was impressed.

Months later, Affleck approached Weiner to ask for help in preparing for a role as a politician in the movie *State of Play*. They met in Weiner's office, and an argument ensued. Affleck was backing Obama in the presidential race, Weiner was for Clinton. The movie never came up. "We just spent too much time talking at each other," Weiner said. "I developed, I must confess, a grudging respect for [Affleck]. He has good political instincts. He said Barack was going to win, and he turned out to be right." The two men became friends and drinking partners. Affleck was charmed by a man prepared to treat him like a political equal (Weiner: "There aren't too many Hollywood actors I would say this about, but Ben would be a good politician."), and Weiner got access to a movie star happy to raise big cash for his bid for the New York mayoralty. Affleck told his friends in Hollywood that Weiner was worth donating to because he was "hard and clean."[11]

He was half right. In May 2011, it was revealed that Anthony Weiner had been sending indecent pictures of himself to women via his Twitter account. At first he claimed that he could not recognize the engorged junk beneath a pair of boxers that he had tweeted to a twenty-one-year-old student, but eventually he did come clean. Andrew Breitbart, the muckraker who broke the scandal shortly before his tragic death, offered me this analysis of what went wrong: "Weiner got sucked into the Hollywood way of thinking, which is that there are no morals and you can get away with anything. . . . [Celebrities] can fool around, and [they'll] just get a feature in *National Enquirer.* Weiner does it, and he loses his career. But it's his fault. Hollywood corrupts politicians and makes them think they're stars."[12]

Weiner quit Congress and went quiet for a year, before resurfacing in 2013 with a fresh bid for mayor of New York. Everything was going swimmingly until it was revealed that even after his resignation he had continued sexting young women under the nom de plume of Carlos Danger. Plenty of the shamelessness of the movie business has found its way into politics.[13]

The dynamic between Affleck and Weiner is representative of the dynamic between Hollywood and politics in general: infused with idealism, pragmatism, honesty, and deception. Both men were showmen, and both, to different degrees, confused celebrity with power. As they flattered and drove each other on to ever greater heights of fantasy, they contributed to the debasement of politics—to its slow descent into tinsel and scandal. This is what has happened to American democracy on a grander scale, both in history and to-day. Hollywood has encouraged the worst in her already very vain politicians.

I

THE DARK KNIGHT RISES

How Hollywood Helped Reelect Obama

Barack Obama's 2012 reelection campaign was a perfect example of how Hollywood can promote, finance, and even define a modern political candidate.

After the battle of 2012 had been lost and won, the journalist Michael Scherer wrote a piece for *Time* magazine that lifted the lid on the president's fund-raising strategy. Team Obama credited part of their success to Hollywood. Scherer wrote:

In late spring, the backroom number crunchers who powered Barack Obama's campaign to victory noticed that George Clooney had an almost gravitational tug on West Coast females ages 40 to 49. The women were far and away the single demographic group most likely to hand over cash, for a chance to dine in Hollywood with Clooney—and Obama. So as they did with all the other data collected, stored and analyzed in the two-year drive for re-election, Obama's top campaign aides decided to put this insight to use. They sought out an East Coast celebrity who had similar appeal among the same demographic, aiming to replicate the millions of dollars produced by the Clooney contest.

The number crunchers settled on Sarah Jessica Parker, the actress who played Carrie Bradshaw in *Sex and the City*.[1]

Team Obama invited ordinary members of the public to donate money for a chance to win a seat at a fund-raising dinner at Parker's brownstone in New York City's West Village. Conservatives, when they heard of the idea, thought it would bomb; surely the contest would be a tough sell to a country going through a recession. Sarah Jessica Parker had played a character who was proud of having spent forty thousand dollars on shoes. And the ad cut for the campaign was fronted by Anna Wintour, the editor in chief of *Vogue* who almost prides herself on being unlikable. Her designer labels and power hairdo were a far cry from Middle American tastes, while her strange, wandering accent accentuated her elitism. "I'm soooo luck-ee in my work," she purred, "that I'm able to meet some of the most incredible women in the world. Women like Sarah Jessica Parker and Michelle Obama." Was Sarah Jessica Parker really one "of the most incredible women in the world"? And was the unemployed mother of four watching the ad from her soon-to-be-repossessed home supposed to be thrilled by Wintour's good luck in knowing her? Anna thought so: "These two wonderful women and I are hoosting [sic] a dinner along with the president in New York City to benefit the Obama campaign. We're saving the best two seats in the house . . . for you!"

After laying out the rules of the competition, Wintour glared out from under her heavy red fringe and said, "Please join us. Just don't be late." It sounded a little like a threat.[2]

"She's not saving the two best seats!" laughed the conservative pundit Glenn Beck on his TV show. "Do you really think Anna Wintour is going to be taking the crappy seats?" Beck pointed out that not only were Parker and Wintour part of the Hollywood aristocracy, but Wintour was also well-known as a boss from hell. A movie had even been made about it, called *The Devil Wears Prada*. "She was the person who actually was in the movie treating all of her coworkers, her underlings, like garbage, waiting on her every whim," said Beck. "She is—she is—what [Barack Obama] says capitalists are like all the time. She is everything she says the Republicans are, and she's an Obama supporter!"[3]

Like many of us writing and talking about the election, Beck wrote off the Wintour ad as a terrible mistake—something that would hurt Obama in November. But he was wrong. Thousands entered the contest, and famous attendees—including Meryl Streep and Aretha Franklin—forked out forty thousand dollars per head to meet the president. The fund-raiser was a success, and Obama's numbers didn't slip from all the publicity.[4] The contest worked as an idea because it wasn't just a lazy stunt (find a Hollywood host, throw together an ad, and try to squeeze money out of people). On the contrary: It was a carefully designed example of Team Obama's "data mining"—statistical analyses of who gives how much to whom and why. The wonks worked out that many female voters like contests, like small dinners, and whatever Glenn Beck might think, they do like Sarah Jessica Parker and Anna Wintour. One person's rich bitch was another person's style icon.

This one story says a lot about how Hollywood helped Obama in 2012. First, it raised him a lot of money. Nothing surprising in that: The moviemakers have always been generous to Democrats. Second, Hollywood helped bolster Obama's image among certain key groups of voters, something that was unusual. In many previous presidential cycles the Democrats had, overall, been hurt by their association with the cosmopolitan, left-wing darlings of Los Angeles. But in 2012, Hollywood's brand of social liberalism caught the zeitgeist rather well—particularly among the young, and especially among women. Harnessing that social liberalism helped Obama keep his desk in the White House in spite of high unemployment. On Election Day he lost the male vote narrowly but won the female vote by a mile—the vote that the Parker and Wintour ad was designed to impress.[5] Hollywood helped Obama to focus the election on the cultural issues that he knew he could win on, attracting to his ticket millions of voters who were alienated by Mitt Romney's social conservatism.

Team Obama understood that, and that's why they made such a big effort to win over the moviemakers. But before they could be put to work for Obama, the Hollywood elite first had to be wooed. And that was harder to do than you might think.

Seducing Hollywood

In 2011, Obama's relations with Hollywood hit an all-time low. Enthusiasm was down and donations were drying up. When he toured the movie industry in 2008, Obama had been invited to the homes of the rich and famous and treated like the second coming of Elvis Presley. But when he visited in September 2011 he was reduced to appearing at the sweaty House of Blues on Sunset Strip. The host was a TV sitcom actor and the entertainment was the Gay Men's Chorus of Los Angeles; tickets went for as little as $250. There was dinner afterward at the Fig & Olive restaurant with Jeffrey Katzenberg, where a chance to chow with the commander in chief went for $35,800. But tickets were still available online hours before the event. One political consultant said that the day's fund-raising drive had been "tough, tough, tough."[6]

The problem was partly philosophical. Obama hadn't lived up to the superhero narrative that Hollywood wrote for him in 2008. While the Tea Party fumed that he was too liberal, the moviemakers insisted that he wasn't liberal enough—that he had wasted a unique opportunity to transform America into something more caring and democratic. In an interview in March 2011, Matt Damon told Piers Morgan that he was particularly upset about the lack of education reform. When asked by Morgan if he approved of the way that Obama was running the country in general, Damon replied, "No . . . I really think he misinterpreted his mandate. A friend of mine said to me the other day, which I thought was a great line, 'I no longer hope for audacity.'"[7] Obama, to his credit, gave as good as he got. At the White House Correspondent's Ball, he told the audience, "I've even let down my key core constituency: movie stars. Just the other day, Matt Damon . . . said he was disappointed in my performance. Well, Matt, I just saw *The Adjustment Bureau*—so right back atcha, buddy."[8]

Nevertheless, "I no longer hope for audacity" was a great line, and it became shorthand for Hollywood's disappointment. A lot of the anger came from older, more politically radical celebrities. Hugh Hefner wanted troops out of Afghanistan ("We are going through the same thing as Vietnam right now"). Robert Redford said Obama had a "failed energy policy." The most common complaint, though, was inaction on gay rights. Barbra Streisand couldn't understand why the president didn't use his executive privilege to get rid of the military's "don't ask, don't tell" policy on homosexuality. Jane Lynch, an openly gay actor and one of the stars of the TV series *Glee*, called him a "huge disappointment" on gay marriage: "We thought the great hope of Obama was going to magically change all that. He's just nicely walking the middle."[9]

Why didn't Hollywood mind so much when Bill Clinton "walked

the middle" in the 1990s? The answer was personality. President Clinton might have been the consummate centrist who reformed welfare and went to war in the Balkans, but he loved the attention of stars and tried his best to be nice to them. Obama was a very different story.

Hollywood was stunned that Obama never called to say thank you the morning after the 2008 election. In select speeches he did acknowledge what the town had done for him, but he failed to send personal thank-you notes or maintain a dialogue with the big players. Maureen Dowd in *The New York Times* put this down to his unusual political background:

> Obama smashed through all the barriers and dysfunction in his life to become a self-made, self-narrating president. His brash 2008 campaign invented a new blueprint to upend the Democratic establishment. So it's understandable if Obama, with his Shaker aesthetic, is not inclined to play by the rococo rules of politics.

Searching for a good simile, Dowd compared the prez to Paul Newman, an actor known for scorning Hollywood's social circuit.

> "I've been accused of being aloof," Newman told me. "I'm not. I'm just wary. . . . With film critics and fans, you have to be selectively insensitive to their insensitivities. . . . If people start treating you like a piece of meat or a long-lost friend or feel they can become cuddly for the price of a $5 movie ticket, then you shut them out."[10]

The comparison struck a chord: producer Harvey Weinstein also called Obama "The Paul Newman of American politics."[11] All those Paul Newman references were classic Hollywood—the industry is so self-obsessed that it can only understand the behavior of presidents by comparing them to film stars. But the allusion also reflects the importance of manners in the movie business. Hollywood is a place where everybody is usually very nice to everyone else—whatever their social status—either in deference to their fame or in the hope that someday they might make it and remember you (that's why waiters' tips are so generous in Los Angeles). So Obama's distance made no sense to people who had built careers on gregarious charm. Never mind that the charm could be two-faced (as Paul Newman feared) or that the president had better things to do than call Robert Redford and beg his advice on solar energy. In Hollywood, everyone is grateful for anything and everything, and they are very loud about it. That's the rule.

Obama broke that rule all the time: just ask Oprah Winfrey.

The talk show queen worked hard for Obama in 2008, and she enjoyed a remarkable degree of access. Journalist Ed Klein wrote, "When she phoned, he dropped everything and took her call. They huddled over strategy. Of all of Obama's unofficial White House advisers, Oprah had unparalleled access, input, influence, and power." Team Obama figured that she was worth it: One study calculated that her endorsement was worth one million votes in the general election.[12]

But when Obama evolved from candidate to president, things changed. His staff wanted to control access to their boss. After all, what was the point of being the president's gatekeeper if some talk show host could just pick up the phone and get straight through to him? Oprah discovered the shift in attitude when she put in a request to interview Obama. Her calls to Michelle went unanswered, and when the administration finally got back to her, she found that she had to do an interview prep with White House staff. An executive within her studios told Klein, "It was a pain as far as Oprah was concerned. Oprah isn't a snob, but she doesn't like having to put up with mid-level clerks. These guys were $75,000-a-year men. Oprah was like, 'Hello, what is this s–t!'"

It sounds a little snobby to those of us on middle-class salaries. Nevertheless, Oprah decided to go ahead with her interview. But when she turned up at the White House, she was confronted with the greatest horror of all: Oprah Winfrey was treated like an ordinary person. Klein:

> When they arrived, Oprah and [her producer] Gayle weren't [welcomed] like VIPs; they were made to wait at the security gate like ordinary visitors. Once inside, they had to cool their heels for a long time before they were shown up to the Yellow Oval Room in the family residence, where Michelle finally made an appearance.

To make matters worse, Michelle boasted about having a big staff ("as if Oprah wouldn't know about that"). And—prepare yourself for a shock:

> Michelle mentioned that the White House cooks made the best pie in the world. But she didn't offer Oprah or Gayle any.[13]

The Obamas actually come across rather well in Klein's account. Obama is too busy running the world to entertain TV stars, and Michelle is delightfully giddy about her sudden elevation: She's a working-class girl made good. But the Oprah fiasco also underscores how un-Hollywood they were in both priorities and manners. If Obama had been unabashedly liberal and pursued the stars' pet causes, they'd have forgiven his distance. If he had been charming and approachable, they'd have forgiven his centrism. But the president let down Hollywood on both counts. So how was he going to win them back?

Hollywood Goes Gay . . . and Obama Follows the Money

Much of Hollywood believed that the biggest betrayal from the White House was on gay rights. Gay rights was a natural "cause celeb": Not only has Hollywood always had a libertarian streak, but the industry draws upon a large amount of gay and lesbian talent. West Hollywood is estimated to be 40 percent gay, making it the sixth gayest district in the United States. So the passage of California's anti–gay marriage Proposition 8 in 2008 had a profound effect upon the movie community. It found itself on the front line of the culture war, with friends and family as the foot soldiers. Understandably, they insisted that the president pick a side.

Dustin Lance Black, the scriptwriter behind the biopic *Milk*, about a gay rights leader, explained to me how the issue of marriage equality created a rare sense of political unity in Hollywood, but also a wide sense of frustration at the slow pace of change coming out of Washington. If a cause was so self-evidently right, why did the president drag his heels?[14] Black wrote in an editorial for *The Hollywood Reporter*:

> The fact that Obama says his position is "evolving" indicates change, but that simply leaves me hoping again. Is this "evolution" akin to a message from a good friend, who, after an argument, has stepped onto an L.A.-to-N.Y. red-eye? He can't fall asleep until he sends that e-mail saying, "Hey, I'm at 30,000 feet (over the swing state of Ohio). Don't worry, I'll make things right when I finally land in (the equality state of) N.Y." Possibly. Hopefully. The problem is, when the president flies, he's on Air Force One, a plane designed to refuel in the air. He can stay up there for as long as it serves him.[15]

The metaphor was strained, the politics unreal. As on so many other issues, Hollywood misunderstood the man they met in 2008: Obama was never a gay marriage advocate. He'd always said that he felt marriage was exclusively between a man and a woman, and expecting him to go beyond that was naïve. The caution reflected political reality: Hitherto, every single referendum held on gay marriage had ended in defeat, and that defeat wasn't just at the hands of the clichéd white, redneck bigots. California's Proposition 8 passed in 2008 thanks to the large turnout of Hispanic and African-American voters that occurred, in turn, thanks to Obama being on the ballot. In an ironic twist, Obama's candidacy was partly responsible for California's ban on gay marriage.[16]

Hollywood's campaign for gay marriage existed within its own bubble. In a town where memories are shorter than Tom Cruise, people easily forgot that the moviemakers had only been agitating for gay rights for a couple of years. The turning point had been the release of *Milk*, a surprise hit that suddenly made it glamorous—even sexy—to support gay rights. *Milk* generated a fashionable passion for them, and the movie community expressed that passion in the only way it knew how: house parties, celebrity endorsements, and by putting on a show.[17]

After Chief Justice Vaughn Walker ruled that California's gay marriage ban was unconstitutional, Dustin Lance Black decided to write a play about it. I say "write"—he actually just invited a lot of very famous people to read out the trial's transcript onstage. The cast was impressive: George Clooney, Morgan Freeman, Brad Pitt, Martin Sheen, and John Lithgow. Financing came from industry insiders Steve Bing, Roland Emmerich, and David Geffen; they put it on in both Los Angeles and New York and broadcast it live. "New Yorkers just got it," said Black. But what New Yorkers? The play was only performed once in New York, and it was followed by an exclusive reception at the Gotham Comedy Club. This was Hollywood putting on a show for Hollywood, and it might just as well have been performed in Black's garden. Probably the only dissenting member of the audience was anti–gay rights campaigner Maggie Gallagher, who came along to see how she would be played by *Glee's* Jane Lynch. She ate potato chips loudly throughout the performance and laughed in all the wrong places.[18]

So if Hollywood really was only talking to itself on the gay marriage issue, why did its views matter to the Democrats at all? One reason was money.

By May 2012, it was becoming obvious that Obama's refusal to say "I do" to gay marriage was hurting his wallet. One in six of the candidate's so-called bundlers—people collecting large donations from others—was gay, and NBC's Chuck Todd claimed on the *Morning Joe* show that gay money had started to eclipse Wall Street money as a major source of cash.[19] The *Hollywood Reporter* noted how commonplace the marriage debate was in Hollywood and how the president's inaction was hurting him. Quote:

> It's safe to say that the longer Obama waits on the issue, the more frustrated the [movie] community will grow with him. Perhaps it won't cost him their votes, but it might slow the flow of cash and public rally appearances.[20]

That report was filed on Tuesday, May 8, 2012. The timing is important.

On Sunday, May 6, Vice President Joe Biden had appeared on *Meet the Press*. North Carolina was about to hold a vote on outlawing gay marriage. When asked what he thought about the referendum, Biden dropped a bomb. He refused to rule out the president endorsing gay marriage in his second term—and added that he personally had no problem with gay weddings at all: "I am absolutely comfortable with the fact that men marrying men, women marrying women, and heterosexual men and women marrying one another are entitled to the same exact rights, all the civil rights, all the civil liberties." Asked why he had changed his mind on the issue, Biden recalled meeting the kids of gay people and seeing "the look of love" in their eyes. But he also name-dropped the sitcom *Will & Grace*—which "probably did more to educate the American public than almost anything anybody's ever done so far." Never has the cultural power of TV and movies been so explicit.[21]

Why Biden did what he did is a matter of dispute. One source told me that he had gone rogue; the White House had no idea what he was going to do and was thrown into chaos when he did it. "All the press suddenly wanted to talk about was gay marriage. Whenever someone went on TV, that's what the journalists would talk about."[22] Certainly, that's exactly what happened. David Axelrod was pushed by Piers Morgan on CNN about whether or not the president and the vice president disagreed, while deputy campaign manager Stephanie Cutter was fairly grilled alive on NBC.[23] Two days after Biden's interview, North Carolina voted 2 to 1 not only to outlaw gay marriage but also civil unions. That morning several aides stopped Obama in the Oval Office and informed him that he had to make a statement on gay marriage or else his campaign would be totally overwhelmed. The debate among the staff lasted a matter of minutes. An interview with ABC was hastily arranged and, on Wednesday, May 9, the president of the United States said on TV that he thought gay marriage should be legal. History had been made, and *Will & Grace* had at least something to do with it.[24]

What was at the forefront of Obama's mind? According to much of the press, and his own campaign, Biden had simply forced him to do sooner something he always intended to do later.

But others suspected a different motive. If Obama had not endorsed gay marriage, the cost to his campaign might have been greater than if he had. Recall that just one day before the president went on ABC, *The Hollywood Reporter* was warning that progay marriage donors were getting itchy feet. If the president had simply repeated his view on air that marriage is exclusively heterosexual unless the states say otherwise, then he would have lost out on a lot of Hollywood money. But by endorsing gay marriage after Biden's interview, Obama cashed in big. And we're talking big. Within ninety minutes of Obama's broadcast statement he had taken $1 million in donations. The legendary TV producer Norman Lear, who had previously held out on giving any money to Obama, let it be known that he and his wife were now donating eighty thousand dollars. "This is the kind of leadership we support," he said, "and we are happy to max out today to his reelection campaign."[25]

The day after he endorsed gay marriage, Obama flew to George Clooney's house in California for a fund-raiser. Stars paid forty thousand dollars each to shake his hand and call him brave. The *Hollywood Reporter* told readers:

> On June 6, the president will be at the SLS hotel in Beverly Hills for an LGBT fund-raiser featuring a performance by Pink. (A sellout now is virtually guaranteed.) Obama will be at another LBGT fund-raiser Monday in New York, featuring a performance by Ricky Martin.

By backing gay marriage, Obama had made history. But he had also made a lot of money.[26]

Aside from being about fund-raising, it was hard not to detect a dash of ego in Obama's gay marriage U-turn. The president offered no practical support for gay rights advocates: He insisted that the matter be decided at the state level and continued to refuse to sign a nondiscrimination executive order. Conservatives also took offense at the language he used when talking about the gay "soldiers or airmen or marines or sailors who are out there fighting on my behalf."

Technically, they fight under the president's orders but not on his behalf—a turn of phrase that irritated some veterans.[27]

But the egotism of discussing the "evolution" of his private beliefs in this way probably raised Obama's approval rating even higher among the moviemakers. It refocused attention upon Obama's unique personality and leadership—and Hollywood could easily identify with his charismatic introspection. What liberal movie star couldn't love a president who had not only come over to their way of thinking but who also was willing to fly over to Hollywood and have dinner with them to discuss it? The sense of personal and political alienation from the White House evaporated overnight. It was just like it was four years earlier. Obama was the moviemakers' man again—a reforming liberal who would help Hollywood make America a better country. It was time for 2008: the Sequel.

Hollywood Throws Around Some Money

Almost every Hollywood skeptic came home. Director Rob Reiner confessed to a sin of doubt:

> "I felt that [Obama] tried to accommodate the other side too much," he told reporters. "[But] I realize now that it was an attempt to try to broker some kind of compromise. I think he realized like everybody realized, that it's virtually impossible. Given all of that, I think he has done an incredible job."

Bill Maher cut a check to the president's super PAC for $1 million. "I think all progressives are disappointed in Obama to a degree," he said. "He is not slashing the defense budget, he is not raising taxes on the wealthy, really. He gave in on the Bush tax cuts." But Mitt Romney—the only alternative to the president—was too awful to contemplate. "It's not even close. You just run back into his arms." It helped that Obama now swallowed his pride and picked up the phone. He called Ari Emanuel, the talent agent brother of Rahm Emanuel, formerly Obama's first chief of staff, to ask what he needed to do to win Hollywood back. Haim Saban, an industry billionaire who made a fortune out of the Mighty Morphin Power Rangers, and who had privately criticized Obama on Israel, was received at the White House and, consequently, gave his blessing.[28]

Michelle also acted as Barack's envoy to the stars. What's striking about Michelle is her ordinariness. In October she appeared on *Jimmy Kimmel Live*. The host asked her what she could do if she was an anonymous civilian for a day, and her answer was touching:

> I would walk out of the door of the White House like a regular person . . . go to CVS, go in there, go shop. I'd buy my toiletries. I'd pay money, I'd get a receipt. And then I'd go sit on a park bench and just watch people.[29]

So what did the First Lady really think about all the mad money she encountered in Hollywood? What, for example, did she think of Will Smith's collection of ornamental doors?

Michelle was a guest at the twenty-five-hundred-square-foot residence of Will and Jada Smith the same day she recorded her interview with Jimmy Kimmel. It was a house built from scratch; every piece of furniture was custom-made. *Architectural Digest* described it this way:

> Ancient cultures are referenced throughout—thanks to the Smiths' collection of antique carved panels, doors, and architectural details from the Middle East, Africa, the American Southwest, and Asia, including the house's monumental front door, which once provided entry to a fort in northern

India. "I have a thing for doors," Jada confesses. "I always think of them as a threshold to something new."[30]

And, of course, a convenient way to get from one room to another.

Through Mrs. Smith's doors passed 250 people paying $2,500 a ticket to meet the First Lady. If you wanted a photo with her, the door price leaped to $10,000. Lunch was included. According to *People* magazine,

[G]uests dined on a roasted grapes and arugula with goat cheese toast salad; a choice of Alaskan halibut with fennel puree, devil's chicken with braised leeks, onions and mustard bread crumbs or Farro Tabbouleh with fall market vegetables.[31]

In her speech, Michelle invoked a very different time and place:

Growing up on the South Side of Chicago, I watched my own father make that same uncomplaining journey every day to his job at the city water plant. And I saw how he carried himself with that same dignity. We all know that dignity, that same pride that a man gets when he can provide for his family.

It was a sentiment that Will Smith could understand—he, too, had come from nothing to become the kind of guy who could import his front door from India. Michelle said that her own family

believed that when you've worked hard and done well like so many of us have, and you finally walk through that doorway of opportunity, you do not slam it shut behind you. No, you reach back and you give other folks the same chances that helped you succeed. And that is how Barack and I know how so many of you were raised.

Michelle actually gave a good working definition of Hollywood liberalism—having lived the American Dream to the full, the moviemakers see it as their duty to expand similar opportunities to others. That's how they reconcile their crazy wealth with their claim to egalitarianism.

One way to help those less fortunate, apparently, was to redistribute their income to the Obama campaign. The party at the Smith house netted an extraordinary $2.1 million.[32] In total, October brought in $13 million from Hollywood. By election night the entertainment community had given more to the official Obama campaign than to Romney by an estimated advantage of 16 to 1.[33]

That $13 million figure doesn't cover the incredible outpouring of funds made possible by the super PACs. Many Democrats—especially in Hollywood—had bemoaned the 2010 *Citizens United* Supreme Court decision that made it possible for activists to donate money to a body that wasn't technically part of an individual's campaign.[34] But the Democrats ended up doing pretty well on it. The Court's decision allowed entertainment industry tycoons like Morgan Freeman to give over $1 million each to Obama's Priorities USA Action, while others became "bundlers" for other people—donors who took money from friends and family and combined it all into one giant gift. The entertainment industry provided forty-one bundlers. And being a bundler came with a quid pro quo: a degree of access to the White House that had been hitherto unavailable. Producer Jeffrey Katzenberg donated $3.07 million through gifts and bundles, making him the third-largest individual Democrat donor of 2012. He was spotted at a White House soiree just before the election mingling with then Chinese vice president Xi Jinping. A little while later the Chinese signed off on an overseas deal that benefited Katzenberg's studio. I'm not implying a link; just noting the coincidence.[35]

Citizens United had a big effect on the culture of Hollywood giving. In the past, stars like Eva Longoria—a star of *Desperate Housewives*—might have just made one-off donations that were worth a speedy phone call of thanks from the Oval Office. But thanks to bundling she was able to bring in nearly three hundred thousand dollars and, again coincidentally, get a prime-time speaking spot at the convention.[36] This was a new kind of giving—a marketing of connections and celebrity on a scale previously unimaginable. In 2012, Hollywood bought itself a whole new level of influence in national politics.

Hollywood Rebrands Obama

The New York fund-raiser with Sarah Jessica Parker and Anna Wintour worked out well for Obama partly because it raked in lots of cash, but also because it helped him to connect with the key demographic of young women. In 2012, Hollywood helped plug the president into a cultural zeitgeist that proved rich in votes.

In the past, Hollywood's social liberalism tended to be a net vote loser for the Democrats. In the 2000s, in particular, George W. Bush's old-fashioned values had led to a revival of the Moral Majority spirit—convincing many Democrat strategists that associations with progay, prochoice, prodope Hollywood were a liability. By 2012, however, the electoral mathematics had changed, and Democrats now gambled that there were enough people turned off by aggressive religious conservatives on the Right to make social liberalism a vote winner.

A new phase in the culture war began in January 2012, when the White House decided that religious employers would be forced to include birth control and other reproductive services in their workers' health care coverage. Rather than running away from the culture war, Obama had decided to fight and win. In the course of the year he defended abortion rights and endorsed gay marriage. And his campaign exploited the enormous gender gap that opened up between male and female voters. In poll after poll Obama ran even or behind Romney among men but far ahead among women. The socially liberal commentator Andrew Sullivan applauded Obama's focus on condoms and gay weddings:

> The more Machiavellian observer might even suspect this is actually an improved bait and switch by Obama to more firmly identify the religious right with opposition to contraception, its weakest issue by far, and to shore up support among independent women and his more liberal base. . . . And if this was a trap, the religious right walked right into it.[37]

They sure did. The Republican Party peppered the election year with bouts of offensive chauvinism. Senatorial candidate Todd Akin of Missouri spoke of a distinction between "legitimate rape" and fake rape, while the senatorial candidate in Indiana, Richard Mourdock, appeared to suggest that pregnancy resulting from rape was "intended" by God. While Mitt Romney was running for president in 2012, some members of his party behaved like they were running for Witchfinder General in 1612.[38]

Republicans complained mightily that the administration and the media were playing the culture war so as to distract from high unemployment and burgeoning welfare rolls. Many of them presumed that it wouldn't work—that the "tastelessness" of Obama's campaign would undo him. In particular, they scorned the ruthless pursuit of the young female vote. Republicans laughed when the Obama campaign released *The Life of Julia*, an online cartoon that depicted the ways in which White House policies helped a woman over the course of her time on Earth. At eighteen, she gets a college tax credit. At twenty-seven she gets mandated birth control coverage. By the time she's sixty-seven, she's livin' *la vida loca* on social security and volunteering in a community garden. For Rich Lowry of the *National Review*, this ad was a mistake by Team Obama to rival the Anna Wintour ad:

> Julia's central relationship is to the state. It is her educator, banker, health-care provider, venture capitalist, and retirement fund. And she is, fundamentally, a taker. . . . She has no moral qualms about forcing others to pay for her contraception, and her sense of patriotic duty is limited to getting as much government help as she can.[39]

The Right was in hysterics when the Obama campaign produced an e-card that read: "Vote like your lady parts depend on it." The White House, they said, had resorted to smut.[40]

But to a new generation of women, contraception, abortion, and reliance on government programs (made all the more necessary by a bad economy) were simply the facts of life. Lena Dunham, writer, creator, and director of HBO's *Girls*, cut an ad called "Your First Time" that horrified conservatives but amused a lot of her own age group. It compared the first time voting with the first time of something altogether more enjoyable: "Your first time shouldn't be with just anybody, you wanna do it with a great guy," she whispered.

> It should be with a guy with beautiful manners. . . . Someone who really cares about and understands women. . . . My first time voting was amazing. It was this line in the sand. Before I was a girl, now I was a woman.

Whether or not folks found this funny or smutty depended upon age and politics. "How could a president with two, young blossoming daughters release an ad as disgusting as this?" asked an editor of Breitbart.com.[41]

But the video eventually gained 2.5 million hits on YouTube. Its thinly veiled crudity might've appalled conservatives raised on *Happy Days*, but it was a perfect fit for kids used to obscenity-laden shows like *Family Guy* or *South Park*. Dunham's ad was part of a wider effort to use the entertainment industry to cast the president as young and "with it." Colleges were visited by singer will.i.am, Kal Penn, *Daily Show* correspondent Olivia Munn, and actor Justin Long. Rock acts like John Legend, Trey Songz, Raphael Saadiq, and Passion Pit provided free concerts in battleground states.[42] Of course, such glitzy, youth-orientated efforts had been tried before—both in winning years for the Democrats (1992) and disastrous ones (1972). What was different this time around was that polls showed that a majority of the electorate sided with the socially liberal message being articulated. The bands were singing in tune with the mood of a substantial number of voters.

It also helps that the campaign started pushing Barack Obama as Batman. Seriously. The most exciting movie release of the summer of 2012 was *The Dark Knight Rises*, and the White House marked the occasion by releasing a photo of Obama and Biden high-fiving each other with the title "Dynamic Duo." The *Washington Examiner* reported that the Obama campaign wanted to use the release of *The Dark Knight Rises* to crystallize the differences between their man and Romney. The villain of the movie is called Bane, and Romney's former company happened to be called Bain, which led to some (pretty thin) comparisons between Mitt and the asthmatic behemoth who levels Gotham City. Democratic adviser Christopher Lehane told the *Examiner*:

Whether it is spelled Bain and being put out by the Obama campaign or Bane and being put out by Hollywood, the narratives are similar: a highly intelligent villain with off-shore interests and a past both are seeking to cover up who had a powerful father and is set on pillaging society.[43]

Poor old Romney was indeed the anti–Dark Knight but not in the sense of being evil like Bane. Rather, he seemed indecisive and insubstantial and far removed from people's everyday concerns. Mark Hamill, the star of *Star Wars*, compared Romney to the shape-shifting alien in *The Thing*, released in 2012: "You look at Romney and I'm sure he's a nice guy, but I think he's like The Thing, he only imitates human behavior. He's not actually human himself."[44]

The Republicans understood the role that Hollywood was playing in defining the candidates. Stuart Stevens told me that it had always been a factor, that many of the candidates he had worked with before were somewhat like old movie stars and that this helped define them in the public's mind: "I'd say Ronald Reagan was a bit like John Wayne . . . Bob Dole was kind of like Humphrey Bogart—smart, funny, old-school." But when I pressed Stevens to describe Romney, rather than offering a movie star reference he gave a string of qualities in search of a central narrative: friendly, optimistic, charming, thoughtful, etc. When pushed a little harder, the best that Stevens could come up with was to say that Romney was "maybe kind of like James Stewart." If so, that only emphasized how out of time his politics were. This was a year when people wanted Batman not George Bailey from *It's a Wonderful Life*.[45]

The problem was that the 2012 election wasn't nearly as much about economics as conservatives hoped. If it had been, Obama probably wouldn't have won: Unemployment was historically high, and the president's approval ratings hovered around the mid-40s for much of the year. Instead, Obama's victory came down to changing demographics and culture. While Romney took the white vote, the president benefited from a huge turnout among Hispanics (now the country's largest ethnic minority at 16.7 percent of the population) and African-Americans. Far from being concentrated along the border, Hispanics had built sizable populations in crucial swing states—which is one reason why Virginia, the capital of the old Confederacy, went twice for Obama. And although Ronald Reagan insisted that Hispanics were Republicans "who just don't know it yet," polling showed them to be stereotypical Democrats, almost liberals. Not only had the credit crunch forced middle-class Hispanics to rely on the state more than ever, but they were just as socially tolerant as whites.[46]

And that's the key to understanding 2012: It was an election that hinged on the dynamics of social change. The young made up an unusually high proportion of the electorate (19.1 percent), and they were far mellower than older voters on social issues. For example, Hollywood's gay marriage campaign might have been self-absorbed and naïve, but its message did reflect how growing numbers of ordinary Americans felt about their gay friends and coworkers. The same day Obama was reelected, three states voted to legalize gay marriage, and two states voted to legalize smoking marijuana. A Pew Research Center's Religion & Public Life Project survey discovered that the fastest growing "religious" group in America was made up of people with no religion at all. Thirty-three million Americans said they were without a specific faith and thirteen million within that number described themselves as atheist or agnostic.[47] The old orthodoxies of presidential contests—that you had to be outwardly religious and culturally traditionalist to win—were coming undone. American voters were drawn more to Obama's liberal Dark Knight narrative than to Republican Jimmy Stewart nostalgia.

Hollywood Wins

On election night, Twitter exploded with celebrity approval for Obama.

Justin Bieber: "alot of emotions right now. congrats President Obama . . . Im Canadian. Im good. #FreeHealthcare :)"

Lady Gaga: "I JUST GOT OFF STAGE IN COLUMBIA!! CONGRATULATIONS MR. PRESIDENT @BarackObama! We are so proud to be American tonight! YES!!! YES! YES!!"

Even One Direction's Niall Horan (the Irish one, for anyone who's not a fan): "Wey hey! Come on @barackobama ! Champion! What a man! 4 more years!"[48]

There were plenty of famous faces at Obama's rally, too: Zachary Quinto, Justin Long, Ashley Judd. Melanie Griffith got so excited that she dropped an F-bomb live on TV.[49]

The stars had good reason to celebrate. For a start, their guy had won. And with that victory came an affirmation that, No, Hollywood isn't an alien planet circling a far Left sun; it does share the values of about half of the American public, so it really can claim to speak for significant numbers of ordinary people. All that conservative snobbery toward the moviemakers and their craft was misplaced. It did matter that Matt Damon was angry. Some people did share Hollywood's views on gay marriage. Sarah Jessica Parker did speak for the silent majority of girls who just wanna have fun. Lena Dunham's first time was a giggle. And Eva Longoria could win an election.

That last point about Eva winning the election is critical to understanding how Hollywood viewed 2012. Much of the industry felt that they had been indispensable to Obama, that he couldn't have done it without them. In three key ways they were right:

1. Hollywood helped Obama raise the money he needed to win.

2. The stars used their celebrity to promote the Obama ticket and help define it.
3. The moviemakers helped to set the tone of the election both by stirring up the culture war and by encouraging voters to regard Obama as a superhero.

Importantly, it wasn't just the election that was changed by Hollywood's involvement; the election changed Hollywood, too. Stars got to play the roles of politicians. Some were ambassadors for their candidate (Eva Longoria), while others enjoyed genuine influence in the campaign and the White House (Kal Penn). Hollywood was also alleged to have enjoyed some kickbacks. Republicans accused the White House of giving producers of *Zero Dark Thirty* (2012)—a movie about the killing of Osama bin Laden—access to classified CIA documents in exchange for an understanding that the film would portray the president in a positive light.[50]

What was historically remarkable about 2012 was the degree to which the movie industry helped a candidate win. As the culture war intensifies, as campaign spending rises ever higher, and as Hollywood becomes more aware of its potential power, we can expect this process to continue, and even to accelerate. Nevertheless, although the current situation feels almost revolutionary, it is one with deep roots in American history. In the next few chapters we'll explore the decades of Hollywood's involvement in political debate that helped to set the context for both Obama's election and reelection. It's the story of a slow-burning romance between movies and politics that has grown hotter over time. A romance that began with the spark of reciprocity.

2

THE COLOR OF MONEY

How Hollywood's Cash Buys Influence

Hollywood is a business: It's about making money. That doesn't mean it isn't capable of great art or that its artists don't have high ideals. But, ultimately, the studios rise and fall on the basis of returns. The ability to generate money in vast quantities is what makes Hollywood such an attractive place to visit for politicians. Not for nothing is it known as Washington's ATM.

At the core of the relationship between Hollywood and Washington is the principle of reciprocity: as the kids sing at the end of *Bugsy Malone*, "You give a little love and it all comes back to you." Moviemakers give money to politicians, and they expect it to come back to them in the form of influence. To give an example of the principle of reciprocity at its crudest (and least idealistic), let's begin with the story of perhaps the most lavish and corrupt political fund-raiser ever thrown in Hollywood history. On paper its purpose was to celebrate Bill Clinton's eight "glorious" years as president. In reality, it was all about money.

Hillary's Big Bucks

August 12, 2000.

The stars' limousines stretched all the way along Mandeville Canyon Road: police checkpoints at every corner; snipers in the trees. Hollywood's powerful and beautiful had gathered together at a 112-acre estate to attend a concert in honor of the outgoing leader of the free world, Bill Clinton. The organizers, Peter F. Paul and Aaron Tonken, put up a huge stage, with classical columns, a jumbo TV screen, and room for a seventeen-piece orchestra. The audience of one thousand sat in directors' chairs and got a free tribute book and a collection of the performers' CDs. On the stage: Cher, Patti LaBelle, Sugar Ray, Toni Braxton, Melissa Etheridge, Michael Bolton, Paul Anka, and Diana Ross. In the audience: Gregory Peck, Whoopi Goldberg, Shirley MacLaine, Anjelica Huston, Brad Pitt.[1] There were some disappointing no-shows. According to Aaron Tonken, Rosa Parks wouldn't appear unless a) she was paid and b) they sent a Gulfstream IV private jet to collect her. "Michael Douglas was supposed to show, and didn't, along with Goldie Hawn and Jack Lemmon. I had paid for them and listed them on the invitation, but the publicist who was supposed to arrange things let me down."[2] Such is life in Hollywood, where everything goes through a third party, and you can never be sure if your guest even saw the invite.

But the "shows" were impressive enough. According to Jeannie Williams in *USA Today*:

John Travolta sat with the president at dinner after the outdoor concert and [thanked] Clinton "for the best eight years of our lives." . . . Hillary, in a pink suit and giant pink pearl necklace, got her share of plaudits. . . . Michael Bolton [launched] into "When a Man Loves a Woman," which he said was a request. The president mouthed "thank you." Jimmy Smits . . . thanked the president for "walking the walk" with the Latino community. Whoopi Goldberg reminded Hillary, "I'm one of your constituents, girl!" (and told her husband, "You kicked a–."). Mary Steenburgen told Hillary, "You killed on Leno last night!" . . . Guests David Hasselhoff and wife Pamela have met Hillary and he calls her "very cool."[3]

Of course Hillary was cool—she was running for the Senate. Mrs. Clinton wanted to be the next senator from New York, and the Hollywood Gala Salute to President William Jefferson Clinton was really all about raising money for her campaign. Party planners Paul and Tonken charged $1,000 a seat and are estimated to have collected over $1 million for Hillary's candidacy.[4] So this was about saying "hello" to old friends and passing the magic mantle from Bill to Hillary. The Lewinsky scandal now behind them, the couple held hands during the tribute, and the president even put his arm over his wife's shoulder—the sort of rare act of familiarity between the Clintons that is worthy of a headline. In his speech, Bill said he was, "really proud of" Hillary and "I hope you will help her win."[5]

On paper, they did. In one night Hillary raked in the same amount of money that it took her Republican opponent a week of touring the country to collect. But it came with a big price tag.

Two days after the event the *Washington Post* columnist Lloyd Grove revealed that party planner Peter Paul was a convicted felon. He had served three years in prison "after pleading guilty to cocaine possession and trying to swindle $8.7 million out of the Cuban government."[6] Cocaine possession is a comparatively run-of-the-mill crime; the federal conspiracy charges that resulted from trying to defraud Fidel Castro deserve further elaboration. The plan, hatched in the 1970s, was to sell agents of the Cuban government nonexistent coffee and then to sink the boat that was supposed to contain it en route to Cuba. Alas, the conspirators failed to bribe the right official at the port of Santo Domingo, and the people who intended to scuttle the ship weren't allowed onboard.[7] Paul pled guilty to conspiracy charges, and the cops found his stash of coke when they raided his home. He served three years before being paroled. He was then caught traveling to Canada using the identity of a dead man and sent back to prison. Out for a second time, Paul reinvented himself as a business manager for celebrities; his biggest client was the long-haired, ripped, romance icon Fabio.

When Peter Paul's criminal past came to light, Hillary Clinton denied ever even knowing him and said that she would return a $2,000 check he gave her back in June 2000. That's when things turned nasty. Paul claimed that Senator Clinton's staff hadn't disclosed that he had spent nearly $2 million on the Hollywood event, including in-kind contributions like gifts and services. Paul asserted that thousands of dollars had been spent to encourage the stars to attend the gala with freebies—flights, jewelry, CDs, etc. All those celebrities were there, he implied, because he bribed them to be.[8]

Hillary's then fund-raising director David F. Rosen had only reported $401,419 in expenditures—which, if the figure was true, would have freed Clinton up to spend more "hard money" on the New York campaign. The federal government decided to pursue a fraud investigation against Rosen. They asked Raymond Reggie—a cosponsor of the gala and brother-in-law of Ted Kennedy, who afterward wound up serving time for bank fraud in an unrelated case—to have dinner with Rosen wearing a wire. His mission: to find out if Rosen knew the extent of the sums spent on the infamous palooza. Rosen failed to implicate himself, but he did have some interesting things to say about Peter Paul's coorganizer, Aaron Tonken. He said:

> I mean, I knew he was doing shady [expletive], like saying to Cher, "Cher, the president just called me and he needs you to perform 'If You Could Turn Back Time' in between Diana Ross and before the . . ." Then he'd call Diana Ross: "The president just called me, and we need you to go before Cher's 'If You Could Turn Back Time.'" And he'd mention, like, specific songs that the president was requesting. That's how he got a lot of them. . . . It turned out to be some shady [expletive]. But who knew?

Attention now turned to Aaron Tonken and, yes, he was indeed a "shady" character.

Tonken was an obese man with attention deficit hyperactivity disorder, obsessive-compulsive disorder, and facial tics that made his head jerk unpredictably, but it was his business practices that drew the most negative attention. He started his career in Hollywood working as Zsa Zsa Gabor's dog walker and met Peter Paul in 1993 while living in a homeless shelter. The two clicked. Paul provided names and phone numbers of famous people, and Tonken used his surprising powers of persuasion to convince them to appear at parties for rich businesspeople. He cut his teeth by getting Charlton Heston to read Bible verses at the wedding of a couple of complete strangers; Heston didn't even know their names. Tonken's genius technique was to leverage one star's ego against another to convince them that they had to turn up not to be outshone, just as Rosen described. Attendance, claims Tonken, was secured by handing out gifts like jewelry financed by "borrowing" cash from money given to him by charities: He owed $1 million at Cartier alone. Tonken would meet potential clients at the opulent, pink Beverly Hills Hotel and offer to bankroll a room for them there. Then he'd go back to the homeless shelter. Tonken distracted himself from his growing web of lies and illegality with cocaine and rent boys. In 2004, he went to jail for fraud.[9]

Paul and Tonken both insisted that the Clintons knew how many goodies had been handed out to buy the attendance of stars—and, in 2005, Rosen found himself in court on charges of underreporting the gala's expenses.[10] Conservatives thrilled at the accusation, because it promised to reveal both the dishonesty of the Clintons and the sad possibility that they had to buy friends.[11]

The court reached a different conclusion. Far from being a media circus, Rosen's trial involved a dull recitation of tax law and accountants' figures. Neither Paul nor Tonken were called to testify, perhaps because—as established con men—their word was worth zip. Witnesses for both the prosecution and the defense concluded that the Clintons didn't really benefit from the Hollywood gala: It netted a paltry $57,000 when expenses were deducted. Jurors took five hours to find Rosen "not guilty." Poor Rosen was left with $1.4 million in legal bills. When Hillary Clinton called to offer him her congratulations on the verdict, he told the press that it was the first time in over two years that she had spoken to him. Peter Paul vowed to continue a separate campaign against the Clintons in private cases. Tonken, meanwhile, seemed rather to enjoy his time in prison. In an interview from Taft Correctional Institution, he told *The Washington Post* that he was not only losing weight but finally conquering that facial tic.[12]

The Hollywood Gala Salute to President William Jefferson Clinton was a disaster. After expenses it had raised little net money and it dragged several names through the mud. So why did it even happen? To return to that balmy August night in 2000, the stars were there to meet the president and, according to Tonken, maybe get some free stuff. The Clintons were there partly out of affection for old friends but also to raise cash for Hillary's senate run. So the profitability of the event for all the guests is obvious. But what did the hosts expect to get out of it?

Peter Paul's answer to this question is very interesting. Paul insisted that he hoped to hire Bill Clinton as a promoter for the company that he cofounded, Stan Lee Media, after the president left the White House. He told a conservative writer the following:

> I'm not ideologically linked to the Clintons and my interest had nothing to do with Hillary's political career. It was clearly a business interest, but a legal business interest. I was merely doing what corporations do. Hire ex-presidents as rainmakers for their global companies. George Bush Sr. did it, Reagan did it, that's what ex-presidents do. And that's what I was doing with Clinton, because he was a popular figure internationally.[13]

Of course, we can't take Paul's word for it. The Clintons deny that there was ever any understanding that Bill would work with Stan Lee Media after leaving office, and Paul is a convicted fraudster.

But what Paul is describing here is the principle that governs a lot of the interaction between politicians and businessmen: reciprocity. Consider the relationship between Bill Clinton and Vin Gupta, CEO of the data and marketing services company, InfoUSA. Gupta was a big donor to Clinton while he was in office, and in return, Clinton invited him to spend the night in the White House. After Clinton stepped down from the presidency, Gupta hired Bill as a consultant for $3.3 million. The figure sounds generous, but Gupta calculated that Clinton's efforts and star power attracted $40 million for his business in return. It has been alleged that Hillary Clinton sold valuable activist lists to Gupta, and only to Gupta.[14]

Examples of reciprocity run from the sublime to the ridiculous. In April 2011, bedding manufacturer Serta announced that it would sponsor Bill Clinton's keynote address to an industry conference. The head of the company said, "To us Clinton represents leadership. This appearance shows Serta is a leader and is taking a leadership position. This singles us out." Some might say that it is beneath a former president to basically endorse Serta's new Perfect Sleeper line, even if it does have a "revolutionary gel foam mattress." But Bill got a fee and Serta got to associate itself with a former president. A president who knows a thing or two about beds.[15]

The idea of giving money in exchange for association with political power is something Hollywood is very familiar with. People in the movie industry often use grand displays of access to politicians as an opportunity to boost their reputations, and even their stock worth. In the office of almost every producer and agent is a so-called wall of fame, a collection of photos of them hand in hand with international statesmen. Big names intrude on every conversation, too. At parties people refer endlessly to "my good friend Bill Clinton" or "my good friend Al Gore." So often is each name dropped that you begin to wonder just how many good friends one politician can possibly have. At one Democratic fund-raiser that I attended in West Hollywood I counted six close personal friends of Al Gore alone (quite an accomplishment for a man with the personality of drying paint). Of course, when a moviemaker drops a politician's name into the conversation, what they are really doing is establishing is their own status: "I'm so important that I've met Al Gore. So if you want to make a movie with anyone, make it with me. . . ."

The bottom line is that at the heart of much of the interaction between Hollywood and politics is money: The moviemakers give their cash and the politicians give them influence and status—which can, in turn, generate more income for the moviemakers. As we shall see, it has ever been thus.

Louis and Herbert Go into Business Together

Six days before the 1932 election, movie mogul Louis B. Mayer threw a gala at the Shrine Auditorium for his pal President Herbert Hoover. America was not in a good place: The Great Depression had set in, unemployment was high, and the mood was revolutionary. But Mayer's party suggested that the country was enjoying a gold rush. Stars of the screen led a torchlight procession into the shrine, wherein Herbert Hoover's disembodied voice boomed out over the airwaves from Washington, D.C. On to the stage walked Lionel Barrymore, Mae Murray, Colleen Moore, Buster Keaton, and Jimmy Durante. They danced, joked, and sang—all accompanied by a twenty-five-piece orchestra. Mayer addressed the overflow crowd and urged them to give four more years to the president: Hoover might have landed them in the Great Depression but he was the guy to get them out.

Mayer's devotion to Hoover was emotional and absurdly grandiloquent. By most voters' judgments, the prez was a busted flush whose name would be forever associated with soup kitchens and the endless lines of the unemployed. But on election eve Mayer told radio audiences that he was close to greatness. "History discloses that, shortly before Abraham Lincoln was reelected, it looked as if he would go down to defeat," he said. Mayer earnestly believed that enough Hollywood razzmatazz could turn Hoover into Lincoln II and pull off a coup on Election Day. He was wrong. Despite the inflow of Hollywood cash—despite the endorsements of child star Jackie Cooper and Tarzan actor Johnny Weissmuller—the country threw out Hoover by a landslide. They preferred Franklin D. Roosevelt, who the Warner brothers had been busy campaigning for.[16]

Why did Mayer go all out for a losing candidate in 1932? The answer is a potent mix of ideology, personal foible, and the desire to make money. Mayer was a man who understood poverty and the power of America to transform a poor boy's life. He was born Lazar Meir in 1884, to a Jewish family in the Russian Empire. Looking for a safer, richer life, the family moved to England in 1886, and then settled in Canada in 1888. As the eldest son, Louis didn't have much of a childhood: His time was divided between protecting his brothers against anti-Semitic bullies and helping his father's scrap business. Mayer Senior came to rely upon Louis's obvious talent for making money; Louis quit education at twelve to work full-time in his family's business and slowly took charge of it. Missing out on a formal schooling didn't seem to bother him much. Years later Mayer said, "If I had my life to lead over, I'd go to work at ten."[17]

Mayer moved to Boston in 1904 and opened a new junk firm. In 1907, he broke into the infant craft of cinema. In the early years of the twentieth century, movies were a working-class entertainment looked upon with great suspicion by America's social and clerical elites. Mayer helped change that. He took over a run-down burlesque theater and turned it into a respectable family one that showed Christian movies with titles such as *From the Manger to the Cross*. His big break came when he secured the exclusive rights to show D. W. Griffith's racist hit *The Birth of a Nation* and made himself $250,000 (around $6 million today). Mayer hated having to share his profits with the production companies, so he decided to move to Los Angeles to make his own movies. Once there, he followed the same formula he had used in Boston: take trashy entertainment and elevate it to a wider audience with artistry, great actors, and family-friendly themes. In 1924 he joined forces with two recently amalgamated studios to form Metro-Goldwyn-Mayer. When the new one opened, Mayer received a congratulatory telegram from President Calvin Coolidge.

We might have expected a man with Mayer's humble background to lean toward the Democrats—traditionally the party of the urban poor and immigrant. But Mayer went Republican instead, out of a mix of ideology and self-interest. Identification with the GOP suited a man trying to get ahead in the 1920s, the dizzy epoch of popular capitalism. After the misery of World War I and the recession that followed, the presidencies of Warren Harding and Calvin Coolidge brought stability and success. Under Harding, federal spending fell from $6.3 billion in 1920 to just $3.2 billion in 1922. Federal taxes were cut from $6.6 billion in 1920 to $4 billion in 1922—with the top rate eventually falling to just 25 percent. Unemployment almost vanished, share ownership rocketed, and the stock market soared. A consumer revolution expanded ownership of cars and radios. "The chief business of the American people is business," said Coolidge—a man who generally preferred to say nothing at all. His frugality with words reflected the frugality of his administration.

Mayer shared this business-friendly outlook, and he understood that it could make him a lot of money. In the 1920s, Hollywood went corporate: It had nearly $1 billion in capital investments by 1921. MGM functioned as smoothly as a factory under Mayer's leadership, rolling out movies in much the same way that Henry Ford rolled out Model-Ts in his giant, nonunion plants. To quote film critic David Thomson, Mayer was

> the first man—maybe the only one—who ever ran a humming factory system that had all its stages and its contract artists at work at the same time, with one picture coming out a week, and the whole thing profitable. In the twenties, he knew the numbers—the size of the audience, the budgets of

the pictures, the overhead, the promotion—and MGM was secure.

So was Mayer: The immigrant boy was the highest paid man in America.[18]

Not that Mayer was right about everything. He disliked Clark Gable at first, because his ears stuck out, passed on *Gone with the Wind*, because Civil War movies rarely did good business, and advised that Mickey Mouse would flop because "every woman is frightened of a mouse."[19] Color photography he called "a fad."[20]

Nevertheless, he was part of the great integration of the movie machine into the Roaring Twenties economy: selling stocks in the studios through Wall Street and raising money via commercial banks. Mayer worked hard to keep the free market free by volunteering his services to Coolidge's reelection campaign in 1924. The payoff was that he always presumed access to the White House would translate into policies that would help MGM expand into overseas markets or avoid pesky antitrust suits. Just like Peter Paul had fantasized that raising money for the Clintons in 2000 would get Bill Clinton's name on his stationery.

Mayer's efforts were part of a wider pattern: The studios realized that as their industry expanded they had to develop a closer partnership with politicians, to ride the political tiger carefully enough to avoid being swallowed by it. Antitrust legislation was one area of concern, another was censorship. The movie industry embraced self-censorship in order to avoid federal regulation. In 1922, in the face of growing public anger at "obscenity" in the cinema, the studios formed their first serious industry lobby—the Motion Pictures Producers and Distributors Association (which became the Motion Picture Association of America in 1945)—and hired Republican Will H. Hays to head it. In 1927, he compiled his famous Production Code, which became voluntarily enforced by the studios in 1934. Rules included: Criminals should always be punished for their crimes; no display of revenge in contemporary-era movies lest it glorify violence; nudity banned; interracial relationships an absolute no-no; and profanity from "damn" upward totally outlawed (with the result that even gangsters would shout "Gosh darn it!" when they got shot). A famous example of a victim of the code was the 1943 feature *The Outlaw*, which was initially denied a certificate of approval because the advertising gave too much attention to Jane Russell's breasts. The moral conservatism of the studios was designed to appease Washington, an acceptance of the power of politicians and of the importance of keeping them happy.[21]

There was another reason for taking part in politics: the desire to belong. Mayer could make all the money he wanted in Hollywood, but the local high society still regarded him as a second-class citizen because of his ethnicity. Jews were barred from many social clubs and, most painfully, from the best schools. Louis "begged" the gossip columnist Hedda Hopper to get his daughters into a school where she counted the principal as a friend. "Mr. Mayer, they won't accept them," Hedda replied. "But they'll take my daughters," he insisted. "Can't you tell the headmistress how important I am?" "It won't do any good," Hopper insisted. "They will not take Jews."[22]

So imagine Mayer's delight when a man as big as Herbert Hoover was prepared to take him into his confidence. Hoover, too, was a self-made man—from a boyhood on an Iowa farm to secretary of commerce in Coolidge's cabinet. When he met Mayer in 1924 the two go-getters hit it off instantly. Hoover needed glamour and money for a potential presidential bid. Mayer needed access to important people in Washington, D.C.[23] They addressed each other as "Mr. Hoover" and "Mr. Mayer," in traditional Victorian style. After their first meeting Mr. Mayer wrote Mr. Hoover to say, "I cannot help but express to you the keen enjoyment I had in the little chat we had together while you were the guest at my studio. I wish the citizens of our glorious country could know you intimately as you deserve to be known." The letter hinted at a promise to assist Hoover reach the White House, and it also carried a request for the secretary of commerce to help with some production problems Mayer was having overseas. "Glad to see you anytime on 24 hours notice," replied Hoover. He was soon helping MGM to establish wavelength monopolies for its newest radio station. Their correspondence reads like love letters between egotists; they sent each other autographed photos of themselves.[24]

Louis and Herbert's friendship reflected a growing symmetry between how politics and movies worked. Politics in the 1920s was run by the party machines on their own reciprocity principle: The local party, Democrat or Republican, would serve its constituents by providing jobs or handouts in exchange for votes. As a result, people were bound to a party less by ideology than by self-interest or ethnic identity, i.e., "The local Democratic Party is open to the Irish, it gives us jobs, therefore we shall vote for it." Once elected, officials had the power to fire the government appointees of all their opponents and replace them with their friends. This patronage system upped the stakes of politics considerably: In 1893, the mayor of Chicago was assassinated by a "disappointed office seeker." President Garfield was shot dead in 1881 by a man who thought he was owed a diplomatic post. National politics became dominated by the machinations of party power brokers—party bosses who used patronage to guarantee delegate votes at a presidential nominating convention and who could then negotiate with all the other party bosses over who was the most ideal or least divisive candidate. Presidents were less "nominated" than they were "spotted, groomed, and selected" by political moguls. The comparison with how actors were turned into stars is inescapable.[25]

Hollywood's version of the party machine was the studio system. The studios held vertical control over their industry by controlling production, distribution, and screening of the films. Studio heads decided which directors and actors were hired, concentrating creative responsibility in the hands of a tiny cabal of men. Moguls like Mayer would find talent, book it, tie it up with a contract, and then control its every move. Discovering the right actors was critical to the success of a studio. The camera had the ability not only to see through a star's eyes but also to show their reaction to events with a close-up, turning the actors from an agent within the story to the focus of the story itself. The stars became to the movies what politicians were to politics: the physical embodiment of an ideal, the product on sale, the object of desire.[26]

"Object of desire" is an apt phrase, for many leading ladies were screen-tested on the "casting couch" before they were allowed in front of a camera—selected for stardom based on whether or not they could perform privately for the moguls. Mayer's MGM was notorious for this. Its corridors were patrolled by ugly predators, such as production manager Eddie Mannix (who beat his mistress so hard that she required multiple abdominal surgeries) and executive Ben Thau, who was so terrifying that it was said that he "pissed ice water."[27] Arthur Freed, producer of family favorites like *The Wizard of Oz*, invited a twelve-year old Shirley Temple to his office, unzipped his pants, and introduced her to his penis. Years later, Temple wrote:

> Having thought of him as the producer rather than the exhibitor, I sat bolt upright. Guarded personal exposure by both brothers and father had left me in relatively pristine innocence. . . . I still had little appreciation for masculine versatility and so dramatic was the leap between schoolgirl speculation and Freed's bedazzling exposure that I reacted

with nervous laughter. Disdain or terror he might have expected, but not the insult of humor. "Get out!" he shouted, unmindful of his disarray, imperiously pointing to the closed door. "Go on, get out!"

In the office next door, Mayer had Temple's mother on the couch and was trying to seduce her. She, too, escaped unharmed.[28] Louis had a taste for older women, especially faded actresses in need of a comeback, or maybe an encouraging spanking, although Judy Garland recalled that he also had a penchant for her teenage breasts, and would gently squeeze them whenever they were alone.[29]

When working out who to put on his casting couch, Louis Mayer employed the same technique that he used to fill his stables with horses. To quote director Clarence Brown:

He didn't know the front end of a horse from its hind end, so he treated it exactly like he treated the picture business. He went out and got the finest breed that money could buy. He went to South America, he went to Ireland, he went everywhere, until he worked up a stable producing horses that were finishing first, second, and third. Mayer told one aspirant male actor, "We have a whole stable of girls here."[30]

And under Mayer's leadership, MGM became the studio that boasted "more stars than in heaven": Greta Garbo, Clark Gable, Katharine Hepburn, Joan Crawford, Judy Garland, Fred Astaire, Gene Kelly. He managed them with threats, love, blackmail, and extraordinary displays of emotion calculated to terrify or romance someone into doing what he wanted. "He could play the part of any star in the studio, and play it better," reckoned screenwriter Adela Rogers St. Johns.

That's how he used to make them do it. Greer Garson didn't want to play Mrs. Miniver, so Mayer called her into his office and played the role himself. He was the best Mrs. Miniver there ever was. He was hypnotic. And Miss Garson played the part.[31]

The mayors had their city machines and the party bosses had their presidential conventions. Louis Mayer had MGM: his republic of dreams. To quote film critic Manohla Dargis:

The MGM lot was 167 acres, or 68 hectares, big, with 30 soundstages, phony jungles and a real zoo that housed the studio's other magnificent beast, the lion that roared before every film. There was a barbershop, a police force and a 24-hour commissary that served chicken soup. There was a house bookie, an opium den and, every Christmas Eve, remembered one employee, "an orgy that would have made Caligula feel at home." The studio did not employ a staff abortionist, however. For that service, its stars and contract players would travel across town to 20th Century–Fox.[32]

All of this Mayer put at the disposal of his pal Herbert Hoover: the party machine and the studio system working in synchronicity. Two systems of extraordinary power exchanging favors.[33]

Louis jumped on the Hoover for president bandwagon in 1928 and pumped money into the effort: a $10,000 donation from Cecil B. DeMille (roughly $250,000 today) and $7,000 apiece from Mayer and United Artists president Joseph Schenck ($90,000 today). He sent studio photographers to take portraits of the Hoovers. In a critical move, Mayer persuaded William Randolph Hearst—a media tycoon whose holdings included newspapers and radio outlets, and who provided a model plutocrat for Charles Foster (Citizen) Kane—to back Hoover at the Republican nominating convention in June 1928, and it was the Hearst machine that helped to hand him the nomination. Mayer was there as a delegate (he was now treasurer of the California Republican Party), and he gave a speech to the convention in which he promised to deliver the movie industry to the GOP in November—as if he were talking about a voting district in New York or Chicago. Then he hit the road to speak on behalf of his guy, with the swagger of a national statesman. Behind Mayer trotted that stable of stars he had so meticulously groomed, ordering them to perform for Hoover at Louis's whim. Louis and Herbert "are practically sleeping in the same bed," complained actress Marie Dressler who was barred from campaigning for the Democrats.[34] Another star who felt that Mayer was neglecting his career staged a protest by donating to Hoover's rival.[35] It was an empty gesture: Hoover took the country by a landslide.

Mayer and his wife were the first guests to stay the night at the White House after the Hoovers moved in. Mayer felt so at home that he even complained over dinner that the gravy was too thick. His achievement was remarkable: He had pulled himself up from the gutter to become the best paid man in America, and was now best buds with the prez. Lying in bed in the White House, he was unable to sleep. "I kept thinking back," he later said, "here was I—an immigrant boy, born in Russia, and I was guest of the President of the United States. I didn't sleep a wink."[36]

Mayer's loyalty was rewarded. First Hoover asked him if he'd like to be ambassador to Turkey. (Why Turkey? It was thought to be the only country that wouldn't protest being sent a Jewish ambassador.) Mayer said no. He was far more interested in getting help to avoid federal antitrust legislation. Some pinhead liberals in Washington weren't so impressed by the studio system and its vertical control of production, distribution, and movie theaters—they thought that amounted to a monopoly. With Hoover's help, Mayer succeeded in getting the Justice Department to arbitrate between federal prosecutors and the studios, and so put off any attempts to break up his monopoly. With Mayer at the White House so often (twice within a ten-day period in June 1929), the other studios started to worry that they might get tapped for antitrust action instead.[37] They suddenly discovered that an enthusiastic engagement in national politics was no longer an indulgence but a necessity. A mogul's relationship with the president could determine whether or not his studio survived the next four years.[38] This was when Hollywood's political involvement really took off.

Embracing the Democrats

It soon became obvious that Louis Mayer had invested all his time and money in a flop. In October 1929, Wall Street crashed. The good times had been based on a speculative bubble; after a period of manic buying financed by unsustainable loans, America panicked, and people rushed to dump bad stock. Hoover's administration bungled its response; the Great Depression began. The roar of the 1920s became a tortured moan in the 1930s. RKO and Paramount studios were put into the hands of the receivers; Warner Bros. lost $22 million in two years. Thanks to Mayer's investment in real estate, MGM remained relatively untouched.[39]

Mayer stuck by Hoover in 1932, but by now he wasn't the only mogul interested in politics. The brothers Warner were bitter adversaries of MGM and just as keen to leave their mark on the political life of the nation.[40] They shared many similar characteristics with Mayer: Harry (born Hirsz), Albert (Aaron), Sam (Szmul), and Jack (Itzhak) were Jewish Poles who emigrated to the United States in the late nineteenth century. They made their break in the movie business by using a projector to show films in the mining towns of Pennsylvania and Ohio. Like Mayer, they resented sharing profits, and so, like Mayer, adopted the vertical business model: They moved into distribution in 1904 and founded a studio on Sunset Boulevard in 1918. They became Warner Bros., Inc., in 1923. After they hired Broadway actor John Barrymore to play the lead in 1924's *Beau Brummel*, they instituted a star system of their own that would later include Barbara Stanwyck, Edward G. Robinson, James Cagney, Bette Davis, and Humphrey Bogart.[41]

Like Mayer, the Warners ran their studio like a factory. Screenwriters had to punch a clock and worked together six days a week in a single building. The writers posted a lookout to sound the alarm if they saw a Warner coming: that was the signal to start typing loudly—gibberish, if necessary—to convince the boss that they were hard at it; the Warners couldn't comprehend that writers weren't always writing, that they sometimes needed time to think.[42] The brothers were capable of mistakes (Harry said of the invention of sound, "Who the heck wants to hear actors talk?"), but their release of *The Jazz Singer* in 1927 established them as successful pioneers. The arrival of the talkies had sad consequences for actors whose voices didn't match their beatific faces, and Jack (who replaced Sam as head of the studio after his death in 1927) was brutal in his willingness to discard old favorites. Throughout the 1920s, one of Warners' biggest stars was the German shepherd Rin Tin Tin. As well as a convincing actor, the canine was a merchandising empire of pins, badges, photos, and statuettes. He was the "spokesman" for Ken-L Rations dog food (they handed out dog biscuits in theaters where his films played), and he sent fans not autographs but "pawtographs"—an inky pawprint on a picture. Jack called him the "mortgage lifter" for his ability to make money. But in 1927 poor Rin Tin Tin was sacked by the studio that claimed to love him. Why? Because sound was the future and "dogs don't talk."[43]

It takes ruthlessness to succeed in Hollywood, and Jack and his brothers had it in spades. Like Mayer, the Warners were convinced Republicans. Unlike Mayer, they recognized that the GOP was not going to be the party of the 1930s. In 1932, Harry Warner summoned his brother Jack to a clandestine meeting at their offices in New York. There Jack found former Democratic presidential nominee Al Smith, industrialist Joseph Kennedy, the chair of the Democratic National Committee, and several of New York governor Franklin D. Roosevelt's advisers. The Democratic Party had done some research into Hollywood politics and, perhaps aware of the rivalry with Mayer's MGM, had decided to try to woo the Warners over to their side—even if the brothers had previously been GOP partisans. Jack was perplexed at his brother's change in loyalties and asked him what was going on. Harry said that he'd seen the polls and done the math: "The country is in chaos. There is a revolution in the air, and we need a change." Jack dropped Hoover just as easily as he dropped Rin Tin Tin.[44]

There were other considerations, too. If Roosevelt was going to win, then the Warners might benefit from having a friendly face in the White House when it came to the constant, lingering threat of antitrust actions designed to take their empire apart. Harry was still fuming at a Senate investigation of a stock sale of his that occurred under Hoover's watch that he felt the Republican should've squashed. And so, with the Hollywood reciprocity formula in mind, they funneled money to Roosevelt in exchange for—they hoped—a little more influence in Washington, D.C. When Mayer threw his torchlight parade for Hoover, the Warners used their radio stations to organize a giant gala for Roosevelt at the Los Angeles Coliseum, which was attended by 175,000 (beat that, Louis!). Every spotlight in the studio was commandeered to light up the sky.

Roosevelt won the 1932 race by a landslide, and Jack was appointed head of the Los Angeles office of the National Recovery

Administration. The Warners sent a train packed with stars to Washington for the inauguration: Bette Davis, James Cagney, Ginger Rogers. Back in 1928, Hoover had offered Mayer an ambassadorship; Jack Warner claimed that Roosevelt did just the same for him in 1932. Jack told everyone that he turned it down, insisting, "I think I can do better for your foreign relations with a good picture about America now and then." Jack's son later disputed the story: "FDR never offered an ambassadorship to my father. I heard him say that he wished it was true, but his old presidential pal never came across. My father was jealous of Louis B Mayer."[45]

Is it possible that the channeling of money, the expensive ceremonies, and the celebrity endorsements could be motivated by petty jealousy between studio moguls? Yes. But more likely, the Warners had made a simple business calculation: The polls showed that Roosevelt was more popular than Hoover, so Warner went with FDR in '32. What's fascinating, though, is the ability of Hollywood's storytellers to turn a story of greed into a story of political idealism. Just like Peter Paul and Aaron Tonken's exploitation of the Clintons in 2000, the Warners pitched their dealings with Roosevelt as something done for a higher cause.

Betty Warner recalls of her father, Harry, "He was an idealist and he had a lot of hope that Roosevelt would transform America. . . . He wanted to help rebuild the country after the Depression." Certainly the Warners promised a "New Deal in entertainment" that would offer movies that both entertained and reflected the realities of life during an age of austerity: no more illusion, no more lies.[46] Harry wrote about film's commitment to "ethics, patriotism and the fundamental rights of individuals" and said that he only desired to make movies that would "advance the public interest and welfare."[47] Cinema was almost a divine instrument: "The motion picture presents right and wrong, as the Bible does."[48] What was wrong was poverty; what was right was Roosevelt's New Deal programs that offered work to the workless. Warner Bros. put the National Recovery Administration's eagle symbol in the credits of its movies.[49] Busby Berkeley's musical *Gold Diggers of 1933* (1933) closed with a sequence titled "Remember My Forgotten Man" that was a grim, expressionist tribute to the long queues of the unemployed left hopeless after the Wall Street crash. Berkeley's *Footlight Parade* (1933) climaxed in drill formations, a display of giant cards that when put together formed the American flag and the image of President Roosevelt. This was sheer, naked propaganda and, like Mayer's torchlight celebration of Herbert Hoover, could rival anything produced in fascist Europe, say, to celebrate the brilliance of Il Duce.[50]

But at the same time that the Warners were professing their love for Roosevelt and his New Deal liberalism, they were actually working to suppress wages in their own studio and resisting the labor unions (Mayer, no better, cut wages by 50 percent in 1933).[51] And when socialism nearly came to California, the moguls put aside their differences to unite against it.

On August 28, 1934, the writer Upton Sinclair sent shock waves through Hollywood when he won the Democratic nomination for governor of California. He was running on a bold reform program that promised to provide pensions for the elderly, end unemployment, end taxes on homes worth less than three thousand dollars, and institute a graduated income tax that included a rate of 50 percent on incomes over fifty thousand dollars. The screenwriters, crews, and poorly paid actors loved it; the moguls hated it—they contemplated moving everything to Florida. When pollsters gave Sinclair even money to win, Louis Mayer flew into action. He set the goal of raising half a million dollars for advertisements, including negative newsreels, that portrayed Sinclair's supporters as foreigners and communists—one of the first set of theatrical negative ads ever made. Mayer came up with a novel way of getting the cash. All MGM employees who made over one hundred dollars per week were required to give a day's salary to the Republican candidate. Some received unsigned checks with an amount written on it and a terse note informing the recipient that this was how much they were expected to donate. Anyone who didn't pay got a visit from Mayer's thuggish squad of collectors, who would pester them night and day for the cash and throw around threats about nonrenewed contracts. This moneymaking scam might have seemed crooked—even un-American—but that didn't stop the Democratic-voting Warner Bros. from copying it. They also demanded that their employees pay up to beat Sinclair. James Cagney led a small number of Warner stars in protest, saying that if he was asked to give a day's salary to the Republicans, then he'd give a week's salary to the Democrats. It made no difference: Sinclair was clobbered by studio money and easily beaten in the fall election.[52]

This was the reality behind the Warner devotion to Roosevelt and his liberal ambitions: It would last only as long as he scratched their backs. If all the reciprocity stopped, so would the money. That was understood.[53]

At first, things worked out well. By 1936 cinema attendance was almost back to its 1930 level, and Warner Bros. recorded a 345 percent fiscal gain over 1935. Nearly every studio was climbing out of the red, and the New Deal's pledge of higher wages and better conditions for workers promised a future in which everyone would have more money and time to spend at the movie house. Warners caught the spirit of the age, with its mix of fun-loving musicals and movies about real people—especially the violent gangster films that sneakily celebrated those who got the better of the banks and the law. According to *Business Week*, "Looking ahead, the movie magnates can see nothing but champagne and nesselrode pudding."

The *Hollywood Reporter* said, with surprise, "Even good pictures made money."[54] It helped that the National Recovery Administration effectively sanctioned the kind of monopolistic practices that the studios engaged in, protecting them from the attention of the trustbusters.[55] The result was that these studios clung on to their dominant market share: By 1939, the top eight studios produced about 75 percent of the features released in the United States, and the top five studios controlled about 80 percent of the theaters in the largest cities.[56]

The problem was that the New Deal had a paradoxical relationship with business. Yes, it created the conditions under which capitalism could revive and flourish. But it also injected something new into Hollywood culture that the studio heads didn't like: social democracy. All that talk of unions and workers' rights slowly filtered down into the ranks of the studio. As we shall see in the next chapter, the conflict that erupted between the employees and their mogul masters would inform much of the anticommunist effort in the 1940s and 1950s.

And trust-busting gained a momentum that was hard to slow. On the one hand, the Roosevelt administration saw corporations as bastions of stability that ought to be encouraged. On the other hand, it liked to think of itself as being on the side of the little guy who was being bullied by his oversized competitors. The Justice Department stepped up a long-running campaign to end the studios' vertical monopoly over production, distribution, and exhibition by invoking the Sherman Antitrust Act. In 1938, Assistant Attorney General Thurman Arnold filed *United States v. Paramount Pictures et al.* in New York Federal District Court in an effort to break up the vertical monopoly cartel.[57] By then Harry Warner's faith in the New Deal had already been tested by what he regarded as Roosevelt's failure to intervene on his behalf in private business matters. One magazine reported, "The New Deal, as Harry sees it, pays off its friends with the Sherman Act and causes him to lose his theatres." He wrote Roosevelt to ask for help but FDR declined to do anything. From that moment on Harry became, in the words of his daughter, "a bitter Republican."[58]

After decades of various suits, in May 1948 the Supreme Court finally ruled that the studios were running an illegal monopoly. It ended their ability to control what was shown in their own cinemas, which led them to divest themselves of many of their theaters. Combined with the growing popularity of television, the inexorable decline of the studio system had begun.[59] Spending lavish sums of money on politicians had offered some benefits—i.e., defeating left-wing upstarts like Sinclair or stalling some unfavorable antitrust verdicts. But ultimately it failed to protect the moguls from either the law or changing tastes. Rather like Peter Paul chasing some fantasy of Bill Clinton joining his company if he could only raise $1 million for Hillary's Senate race, the moguls had foolishly imagined that their bank accounts and their personalities could win any politician of any stripe over to their way of thinking. But history isn't so easily controlled by one individual's willpower, even if the movies try to convince us that that is the case. As receipts shrunk at MGM in the 1940s, Mayer's star began to fade. After three years during which MGM did not win an Academy Award, confidence in his ability to produce films of quality that could also make money dwindled. He was sacked from his job in 1951; to his disgust, he was replaced by a liberal Democrat, Dore Schary. Furious at the decline of his industry and angry at the world, Mayer moved further to the right. In 1954, he made a speech praising Joe McCarthy and his campaign against the Reds. "The more McCarthy yells, the better I like him," he said. "He's doing a job to get rid of the termites eating away at our democracy." Ignored and without clout, Mayer passed away from leukemia in 1957.[60]

What Hollywood Wants from Washington

The political history of Louis B. Mayer and his rivals, the Warners, reminds us that Hollywood is a business, and when many movie-makers give money to politicians they expect something in return. Of course, their motivations are personal and complex, and often articulated as high ideals. But the principle of reciprocity—which governed the prewar party machine and the studio system—is inescapable.

As it was in the 1930s, so it remains today. Many of the studio executives who gave thousands of dollars each to Barack Obama did so in part because they assumed it guaranteed them a reciprocal relationship with the White House. What did they want in return for their money? Just as Hollywood was concerned with the threat of trust-busting in the 1930s, so in the twenty-first century the moviemakers have seen their monopoly over the distribution of its films threatened by the Internet. Nowadays you don't have to go to a cinema to see a movie: At the click of a button you can download it from a shady Web site for free. Moviemakers have lobbied hard for legislation to censor and shut down these pirate Web sites, and many of them supported Obama in the hope that he'd prove an ally in their cause.

When Hollywood-backed legislation on piracy stalled in Congress in early 2012, Chris Dodd, a former senator turned head of the Motion Picture Association of America (MPAA), gave an interview to Fox News in which he gently reminded President Obama of the reciprocity principle:

Those who count on quote "Hollywood" for support need to understand that this industry is watching very carefully who's going to stand up for them when their job is at stake. Don't ask me to write a check for you when you think your job is at risk and then don't pay any attention to me when my job is at stake.

Translation: Back the bill or Barbra Streisand won't sing for you anymore.[61]

To be sure, there's nothing unusual about this attitude. Car makers, oil men, and bankers all give money to politicians on the basis that they expect to get something nice for their industry back in return. What makes Hollywood different is its ability to dress up something transactional as something idealistic. This is not to mean that there aren't real idealists in Hollywood who give money to the causes they believe in (we'll meet many in this book), and nor does it mean that the personal relationships between moviemaker and politician are entirely cynical. But it does mean that Hollywood people have the ability to do something for materialistic reasons, pretend to be motivated by idealism, and somehow—thanks to all those spotlighted skies, autographed letters, gala performances, and gushing tributes—convince themselves and half the world that they are doing what they're doing for love of country.

Mayer and Warner became Republican or Democrat for exactly the same reasons: They thought it would help line their pockets. But they managed to turn that reciprocal arrangement into a love story—and somewhere along the line they started to believe the romance was real. Of course, for many Hollywood activists it is real—and never more so than in the 1960s and 1970s.

Cut to Burt Lancaster's house in 1963 . . .

3

EASY RIDERS

How Hollywood Became a Poisoned
Chalice for Liberal Reformers

n May 1963, Martin Luther King Jr. paid a visit to the home of
Burt Lancaster. The civil rights leader gave a speech to an audience of stars about the evils of Southern segregation and the brutal response to his peaceful protests: skin lacerated by water
cannons; children bitten by police dogs; potbellied sheriffs crack-
ing skulls with clubs. The audience listened in horrified silence.
Afterward they handed over seventy-five thousand dollars to help
support King's good work. But it wasn't enough just to give money;
they also wanted to give their time and—most important—their
fame to the cause. On July 26, they reconvened under the title of
the Arts Group at Marlon Brando's house to talk logistics for joining King's forthcoming March on Washington. Early members included Tony Curtis, *Name of the Game* star Tony Franciosa, Billy
Wilder, and Burt Lancaster. Later they would be joined by Shirley

MacLaine, Dean Martin, Frank Sinatra, Steve McQueen, Paul Newman, Joanne Woodward, Sidney Poitier, and Harry Belafonte. The stars elected Charlton "Moses" Heston to lead them to Washington. Why him? Heston later put it down in part to his union work: "I suppose I was elected because of the time I put in with the [Screen Actors Guild] . . . or maybe just because I'd gotten all those folks through the Red Sea."[1]

The actors were wise to their star status and what it meant to the public, and they were determined to use it to advance their cause. According to minutes of the meeting, someone said, "We know that motion picture personalities are to a great degree the style, fashion, and mores pacesetters of the impressionable masses of the country. As someone in Torrence said: 'If integration is good enough for Marlon Brando, it's good enough for me.' "[2]

That statement goes to the heart of how a lot of Hollywood stars see their role in the politics—as trend makers. It's a fundamentally arrogant worldview, dividing America between pacesetters and followers, with Hollywood as the engine for social change. But it's hard to resent the Arts Group's vanity when it was lent to such a noble cause. In August 1963, the stars boarded a private jet and flew out to join the March on Washington. Their involvement was actually pretty low key: *Variety* reported that they gave "a relaxed and peaceful 'country fair' mood to the huge demonstration." Joan Baez and Bob Dylan sang, Belafonte spoke, Burt Lancaster (who arrived that morning from Paris) brought a list of fifteen hundred supporters living abroad. Most of the actors weren't even recognized until a group of young girls spotted them and started "shrieking at Lancaster, Belafonte, Poitier, Newman, and Heston." The really big draw was Martin Luther King Jr.; the stars were just extras.[3]

But the march was the beginning of a new wave of Hollywood activism, of actors using their fame to promote an issue that they cared about. Likewise, politicians and activists became more and more aware of the usefulness of star power. The Native American rights movement, for example, was pleased to have Marlon Brando join its ranks. In 1964, Brando participated in high-profile "fish-ins": Activists camped out along riverbanks and "illegally" fished in waters that they claimed had been stolen from them in historic treaties. In early March, Brando was arrested for catching two steelhead trout as part of a protest with the Puyallup tribe. According to historian Sherry L. Smith, "The decision to enlist Brando proved to be gold. The nation noticed. And the lessons were clear: to get widespread white attention, get white participation; to get widespread media attention, get celebrity participation."[4]

As we discussed in the last chapter, money is the motor for much of the relationship between politics and Hollywood. But we shouldn't be cynical; many moviemakers have deep commitments to causes beyond themselves and have proven indispensable to environmentalism, minority rights, or putting people in office. The golden age of activism ran from about 1963 to 1974, and most of the causes that came out of Hollywood were unashamedly liberal. During this period, stars and politicians worked as allies to a degree that's never quite been matched since. This national engagement with ideas continues today, but the cultural revolution of the late sixties and early seventies made it an era in which a) stars were more willing to think aloud in public and b) politicians and the media were a little more prepared to listen. For Hollywood politics it was a time of innocence and articulacy. Unfortunately, the combination of naïveté and outspokenness could also be a vote loser. As we shall discover, the celebrity endorsement is a double-edged sword.

One of the things that made that era possible was the collapse of the studio system. To really appreciate how radical the 1960s and 1970s were for Hollywood, we need to remember how conservative the previous time had been. The big moguls of the prehippie era were keen on promoting ideas, too—but theirs were ideas that preserved old orthodoxies rather than encouraged cultural change. It was the age of McCarthy.

Hollywood's Conservative Era

Before the 1960s the studios were both conservative and cautious. One of Hollywood's biggest myths about itself is that it opposed fascism in all its forms from the first moment that Mussolini reached for the skies with his right hand. This is wrong.[5] Columbia producer Walter Wanger (perhaps most notorious for shooting his wife's agent in a fit of jealous rage) was a big fan of Il Duce and insisted that he only wanted to help the downtrodden Ethiopians whose country he had kindly invaded in 1935. Louis B. Mayer met with Mussolini's son Vittorio while the mogul was traveling in Italy, and they amicably discussed the possibility of setting up an Italian film company in Hollywood. In 1937, the mini–Il Duce visited Hollywood and was entertained by the press baron William Randolph Hearst (who published Vittorio's pieces in his newspapers), Walt Disney, and a Fox executive. Only a sustained letter-writing campaign by anti-Fascists eventually convinced MGM to tear up plans for the Italian venture, which caused a furious Vittorio to denounce Hollywood as a "Hebrew Communist center."[6]

Hearst lodged with Hitler during the Nuremberg rally of 1934, and he assured Mayer that the Nazi was misunderstood.[7] Mayer's producer Irving Thalberg toured Germany that year and returned with the conviction that "Hitler and Hitlerism will pass; the Jews will still be there" (although he admitted that a few would probably lose their lives). When Hitler's propagandist director, Leni Riefenstahl, visited America in 1938, Walt Disney rolled out the red carpet.

When Leni's fuhrer invaded Austria, Fox, Paramount, and MGM not only kept their offices open in Vienna but dismissed Jewish executives and employees in order to keep the Germans happy. In a 2013 book, Ben Urwand revealed that the German consul in Los Angeles, Georg Gyssling, enjoyed such influence over the studios that he was able to call up Warner Bros. and demand that pictures that dealt with anti-Semitism be edited to remove their political content. Urwand described the relationship between Warner and Gyssling as a "collaboration."[8]

Considering that all three studios were headed by Jewish moguls, it's an extraordinary black mark on their record.[9] But then, it should be remembered that Hollywood also catered to domestic racism. In the 1940s, scriptwriter Bernard Gordon inserted a black taxi driver into a script and a producer crossed him out. Why? "It would only cause trouble in the South, where theatres would refuse to play the film."[10]

Prior to 1938, no anti-Nazi films were made by the studios. Walter Wanger's independently made and money-losing *Blockade* (1938) offered a veiled comment on the Spanish civil war, but it was only with *Confessions of a Nazi Spy* (1939) that Warner Bros. broke the embargo. It tells the story of an FBI agent, played by Edward G. Robinson, who leads a crackdown on a German spy ring, and the movie deserves plaudits for the frank way with which it deals with the Nazi Party's repellent views toward racial minorities and freedom of speech. The Warner brothers—Harry in particular—were vocal opponents of the Third Reich and outspoken in their opposition to Fascism. But they were not, again contrary to myth, making an explicit case for intervention in Europe. At the end of *Confessions of a Nazi Spy*, a hero describes America as "separated by vast oceans from the bacteria of aggressive dictatorships and totalitarian states." "This ain't Europe, and the sooner we show 'em the better," says another character. It's hard not to read this as a case for isolationism, for saying that America needs to insulate itself against the foreign "bacteria" of totalitarianism.[11] Moreover, the Warners saw that bacteria as belonging to both Left and Right. "You may have heard that communism is rampant in Hollywood," Harry told the American Legion in 1938, "I tell you this industry has no sympathy for communism, Fascism, or Nazism, or any other kind of ism other than Americanism!"[12]

Of course, the Warners probably did believe in 100 percent Americanism all the way. But they also had just cause to shout louder than anyone else about it. It was necessary to assuage the prejudice of America's elites. In 1941, a U.S. Senate subcommittee staffed by isolationists determined to stay out of the European conflict called witnesses to hear whether or not Hollywood was using its clout to drive the country toward war. There was an unpleasant, barely disguised implication that the movie industry was dominated by left-wing Jews—more "bacteria" in the body politic. Republican senator Gerald Nye:

> Those primarily responsible for the propaganda pictures are born abroad. They came to our land and took citizenship here entertaining violent animosities toward certain causes abroad. Quite natural is their feeling and desire to aid those who are at war against the causes which so naturally antagonize them. If they lose sight of what some Americans might call the first interests of America in times like these, I can excuse them. But their prejudices by no means necessitate our closing our eyes to these interests and refraining from any undertaking to correct their error.[13]

Harry Warner's testimony offered a nuanced rebuttal. Yes, he was in favor of aiding the British against the Germans, and yes, he regarded Nazism as something that had to be fought and beaten.

But the senators who questioned him had not even watched the movies they detested (literally: Senator Bennett Clark of Missouri said, "I have not seen any of them [and] I am not going to see any of them!"), and what is more, the pols clearly misunderstood how the free market works. Harry Warner testified: "Millions of average citizens have paid to see these pictures. They have enjoyed wide popularity and have been profitable to our company. In short, these pictures have been judged by the public, and the judgment has been favorable." In Hollywood terms, that's how you know if an idea has merit: whether or not the public will pay to watch a film about it.[14] Harry Warner's failure to convert the Senate committee to his philosophy proved unimportant: War broke out before it could reach any conclusions.

World War II transformed Hollywood's outsider image; the conflict gave it the opportunity to act as the mouthpiece for national unity and the American Way. The studios gifted their personnel, equipment, and expertise to making training films for the army (that's how Ronald Reagan, then in his thirties, spent much of the war).[15] Many stars put their careers on hold to fight overseas: Henry Fonda, Douglas Fairbanks Jr., Clark Gable, Jimmy Stewart. Those that stayed at home did their bit, too. In 1942, Bette Davis and John Garfield rented an abandoned building on Sunset Boulevard and turned it into a twenty-four-hour, seven-days-a-week celebrity staffed canteen to serve military personnel. It was a rebellion against the star system. James Cagney protested that exposing actors to ordinary people like this for long periods of time reduced their glamour. The edifice upon which stardom was built—distance from the fans—was at risk. But other artists welcomed the chance to do something practical for Uncle Sam. Frank Sinatra, Dinah Shore, and Bing Crosby sang; Marlene Dietrich, Betty Grable, and Hedy Lamarr served as hostesses. The canteen was desegregated: Blacks could dance with whites. Bette Davis received tons of hate mail from irate racists. But why discriminate between black and white soldiers, she wrote back? They both take the same bullets.[16]

The studios were doubtless as patriotic as the average American, but they liked to keep an eye on profit. For them there was no distinction between being 100 percent American and making a buck out of it—recall Harry Warner telling the Senate committee that the best test of a film's worth was whether or not people went to see it. In this sense, World War II was business as usual for the studios.[17]

Take *Casablanca* (1942). It's tempting to imagine that when glorious movies like that are made, the moviemakers understand that they are handling something special—that they know they are witnessing the birth of great art. In reality, *Casablanca* was rolled off the production line just like any other feature. Warner Bros. bought the rights to an unproduced play, *Everybody Comes to Rick's*, and sent it off to Julius and Philip Epstein to write a first-draft screenplay. When the Epsteins were called to Washington for war work, it was passed along to Howard Koch, who was famous for producing Orson Welles's *War of the Worlds* radio news broadcast. Even as Koch was working on the script, Jack Warner was casting and setting a production deadline for 1942. He offered the role of Rick to George Raft, and considered cutting the budget and giving it to Ronald Reagan instead. But then Warner did a star transfer deal with Selznick International Pictures and got Ingrid Bergman in exchange for Olivia de Havilland. Humphrey Bogart landed the part of Rick. By now Koch had discovered to his fury that the Epsteins were back working on an alternative script. Bogart and the director argued on set, and music director Max Steiner tried to have the song "As Time Goes By" removed from the score. He loathed it.[18]

At the time, few people—including the critics—understood how important a movie *Casablanca* was. Bogart's Rick, the laconic, cynical bar owner, is a liberal-turned-isolationist (we know that he fought for the Republicans during the Spanish civil war). His lethargy is transformed into action by the thuggery of the Nazis, and he sacrifices the chance of happiness with Ingrid Bergman for the sake of a free Europe. *Variety* wrote: "Film is splendid anti-Axis propaganda, particularly inasmuch as the propaganda is strictly a by-product of the principal action and contributes to it instead of getting in the way."[19] *The New Yorker* called it "pretty tolerable."[20]

It's interesting to note that while plenty of audiences love *Casablanca* and have memorized whole chunks of the script, Hollywood's memory has proven far shorter. In 1982, a mischievous screenwriter sent the script of *Casablanca* to every single literary agency in Los Angeles. He changed the title to *Everybody Comes to Rick's* but kept the rest of the text the same. One quarter of the agencies got the joke. The rest failed to recognize one of the greatest movies of all time. Three wanted to sell the script to a studio but only two as a motion picture. Eight saw a similarity to *Casablanca* and suggested that he draw out some contrasts to make his more original. The rest rebuffed the script, ignored it, or wanted to rework it. "Never send a screenplay unsolicited again!!!!" said the Larry Karlin Agency, "I gave you five pages to grab me—didn't do it." One agent's assistant had these criticisms: "Too much dialogue, not enough exposition, the story line was weak, and in general didn't hold my interest." A fellow at John La Rocca & Associates added: "I regret to say that we will not be able to help you with your script. I strongly recommend that you leaf through a book called *Screenplay* by Sid Field, especially the section pertaining to dialogue."[21]

Casablanca's solid box office performance contributed to the general revival of Hollywood's fortunes. Approximately eighty-five million cinema tickets were sold each week in America during World War II. The war was a time when Hollywood's desire to prove its patriotism and its hunger for profit found perfect synergy, and the experience left a mark upon its character. Once the war was over the studios felt emboldened to promote an uncompromising vision of the unique genius of America—a message that would destroy many lives. By 1951, Howard Koch—the man who in 1944 received an Oscar for coscripting *Casablanca*—had been blacklisted as a Communist and forced to move to Europe to find work.[22]

The enemy in wartime was the Fascists threatening to destroy America from without. In peacetime it became the Communists threatening to destroy America from within. The studios hated Marxism for two reasons: a) it undermined the free market system that they believed in; and b) it threatened their profits. The 1940s saw terrible labor battles between the studios and their set workers and screenwriters over pay and conditions, which the studios interpreted as a sign that their industry was being infiltrated by Reds. The moguls hired goons to break the strikes, which, in turn, led to violence against those who refused to put down their tools. One union leader admitted to breaking the arms of sixteen scabs: "In many respects we out-thugged the thugs." Some employees wrote to the Warners accusing them of fascism, another wrote a letter with "God bless you" underlined several times.[23] So intense were the battles that it was feared there were moves afoot to take control of Hollywood from within, to use the muscle of organized labor to tell moguls what to put in their movies. The president of the Screen Actors Guild, one Ronald Reagan, reasoned that Hollywood's artistic power would make it an invaluable weapon should the Reds seize control of it:

The Communist plan for Hollywood was remarkably simple. It was merely to take over the motion picture business. Not only for its profit . . . but also for a grand world-wide propaganda base. In those days, before television and massive foreign film production, American films dominated 95 percent of the world's movie screens. We had a weekly audience of around 500,000,000 souls. Takeover of this enormous plant and its gradual transformation into a Communist gristmill was a grandiose idea. It would have been a magnificent coup for our enemies.[24]

Reagan's fears about the extremism of his labor opponents were not without foundation. He got death threats from trade union militants and was advised to carry a gun provided by the local police. His wife told a friend that "there had been more than one night that she awakened to see him holding the gun, sitting in bed having thought that he had heard noises in the house." Reagan later recalled that an anonymous caller warned him that "a squad was ready to take care of me and fix my face so I would never be in pictures again." Just before he boarded a bus to cross a picket line, in 1946, a bomb went off and destroyed the vehicle. A cop was stationed outside his house 24/7. "I mounted the holstered gun religiously every morning," Reagan remembered. "I learned how much a person gets to lean on hardware like that. After ten months of wearing it, it took a real effort to discard it."[25]

The moguls cheered him on. In 1944, Hollywood players including Walt Disney, John Wayne, Gary Cooper, and Cecil B. DeMille founded the Motion Picture Alliance for the Preservation of American Ideals (MPA) to combat Communist influence in movies. "In our special field," they wrote,

we resent the growing impression that this industry is made of, and dominated by, Communists, radicals, and crackpots. . . . Motion Pictures are inescapably one of the world's greatest forces for influencing public thought and opinion, both at home and abroad. In this fact lies solemn obligation. We refuse to permit the effort of Communist, Fascist, and other totalitarian-minded groups to pervert this powerful medium.[26]

The MPA asked the libertarian guru Ayn Rand to produce a new movie code for the industry. Each chapter opened with an instruction that read something like Don't Smear the Free Enterprise System, Don't Deify the Common Man, and Don't Show That Poverty Is a Virtue and Failure Is Noble. Rand wrote, "It is the moral (no, not just political but moral) duty of every decent man in the motion picture industry to throw into the ashcan where it belongs, every story that smears industrialists."[27] Rand eagerly reviewed all the movies that had been made in the 1930s and 1940s and identified those that included a Marxist message, even if no one else had ever spotted it. She condemned the smash hit *The Best Years of Our Lives* simply because it urged bankers to give ex-servicemen collateral-free loans.[28]

In 1947, the MPA invited the House Un-American Activities Committee to investigate the influence of communism in the movie industry; HUAC was happy to oblige. Walt Disney, one of the friendly witnesses, told the inquest that Communist-dominated unions had "smeared me" and tried to ruin his international reputation because he wouldn't make "Commie propaganda." He also revealed that he had sold just one cartoon to the Soviet Union—*Three Little Pigs*—but that they returned it unshown. "It didn't suit their purposes," he surmised, because the pigs were property owners.[29] Actor Adolphe Menjou said, "I am a witch hunter if the witches are Communists. I am a Red-baiter. I would like to see them all back in Russia." Jack Warner delivered a performance in which some observers detected a note of fear: He was determined that his studio wouldn't be associated with the Red menace. So, when asked, he threw out names of "Communists" who he had had fired from his lots. Actors Ronald Reagan, Robert Montgomery, Robert Taylor, Gary Cooper, and George Murphy revealed that they had gone through every script they could get their hands on, vetted every actor, and tried their damnedest to find evidence of Marxism. And, they implied, they had found plenty. Eleven "unfriendly" witnesses were called, and ten of them refused to answer the following question: "Are you now or have you ever been a member of the Communist Party?" Actually all of them should have answered yes: they either were or had been in the past. But, citing the First Amendment, they denounced the investigation as an invasion of their right to belong to any organization they liked, and HUAC charged them with contempt.[30] They became known as the Hollywood Ten.

Initially, the MPA was greeted with suspicion and anxiety in Hollywood, and many actors came out against HUAC's investigation. The mood among the moguls was mixed—even Louis B. Mayer was nervous about driving away talented writers and performers and resented the government's intervention in his industry. Studios probably would've settled for a national ban on the Communist Party rather than a full-scale witch hunt.[31] Stars organized a protest against the hearings. "We sat in the Committee Room and heard it happen," said Humphrey Bogart, one of the public dissenters. "We saw it. We said to ourselves: it can't happen here. We saw American citizens denied the right to speak by elected representatives. . . . We saw the gavel of the Committee Chairman cutting off the words of free Americans!"[32]

But the tide was with the right-wing. On November 17, 1947, the Screen Actors Guild voted to make its officers take an anticommunist pledge. On November 24, the House of Representatives voted 346 to 17 in agreement that the Hollywood Ten were in contempt of Congress. The Motion Picture Association of America announced that the ten would be fired or suspended without pay and would find no work within the industry until they had been cleared of contempt and sworn that they were not Communists.[33]

The blacklist spread and spread: Refusal even to comment on another person's politics could lead to losing work. Others were forced to sign loyalty oaths by the guilds and studios. Liberals who went to Washington to plea on the Hollywood Ten's behalf now backtracked.[34] Five months after the trip, Bogart recanted in *Photoplay* with an article titled "I'm No Communist." Frank Sinatra put a two-page ad in *The New Republic* saying the same.[35] Charlie Chaplin went to Europe to promote his new movie in 1952 and didn't return for twenty years; FBI chief J. Edgar Hoover had Chaplin's visa revoked because of his left-wing politics. "Fear and psychosis pervades the town," one director said of Hollywood.

> Producers are asking for and getting pictures without ideas.
> In the frantic effort to offend no one, to alienate no groups,
> to create no misgivings in Congressional minds, studios are
> for the most part obediently concentrating on vapidity.[36]

Politically, Hollywood liberals were emasculated. Of course, they continued to work for presidential candidates and other mainstream efforts. But the 1950s were not a time for promoting radical causes. So people focused on their careers instead.[37]

The Liberal Turn

By the late 1960s, the Hollywood blacklist was gone and the victims of McCarthy were not only delisted but rehabilitated and working in cinema again.[38] In 1968, Haskell Wexler—a left-wing cinematographer who had fought against studio conservatives in the 1950s—made an artistically important movie in Chicago called

Medium Cool. The title refers to the medium of television, supposedly unsuited to the violent heat of real life, and details a TV cameraman's political awakening. The novelty of Wexler's project was that he mixed fiction with fact, intercutting scripted scenes with documentary footage of racism, poverty, demonstrations, and police brutality. This was a different way of reflecting on contemporary America. Before the 1960s, cinema was staged, almost theatrically, with carefully constructed plots acted out on carefully constructed sets. That suited the ordered mind-set of corporate, conservative America, but Wexler wanted to refashion cinema into a medium that could capture the chaotic truth of the moment. To be more "real," films had to look more real—even if that reality was actually manufactured.[39] We call this paradoxical style cinéma vérité, and its brief popularity is inseparable from the explosion of radical politics that took place in America in the 1960s and 1970s.[40]

Hollywood's politics changed dramatically in the sixties for three interconnected reasons. First, the studio system collapsed thanks to antitrust action, the rise of TV, and declining box office receipts. As the moguls lost power and faded away (or simply died), so they lost control over the private lives of the stars. That freed young actors up to dress, behave, and think the way that they wanted to. Second, the sixties were dominated by political questions so provocative that they demanded a moral response from the moviemakers. They refused to say no comment to questions about Vietnam or civil rights—a new generation of stars wanted to take part in the great debates of their day. Finally, the decade saw a dramatic shift in aesthetic tastes. Before the 1960s young Americans tried to behave like their fathers and mothers. Male heroes such as Jimmy Stewart wore suits and hats; leading ladies such as Grace Kelly dressed not only for dinner but even for breakfast. From the late 1950s onward, however, America fell in love with adolescence. The new icon was James Dean: teenage, rebellious, and yet childlike in his innocence. Once America worshiped parental authority; the American dream for many middle-class folks was to grow old in opulent surroundings with a pipe and an Andy Williams sweater. Now it was to "live fast, die young, and leave a good-looking corpse."[41] By the end of the sixties, with plenty of bodies arriving home from Vietnam, youth had become all the more precious when the government was so willing to sacrifice it in war.

To illustrate how all of this came together, take the case of Paul Newman—the man who Maureen Dowd and Harvey Weinstein said was so like Barack Obama. Newman had been a direct witness to the suffocating conservatism of the 1950s: His cousin had lost his job in the nuclear industry because he had a Russian wife. In the more open-minded 1960s, Newman was determined to make a difference. And why shouldn't a star take a headline role in national politics? Talking to *Playboy*, he expressed the sentiments of frustrated Hollywood activists:

> The world situation affects us, as movie people, as much as it does everybody else. Naturally, we've got to be careful about using our disproportionate "image power" to sway public opinion. . . . But you've got a choice. Do you abdicate the responsibilities of citizenship merely because you carry a Screen Actors' Guild card? Or do you dig deep and become as knowledgeable and expert as you can? . . . As a feeling, thinking American, I have to get involved.[42]

Vietnam was a good place to start. In November 1967, Senator Eugene McCarthy of Minnesota declared that he would challenge President Lyndon B. Johnson in the upcoming presidential primaries. He was running on an antiwar ticket, protesting the war in Southeast Asia that had left tens of thousands of young Americans dead. Newman wanted to help:

I was so fed up with the present Administration that I couldn't resist going to work for [McCarthy]. I found him to be a dedicated, courageous human being. It took guts to lay his cards on the table, to oppose a president who belonged to his own party.[43]

Newman's contact within the campaign, Tony Podesta, sincerely believed that the star helped put McCarthy's candidacy on the map. When Newman first arrived in Claremont, New Hampshire, to campaign, Podesta worried that no one else would show up.

Until that point, McCarthy was some sort of quack not too many people knew about, but as soon as Paul Newman came to speak for him, he immediately became a national figure. . . . Once we figured out what was going on here, we began to advance [Newman] harder than we advanced the candidate. . . . There wasn't anybody who had the kind of electricity Newman did. We didn't get those kinds of crowds for McCarthy.[44]

It's a very tall claim, that a Hollywood actor made viable one of the most important candidacies in political history. But it's supported somewhat by the memories of Curtis Gans, the director of McCarthy's campaign:

Yes, we had Paul Newman in New Hampshire, along with Tony Randall, Myrna Loy, Dustin Hoffman, and Paul Simon. I don't think it's what made the campaign do so well, by any means. But it was useful in two ways. First, we used famous voices for radio broadcasts and people might listen harder to a famous voice. . . . Second, we used those people when going door-to-door. There was great shock value for the New

Hampshire housewife or whatever when they opened the door and there was Paul Newman.

In other words, the McCarthy people quickly discovered the publicity value of Newman—and they scripted and used him in a highly choreographed manner. Crucially, they got away with it because this was a cause-oriented election. Gans:

It wasn't about personalities, it was about Vietnam. So the glitz wasn't distracting.

In future elections, that wouldn't always be the case.

McCarthy took 42 percent in New Hampshire—not a win but enough to spook Lyndon Johnson into quitting the race. So, by Podesta's reckoning, Paul Newman brought down a president. The McCarthy "victory" also encouraged Robert Kennedy to throw his hat into the ring, which created an early battle of the star endorsements. Gans recalls:

The Kennedys were recruiting Hollywood people early on; getting actors on board was always important to them.[45]

One friend of Bobby's was the TV actor Robert Vaughn, one of the first stars to compromise his reputation as a popular entertainer by speaking out against the war in Vietnam.[46]

Memories of 1968 produce mixed emotions. It was a year of tragedy: Martin Luther King shot dead in Tennessee, Bobby Kennedy in California, the war overseas, the bloody demonstrations at home, and—for liberals—the awfulness of Richard Nixon winning the White House. But while it was a year of dashed hopes, at least it had hopes. McCarthy's campaign had been a "children's crusade" fueled by young activists, and when critics compared him to the Pied

Piper of Hamelin stealing the children away over the riverbank, he responded with characteristic wit: "What [the Piper] did with the children was not to lead them to destruction but into a cave, and it was not to punish them but to punish the townspeople who he felt did not deserve them."[47] McCarthy stroked the ego of his children, confirming in them a sense of moral superiority over their parents that was not entirely deserved. The writer Kurt Vonnegut called them, "The most conceited generation in history. They're bright, but I'm not sure that they're competent."[48]

The mix of smarts and innocence made America's youth perfect consumers for a new kind of socially aware cinema and, slowly, Hollywood gave it to them.[49] It was far more honest than what came before. *Midnight Cowboy* (1969) dealt with homosexuality and prostitution. *Bonnie and Clyde* (1967) featured violence so raw that it closed with its heroes' bodies being torn to shreds by bullets. *The Graduate* (1967) had Dustin Hoffman falling in and out of bed with a much older woman. *Easy Rider* (1967) was a cowboy movie with bikers substituting for Western archetypes. The riders indulge in free love and drugs and initiate a square, played by Jack Nicholson, into the way of the road—before they are picked on by rednecks and murdered in the rural South. The film conveys the ambiguities of the era. In the final reel, Billy, played by Dennis Hopper, thinks their odyssey has been an enlightening success. Wyatt, played by Peter Fonda, says, "We blew it." The conversation achieved totemic quality in a movie that was filmed in early 1968, between Mardi Gras and the assassination of Bobby Kennedy, a period when America came so close to some sort of redemption but, ultimately, "blew it."[50]

The old moguls who were still around loathed these movies. Jack Warner saw a rough cut of *Bonnie and Clyde* and hated it; Warner executives agreed and tried to bury it with a limited release. Early critical reaction was repulsion: Here was a movie that asked us to sympathize with criminals yet also take some vicarious pleasure in their slaughter. A handful of reviewers disagreed. Stefan Kanfer in *Time* hailed the arrival of a "New Cinema" and declared, "In both conception and execution, *Bonnie and Clyde* is a watershed picture, the kind that signals a new style, a new trend." Its young audience had no memories of the 1930s and so saw its protagonists as heroes rather than the coldhearted villains that they really were. It helped that the leads were played by two beautiful young things: Warren Beatty and Faye Dunaway. Their violence was gritty and unpleasant, but also stylized and—yeah—kinda cool. *Bonnie and Clyde* slowly turned into a success, generating over $50 million in domestic receipts on just a $2.5 million budget. It made star and producer Beatty into a very rich man. Because Warners had expected a flop, it offered him 40 percent of the gross instead of a fee. And that's why he was able to devote so much time to politics in the 1970s.[51]

Easy Rider was a crazy hit, too. It made $41 million on a $360,000 investment. The executives threw up their arms in disgust and surrender at the success of these films.[52] They didn't understand young people anymore, so they let them make whatever crazy movies they wanted. We have much to thank for their old-timer ignorance: the directing careers of visionaries like Arthur Penn (*Bonnie and Clyde*), Hal Ashby (*Harold and Maude*, *Being There*), Francis Ford Coppola (*The Conversation*, *The Godfather*), Martin Scorsese (*Mean Streets*, *Taxi Driver*), and Peter Bogdanovich (*The Last Picture Show*, *Paper Moon*). Sometimes the studios tried to intervene and inject some of its conservative instincts. When Paramount purchased Mario Puzo's novel *The Godfather*, executive Robert Evans wanted a conventional cast. He named Laurence Olivier for the Godfather. (His agent replied, "Lord Olivier is not taking any jobs. He's very sick. He's gonna die soon and he's not interested." Olivier lived for another eighteen years.) He also demanded Burt Reynolds as Sonny and the decidedly un-Italian Robert Redford as Michael Corleone. When Al Pacino finally secured the Michael role after much effort by director Coppola, Evans referred to him dismissively as "the midget." Executives hated Pacino's performance (they asked if he was going to do anything) until they saw the restaurant scene in which his character assassinates two men with a gun hidden in the john. They also complained that the movie was poorly lit (intentionally, on the part of Coppola, but Paramount thought the reel they'd been sent was defective).[53] For all their moaning, the movie was the first real Hollywood blockbuster since *The Sound of Music* in 1965. It earned $81.5 million in its first release and eventually beat *Gone with the Wind* as the top rentals earner. Suddenly Hollywood was less critical of the counterculture.

Just as the directors were now freer to do what they wanted, so the stars were at liberty to lead their own lives. That meant sex, drugs, and rock and roll—and politics.

Enter the Beautiful People

On April 16, 1972, Hollywood's youngest and brightest stars threw a party for the antiwar presidential candidate, Senator George McGovern. Warren Beatty, who had been working across the country for McGovern, organized a concert in his honor at the seventeen-thousand-seater Inglewood Forum. It was a sellout, raising over three hundred thousand dollars in one night—about a third of the minimum spend necessary to win the Democratic California primary. Performers included Carole King, James Taylor, and Barbra Streisand. Seats went for as little as four dollars, but anyone who paid one hundred dollars for the expensive seats got a big surprise: They were ushered in by Gene Hackman, Goldie Hawn, Jack Nicholson,

Julie Christie, and Sally Kellerman. The politics of the performers were innocent, even vapid. An interviewer cornered James Taylor and asked him why he was voting for McGovern. "He seems to me the most honest," the singer replied. The interviewer pressed for more detail, but all Taylor said was, "It probably can't be verbalized. I just feel that way." Jack Nicholson was even more modest. On behalf of the actors present, he said, "Most of our political involvement is very superficial, including my own." However, he added, "It is no crime to support the best man."[54]

McGovern was "the best man" to many young liberals because he seemed untarnished by compromise. He wanted out of Vietnam, and out as soon as possible. His appeal lay in his character, in a degree of honesty that came far more naturally to him than to most other politicians. McGovern was the antipolitician: He excited on the level of ideas rather than personality. Running against better-known candidates with far more money, his insurgent campaign made the best of the little that it had.[55] One of its advantages was Warren Beatty, who had been a devotee of McGovern's since Robert Kennedy first introduced them in 1968. Beatty tried to get as many of his friends to support George as possible. "He was one of the three or four most important people in my campaign," McGovern recalled, "and he never sought credit."[56] Nonetheless, his presence on the team was inescapable, and while stars such as Beatty brought attention and money, they brought along some trouble, too.[57]

At the Inglewood fund-raiser, McGovern's noncelebrity backers were worried that the stars eclipsed the candidate. Beatty's goal was to raise money for his man, and many of the performers wouldn't have felt comfortable with being so explicitly political, so he stuck to the line that the event was just a concert. But the ordinary McGovernites couldn't see the point of gathering seventeen thousand people just to sing along to some folk songs. As one of them told

The New York Times, "We've been trying to point out to them that George McGovern is not likely to sing his way into the White House. There is a definite political component here."[58] But most folks in the audience just wanted a good show. "I'm a Republican for Carole King," said a sixty-five-year-old sitting alone. *The Village Voice* reported:

> "I kissed Jack Nicholson," shrieked a teenybopper, her bare midriff quivering with excitement. "Warren Beatty hugged me," one-upped her friend, whose skin-tight hip huggers barely stretched across her 31-inch bottom. "Has anyone seen Elliott Gould?"[59]

Problem number one with Hollywood activism: There was no guarantee that a star's endorsement would actually translate into votes.

Problem number two was that the celebrity endorsement required careful management. When actors appear onstage alongside a politician, the audience doesn't see them as a private individual—they see them as an extension of a public personality. You wouldn't want Bela Lugosi advertising a blood bank or Anthony Perkins a motel. One man who learned that on the McGovern trail was Leonard Nimoy, most famous for playing Spock in the *Star Trek* series and movies. He told me that he was highly conscious of being perceived of by the campaign as a little too "alien" to be used too prominently. His character might have lent itself well to discussions about science or progress, but, ultimately, he was always a Vulcan to everyone he met, and that meant some careful calculations had to be made about how to use him. This sensitive exploitation of image reflects how canny the McGovern campaign could be, despite its reputation for amateurism.[60]

And problem number three was that overreliance on star power could stir a backlash. After a while, McGovern started to get labeled as the candidate of "the beautiful people," a man who was only interested in the opinions of smart types with good bone structure. After the Hollywood concert, news anchor Harry Reasoner used his show to attack celebrity activism as beneath the democratic process. He said, "Presidential candidates should leave endorsements to makers of false teeth cement."[61] Being shown to your seat by Goldie Hawn might've been thrilling, but it wasn't exactly enlightening.

Nothing could keep the liberal stars away from George McGovern, and—being a pioneer of this kind of activism—McGovern didn't understand the potential consequences of welcoming them onboard.[62] Warren Beatty and Shirley MacLaine, brother and sister, threw themselves into the campaign, body and soul. "I don't dabble," explained Beatty. "Dabbling is a sort of waste of time." MacLaine: "I paid for all my hotel rooms, airfare, everything. I must have been $250,000 in and refused to let anybody pay for anything. I gave up several big movies. I mean, my career went in the toilet. When your agent wants to quit you, that's pretty serious."[63]

What motivated actors like Shirley MacLaine to get involved was the mix of frustration and empowerment that had come out of the 1960s. Yes, they had lost the White House to Richard Nixon. But the decade had also created so much potential for articulate idealists. Shirley told a journalist:

> I decided the only option for someone who really cares—and
> I really care—was to go into communications. That's why I
> wrote, and that's why I'm going into television. What I'm
> most interested in is manipulating the system. And today the
> communications are more important than the politics. And
> maybe the communicators are the new politicians. I mean,
> if John Wayne can really influence Nixon and Kissinger on

Cambodia, or if Bob Hope can really become a symbol of vote getting, then I will unabashedly use my celebrity to try to influence people. I think this is a proper use of power. I mean, what good does my turquoise swimming pool in California do anyone else?

All very smart and laudable, but what causes would MacLaine pursue? Alas, not always very popular ones. "The question of overpopulation should not be left to old ladies in sneakers or seminars in Ivy League schools," she told a luncheon with Democrats. "I think we ought to put luxury taxes on diapers and rattles, too, and stop giving tax exemptions for children." Like many Hollywood liberals of her generation, MacLaine seemed attracted to "right-on" causes with little concern for how "out there" they might seem to the average voter: New Age spirituality, affirmative action, wealth redistribution, population control.[64] Nevertheless, her politics gave her a status that elevated her above a mere actress—and made her a new kind of international star. So global was her brand that she even claimed to have met and had an affair with the prime minister of Sweden, Olof Palme. Shirley says she first became attracted to him when she realized he was a reincarnation of Charlemagne.[65]

Many of these liberals were as much in revolt against the legacy of the studio system as they were the Nixon White House. By redefining themselves as actor-activists rather than stars, they were claiming greater control over their own identities. Take Jane Fonda. In the 1960s, Fonda was cast as a classic Hollywood sexpot—the beautiful, desirable, unthinking star of *Barbarella*. She and her then husband, Roger Vadim, lived alternately in a St. Tropez villa and a 130-year-old farmhouse west of Paris, all staffed by a family of Italian servants. When Fonda saw the light and embraced radicalism, she changed husbands, continents, and furnishings. In the early 1970s, a journalist visited her new residence in Santa Monica, which she shared with the socialist agitator Tom Hayden: a "color-less two-family Cape Cod house" in which the couple occupied the top floor.

> The décor is preserved 1967 Psychedelic. Every ancient wooden wallboard and leak-stained ceiling has its individual hue of bright green, blue, red or yellow. The connubial mattress rests on the bare bedroom floor. Jane's gold Oscar, inscribed for "Klute," is a bookend.

How different all this was from the glamorous, micromanaged world of the 1930s star. Jane Fonda, with her psychedelic colors and floor-level mattress, was an actress that no mogul could tame.[66]

Fonda wanted to end the Vietnam War. She toured the United States with a group of performers doing a show for GIs called Free The Army (aka "Fuck The Army" by both performers and spectators) in which they acted out antiwar skits about drugs, race, violence, and Richard Nixon. Fonda also traveled to North Vietnam, where a photo shoot at an Vietcong antiaircraft gun sunk her reputation among veterans.[67] It was, she later insisted, all an innocent mistake. Her hosts had been singing songs about peace, clapping, and laughing; Fonda took the weight off her feet by sitting on the gun.[68] When asked about the impact of all this work on her day job, Hanoi Jane responded with words similar to Shirley MacLaine's: She didn't give a damn. "I would hope that my career would never be separate from my life. I hope that the two can be joined together. But if, because of my political activities, I were prevented from working in Hollywood. . . . I would work elsewhere. That is all."[69]

The liberty that these women espoused in relation to their careers and politics extended to their sex lives. In the days of studio control, sex was a choreographed sequence of public marriages and private affairs—anything out of the ordinary was taboo. When

Casablanca star Ingrid Bergman fell pregnant after an extramarital affair with an Italian director in 1950, she was denounced on the floor of the Senate, and her U.S. career was ruined. But by 1970, everything had changed. Donald Sutherland told *Playboy* about his love affair with Fonda, explaining, "It was a time when we were both experimenting—emotionally, politically, personally—it was like being in one big bowl of soup together, it was terrific. You couldn't ask for a more generous, exciting, funny, sensuous woman than Jane."[70] Of course, what was exciting and funny to Hollywood's liberals could come off as weird to Middle America. A new, pejorative concept of a "Hollywood elite" began to emerge—a popular, mean-spirited notion that these sincere actors were in fact self-indulgent and silly. They didn't help themselves. Jane hung out with members of the violent Black Panther movement, posting their bail and letting them hold press conferences in her apartment.[71] It was what the writer Tom Wolfe dubbed radical chic, a movement that mixed society's highest with the fashionable plights of its lowest: wealthy, glamorous people throwing open their cocktail parties to Black Panthers, hippies, environmentalists, Mexican farmers, urban terrorists. It was conspicuous in its compassion. Revolutionary politics became ornamentation; another good talking point at a champagne reception.[72]

Radical chic did not mark the beginning of a new social order. On the contrary, it made liberalism even more unelectable than before. George McGovern won the Democratic nomination thanks to Beatty and his friends, but he went down in a humiliating 2 to 1 defeat in the general election against Richard Nixon. It didn't help that he was called the candidate of amnesty, abortion, and acid (a label that was—we now know—invented by McGovern's own running mate).[73] The badge wasn't accurate. Although McGovern did want a blanket pardon for Vietnam draft resisters, deserters would be treated on a case-by-case basis. He backed reduced penalties for marijuana possession but never legalization. And he thought abortion was morally wrong; Shirley MacLaine helped him defeat a motion at the Democratic convention to abolish state laws against it. McGovern was, arguably, a conservative in spirit: He wanted an end to intervention overseas and a return to the limited government of the early republic. But his association with radical chic distorted the public's impression of him and allowed his opponent to play the politics of the culture war. He might have come to regret that Hollywood fund-raiser in Inglewood.[74]

Within their own bubble, the Hollywood liberals seemed hip—but what Middle America really regarded as cool in 1972 were the squares that lived ordinary lives with the barest minimum of pizzazz: Okies from Muskogee. "Idealism, Old Hollywood-Camelot style," ran one *New York Times* analysis of the election results, "doesn't have the charisma it once had. George McGovern made what he clearly thought was the most idealistic (and charismatic) of appeals when he emphasized his special concern for the problems of Chicanos, minorities groups, and anti-establishment youth." But the average voter isn't a Chicano, a minority, or an anti-establishment youth, so he or she gravitated toward the middle-of-the-road, reassuring politics of Richard Nixon. "No, charisma just isn't what it used to be in the Old Hollywood-Camelot days. And only our conservatives were alert enough to change and to profit by it."[75]

The liberal stars were depressed by McGovern's defeat. Shirley MacLaine said that she

> took a trip across America by car. I'd seen lots of other countries, but that was the first time I'd really seen America. What I saw was a lot of disillusionment, mistrust and despair. I got back to Los Angeles, looked at myself in the mirror and saw the same thing. I'd gained 30 pounds, let my hair go and looked awful.

Shirley's mood got blacker until "I decided to do something about it. The first thing I did was to go to China." Visiting the communist dictatorship seemed to cheer her up a bit, but she still returned to find a paucity of parts for women in Hollywood. The irony was that the 1960s liberated actresses from one kind of typecasting only to straitjacket them in another:

> You should see the scripts I get. Ninety percent of them have notes that say, "The best hooker you'll ever play." . . . Recently I got a script about a forty-two-year-old woman trying to get out of her marriage. I got three bad scripts on Victoria Woodhull, the early woman's rights advocate. I got a script on Karen Silkwood, the girl who tried to blow the whistle on contamination in nuclear plants. . . . Oh yes, and I got a script on a woman who has an affair with her son. He kills and eats her. I thought that could make a musical comedy.[76]

Shirley should've made the Karen Silkwood movie. Meryl Streep did, in 1983, and it received five Academy Award nominations.

Friends of Fidel

Stars can give a politician money and attention and even become a key part of their campaign. Some of them do a good job of playing the activist, and can be prepared to surrender their careers to help change the world. But associating with celebrities also can do a politician more harm than good, making them appear elite, out of touch, even dangerously radical.

Perhaps if McGovern had won in 1972, the stars would've been vindicated. Perhaps if they had backed a less radical candidate, they might have seemed smarter and more sensitive to the public mood. But Hollywood liberals often demand a degree of left-wing purity that puts them on the side of politicians who are not to the taste of ordinary voters.

What started in the 1960s continues today. I spoke with the writer and director Michael Laughlin, who is responsible for fabulous sci-fi B-movies such as *Strange Behavior* (1981); he was socially active back then and offered this pithy observation:

> With actors, the reality is within themselves. They think that whatever idea they've had on the freeway is the best in the world . . . and the attention that politicians pay to them just encourages the arrogance. . . . The attitude is "I care, I understand. I know how to save the world." And they really believe they do, you know.[77]

I'll close with a distasteful example of what Michael means.

Shirley MacLaine was impressed by her trip to Red China, then at the tail end of a bloodthirsty cultural revolution that took millions of lives. "People related to each other in a way I had never seen before," she wrote. Shirley put this down to "self-criticism," the Maoist obsession with publicly confessing to bourgeois thoughts and behavior. Maybe it reminded MacLaine, fondly, of a method acting class. "Perhaps honest group communication reduced the need for individualistic artistic expression in the New Society," she suggested. That contrasted nicely with America's "climate of anger, violence, crime, and corruption . . . and her free-wheeling abuse of freedom. China makes you believe that everything is possible."[78]

A Chinese dissident might've pointed out to MacLaine that the self-criticism was actually a tool of terror, or that the Red state practiced its own kind of violence—albeit a socialist one with a lot of operas about collective farming. Given how innocent she could be, it wasn't long before Shirley was invited to Cuba for an audience with Fidel Castro—something she jumped at the opportunity to do.

Alas, she wasn't the last celebrity to make this ill-planned trek to Havana.[79] The Communist authorities appreciated the propaganda value of celebrity and, through middle men in Los Angeles, reached out to stars to offer them tours of the island, and even one-on-ones with Big Brother himself.

- In 1998, Jack Nicholson met with Fidel and reported, "Fidel Castro is a genius. We spoke about everything. Castro is a humanist like President Clinton. Cuba is simply a paradise!"
- Chevy Chase: "Socialism works. I think Cuba might prove that."
- Harry Belafonte: "If you believe in freedom, if you believe in justice, if you believe in democracy, you have no choice but to support Fidel Castro."
- On meeting Castro, Naomi Campbell described it as "a dream come true."[80]
- In 2013, Jay-Z and Beyoncé celebrated their fifth wedding anniversary in Havana.

Another big fan of Fidel's is Danny Glover, the costar of *Lethal Weapon* and a committed socialist. He also met Venezuela's deceased president Hugo Chávez, campaigned for John Edwards, and got arrested for protesting outside the Sudanese embassy in Washington. Glover has been at the center of a long-running campaign to free Gerardo Hernández, one of five men convicted of spying on the United States on behalf of Cuba. Since 2010, Glover has visited Victorville prison in California to spend time with him, out of solidarity. It's quite a schlep—a long car ride from the nearest airport, followed by endless security searches. And what do they talk about once they meet? Heaven knows, but if Hernandez offers Glover an invite to Cuba, then he would be wise to turn it down.[81]

How does the Communist regime treat its guests? Very well, by most accounts, if you don't mind being videotaped having sex. In 2005, Cuban intelligence defector Delfin Fernandez told a Madrid TV show that his former job was to try to get as much dirt on the celebrity guests as possible. "Most people have no idea they are being watched while they are in Cuba," he said. "But their personal activities are filmed under orders from Castro himself. Child sex, drug use, orgies, those are the sort of things they want to tape, anything—shall we say—'ethically incorrect.'" Sometimes this is followed by a blackmail effort. It doesn't always work. When the Cuban agents confronted Spanish director Pedro Almodóvar with proof of his homosexuality, he just laughed. "Everybody already knows I'm gay!" he said. "So go right ahead! Knock yourselves out!"[82]

Nothing sums up Hollywood politics' peculiar mix of good intentions and bad decisions than the love that some stars have shown Castro. It is even more extraordinary when moviemakers look at a totalitarian dictator and see an equal. "Fidel, I love you," Francis Ford Coppola reportedly said in a letter he wrote to Castro to ask if he might film *Apocalypse Now* in his country. "We both have the same initials. We both have beards. We both have power and want to use it for good purposes." Fidel and Francis: two red peas in a pod.[83]

4

THE SOCIAL NETWORK

How Politics Helps to Make Movies

It was Bob Dowling, a former editor of *The Hollywood Reporter*, who taught me about the airport trick—an old ruse for ambitious young people to pitch their ideas to the rich and famous. Bob: "You go to the airport and see if there are any limos waiting to collect someone. If there is, then it means someone important is coming in on the next plane. So you go to the gate, see them arrive, go to the exit and then . . . accidentally walk into them. And you say, 'Hi, remember me? We met at Whatever's party.'" The big shot probably understands that you were waiting there all day on the off chance of meeting them, but the Hollywood etiquette is to not walk away but to respect the effort and indulge the stalker in conversation. "At some point, they'll say, 'What are you working on?' And there's your chance to pitch." Nine times out of ten the conversation leads to nothing. But occasionally it pays off—and when it does, that can mean the difference between waiting tables and eating caviar.

The airport trick is an example of the kind of desperation and cunning that it takes to make it in Hollywood. It's also an example of how networking lies at the heart of the movie industry—and political activism is another way in which people get to mingle and swap business cards. The last two chapters have dealt largely with how Hollywood has changed politics; now we're going to consider how politics has changed Hollywood, by creating new networks of influence. Washington has invented new ways for wannabe moviemakers to get ahead.

They say that in the movies "it's as much about who you know as what you know." That might be a cliché, but like a lot of clichés, it happens to be true. Imagine you're a scriptwriter. Only half the work is done when you've finished writing the screenplay for your zombie teen romance (don't sneer—this movie has actually been made and is called *Warm Bodies*). Now you have to print it off, go out into the bright LA sunshine, and sell it to someone. You could start by pushing it through agents to studios, but that presumes: a) you have an agent, and b) he/she is actually any good. Lacking either of those, you're going to have to generate a buzz all by yourself.

Luckily, Hollywood is an industry that's open to new ideas. One of Hollywood's rules of etiquette is that everyone has a right to pitch and everyone has a responsibility to listen. You can't pitch too aggressively, as a hard sell is considered bad manners. No, you have to slip it discreetly into the conversation—a conversation that should occur casually, as if the meeting was pure accident. The usual settings are a chance encounter in a restaurant, or while waiting in line or even sitting in adjacent cars during a traffic jam. As Bob Dowling described it, first there's the casual introduction and then—always—there's the obligatory, "What are you working on?" "The scriptwriter has to introduce themselves ('Hi, you might not remember me but we met at . . .') and then there's a small conversation about how everyone is ('I'm fine, how are you?'). And then, when the small talk is over, the bigger guy asks, 'So what are you working on?'—and that's your chance to pitch the script."

So why do the big shots engage the little people in this obviously contrived conversation? First, because everybody starts at the bottom in Hollywood, so everybody remembers how it once felt to be desperate for an audience. Second, it's because the big shot can never discount the possibility that the guy who pesters them at the airport is indeed sitting on a script worth millions. Nobody can afford to not hear a pitch, just in case it's any good.

How does politics feed into all of this? Bob Dowling put it to me this way. Imagine you've been invited to a fund-raiser for a politician. The room is laid out in order of how much you paid; Bill Clinton is at the front, Steven Spielberg is at the closest table for, say, $25,000. Then sitting at the $15,000 table are the big-money producers. Behind them at the $2,500 table are the big agents. At the $1,000 table are the little agents. And at the back you can buy your way in for just $100 and sit at the table near the door.

Now, if you're a budding screenwriter, you can leave your table and go up to the little agents' table and say, "I've got a script to pitch." They like it, and then they leave and go up to the big agents' table and pass it on. The big agent then goes up to the producer table, and then the producer might take it to Spielberg. In other words, all you have to do to get access to a big shot director like Spielberg is to be a Democrat for a day, and all for the small price of $100.[1]

This is one more reason why there are so many Democrats in Hollywood. Of course, there are Republican events in Los Angeles—but the regular GOP get-together is just once a month in a small bar, and the serious fund-raisers are strictly invite-only. Hollywood is a Democrat town, so it can pay off big time to be a card-carrying liberal.

Politics as a networking tool finds its origins in the 1980s, when Hollywood political activism professionalized and started to ape the corporate management style that was taking over the movie industry. Of course, many liberal activists in Los Angeles are motivated by idealism. But in a business in which fantasy and money are intrinsically linked you can change the world and advance your career all at the same time.

How the Networks Emerged

To understand how Hollywood's political networks came into being, we first have to understand how its business model has changed over the years. In the late sixties the studios were in serious trouble. Television was eating into its audience share and profits were tumbling. The studios needed someone to ride into town and save them from bankruptcy. Wall Street obliged, buying up some Hollywood stocks and rolling them into complex portfolios that included funeral parlors, mines, parking lots, and holiday resorts. The new investors were less interested in high art than in making a fast buck. They tended to side with the so-called suits who manned the distribution wing of Hollywood against the artists and moguls who ran production. The suits sold off acres of studio lots, turning them into real estate or theme parks and generating enough income to keep things going through the bad times. Meanwhile, they diversified their interests into other media: television, radio, magazines, toys, books. By the end of the 1980s, mergers had allied former rivals in a bid to build new entertainment monopolies: Time/Warner, Viacom/Paramount, Sony/Columbia, Disney/ABC, etc. It wasn't long before the Japanese moved in and significant parts of the U.S. media became global concerns.[2]

Big money saved the movies, but it had a hidden cost. As Sharon Waxman writes:

> Gone were the moguls of old, those self-made, self-styled tyrants and visionaries who made films that suited their image of themselves, their families, and the country as a whole. . . . By the mid-to-late 1980s the studios were becoming more like other corporations, run by men in suits with master's degrees in business from Harvard and other fancy universities. They tended to regard movies as products; they scrutinized the balance sheets for profit margins. What those bosses sought most of all were reliable profits and growth. . . . This meant sticking to tried-and-true plot formulas, using market research companies to "predict" profits and weekend box office, hiring movie stars with proven track records, and, as much as possible, appealing to the mass audience by avoiding controversial topics.[3]

Actually, the moguls of the 1930s and 1940s also kept an eye on profits and were reluctant to make political movies that would alienate viewers—hence the dearth of anti-Nazi films before 1938. What the corporate takeovers really did was to kill off the brief, beautiful radical buzz of the 1960s and 1970s, which gave us *The Godfather*, *Easy Rider*, and *Bonnie and Clyde*. Of course, bold and innovative filmmaking would continue, but it became the exception rather than the artistic norm. Money flowed toward the unthreatening, the ubiquitous, the conformist. Anything with a message was treated as either a risk that should be avoided or an "issues" movie designed to win awards rather than make money, such as the first film to deal with AIDS, feature a lesbian in a lead role, or to have a cast made up entirely of African-Americans. (And even the endorsement of the big-name producers and directors couldn't guarantee that proper attention would be paid. It took George Lucas twenty years to get the World War II actioner *Red Tails* made—he claims because it featured an all-black cast.)[4]

What every studio now wanted was a blockbuster to justify the Wall Street investment. Steven Spielberg gave Universal their golden ticket in the summer of 1975 with a movie about a psychopathic fish. *Jaws* was no *Citizen Kane*. It had a number of jump-out-of-the-seat moments, a scary score, and a star who wouldn't swim off set in a tantrum—but it was really an old-fashioned B-movie pic. What elevated it above the rest of the lazy summer fare was a TV advertising campaign that spread the word and helped keep the movie at number one for fourteen straight weeks. *Jaws* was the first film ever to gross over $100 million, and it signaled to the suits that television was no longer cinema's enemy but its friend: Advertising the hell out of one movie could make up for an entire summer of flops.[5]

Another wondrous hit was *Star Wars* (1977). Director George Lucas initially had doubts about his film. He feared that the colorful aliens and two-dimensional plot would only appeal to children: "I've made a Walt Disney movie," he moaned. "It's gonna do maybe eight, ten million." When he showed his first rough cut, only Steven Spielberg and a *Time* critic liked it; Fox was unimpressed. Nevertheless, Lucas was both artistically and commercially savvy. Not only would his movie go on to make something on the order of $460 million, but he had declined a higher fee in exchange for rights over sequels, TV, and merchandizing. He set himself up for life.[6]

Lucas and Spielberg were making movies for families, particularly for kids. Merchandizing meant selling themed lunch boxes, costumes, beach towels, and action figures. Plots could be politely called mythic (man versus fish, rebels versus empire) but were really just simplistic. The celebrated critic Pauline Kael was unimpressed by *Star Wars*:

It's enjoyable on its own terms, but it's exhausting, too: like taking a pack of kids to the circus. An hour into it, children say that they're ready to see it again; that's because it's an assemblage of spare parts—it has no emotional grip. *Star Wars* may be the only movie in which the first time around the surprises are reassuring. . . . It's an epic without a dream. But it's probably the absence of wonder that accounts for the film's special, huge success. The excitement of those who call it the film of the year goes way past nostalgia to the feeling that now is the time to return to childhood.[7]

Kael was right. After the moral uncertainty of the 1960s and 1970s—the wars, the revolutions, the assassinations, the parade of coffins—people wanted fun. They wanted to become kids again. The future would bring *Superman* (1978), *Raiders of the Lost Ark* (1981), and *ET the Extra-Terrestrial* (1982).

The target audience of Hollywood got younger as the movies got dumber (and vice versa). The audience is always a moving target, switching age groups and genres depending on cultural tastes at any given moment (there is, today, a revival in movies aimed at the middle-aged). But when *Star Wars* was released, 62 percent of the film audience was aged between sixteen and twenty-nine. Between 1977 and 1979 the number of tickets sold to twelve- to twenty-year-olds increased by 8 percent, while the number sold to twenty-one to thirty-nine-year-olds decreased by the same number. The suits, who were fast becoming the people who called the shots in the studios, came to see the teenage market as the path to a blockbuster. This is part of the reason why recent summers have been dominated by either romance for girls (*Twilight*) or shoot-'em-ups for boys (*Transformers*).[8]

If the 1980s movie industry became more corporate and risk-averse, Hollywood's politics trended in a similar direction. The stars began to consolidate their political activism into powerful individual brands. It might seem strange to outsiders that Hollywood people should regard their charitable or political fund-raising as something in need of branding, but for those in the industry it was the norm. In their day-to-day lives stars are surrounded by staff who take care of every part of their existence: the agent for business; the personal assistant for the diary; the chauffeur for driving; the guru for chakra maintenance. It was entirely logical that moviemakers would hire activists to take care of their politics, too—their very own Ralph Naders.

Barbra Streisand set the trend when she hired Marge Tabankin. Tabankin had been a student at the radical Saul Alinsky's Industrial Areas Foundation in Chicago, Illinois, worked as the head of VISTA (the domestic wing of the Peace Corps, which does antipoverty work within the United States), traveled with Jane Fonda to North Vietnam, served as executive director of the Arca Foundation for civil rights, and was the first female president of the National Students Association. In the 1980s she landed the role of running the Streisand Foundation, which essentially meant that she handled fund-raising for Barbra, and the distribution of her contributions and endorsements.[9]

Barbra had bought herself one of the most skilled political networkers in the country. Today, the price of her consultancy, Tabankin told *The Atlantic*, is about 10 to 15 percent per payout. That price tends to "hit a ceiling" of around $100,000 per client, and she puts the average Hollywood consultant's annual salary at about $250,000.[10]

One of Tabankin's achievements was to put together the Hollywood Women's Political Committee, which spent the 1980s running workshops, seminars, and training events for wannabe activists—as well as collecting and doling out funds to various chosen political projects. Members included Streisand, Jane Fonda, Cybill Shepherd, and Glenn Close.[11] There was an unspoken understanding that an invite to an HWPC event meant getting access to women who could help you get ahead.[12] One of its earliest members, Barbara Corday (a TV executive who helped create *Cagney & Lacey*), told a journalist:

> Virtually all the members are in the entertainment business, but it's political: we support candidates and do other political work. It's not an organization set up to network for women, but clearly since you're in it with other women who are in the same business, there is a certain amount of networking. Friendships develop.

As we shall see, the most important friendship was with the Clintons.[13]

By the early 1990s Barbra's friend Marge wasn't the only professional activist in Hollywood. The former Democratic Party operative Andy Spahn handled political affairs at Dreamworks for the powerful trio of Steven Spielberg, Jeffrey Katzenberg, and David Geffen; he fielded three thousand requests a year for political support from Geffen alone. As a gatekeeper, Spahn reduced the trio's workload but—inevitably—also accrued enormous power for himself.[14] Likewise, Bill Clinton's former entertainment industry contact Donna Bojarsky coordinated the political work of Richard Dreyfuss. Interestingly, Dreyfuss told *Los Angeles Magazine* that Bojarsky's role was partly to "[introduce] me to certain things" but also to help him say no to things, too. Remember that in Hollywood no one likes to be heard saying no to anything: Tabankin, Spahn, and Bojarsky were the people who dealt in negatives so that the moviemakers didn't have to.[15]

These were the days before the McCain-Feingold campaign finance reform bill of 2002, which put limits on donations and eliminated soft money. In the 1990s, Hollywood's contributions zoomed upward in parallel with its movie budgets—the Wall Street mentality reached all quarters. Haim Sabam, the Mighty Morphin Power Rangers entrepreneur, gave more than $7 million to pay for the construction of a new Democratic Party headquarters in Washington, D.C., and gave $10 million to the Democrats in the 2002 election cycle. In that same cycle the producer Steve Bing shelled out an estimated $8.7 million. Renowned and valued as a man who signs checks to politicians without seeking glory in return, Bing has, however, had his fair share of PR difficulties. He had a much-reported dispute with the actress Elizabeth Hurley over the paternity of a child that did not turn out to be his. He also sued the billionaire Kirk Kerkorian after Kerkorian got an employee to take some used dental floss from Bing's garbage to prove that he was the father of Kerkorian's ex-wife's daughter.[16]

It didn't take long for the most corporate wing of the industry to join in with the new spirit of coordinated giving. Creative Artists Agency and United Talent Agency built a whole new department to match stars with appropriate causes, which were chosen according to how the actor's image matched the particular issue. Other agencies retained third-party firms such as the Global Philanthropy Group, which offered "comprehensive philanthropic management." Slowly but surely, Hollywood activism started to match the carefully coordinated, brand-orientated culture of the studios' new management.[17]

Recall Bob Dowling's description of how a fund-raiser works as a networking opportunity, how it can help a scriptwriter reach Steven Spielberg. Such events, held almost exclusively by Democrats, became more and more common throughout the eighties and nineties. "This is the way society works in L.A.," a Hollywood executive told Bernard Weinraub of *The New York Times* in 1991. "It's like a mating ritual. People have to come up with new and different ways to make money. In a given week I get 15 invitations to events, which I don't even open. You have to find new ways of getting people's attention." Weinraub was investigating the invention of a tasteless new institution, the Hollywood Hunger Banquet. The idea was that celebrities and industry insiders meet, draw lots, and then dine in ways that reflect the unequal distribution of the world's resources. The caterer explained:

> About 75 people will be served by waiters, have a three-course meal, stuffed breast of chicken, sun-dried tomatoes and radicchio, salad with shrimp, and a wonderful dessert and wine, all these guests sitting on nice chairs with cloth napkins and linen and crystal. The middle percentage will sit on benches at wooden tables; they'll have paper plates with rice and beans and tortillas. And then the rest, the majority, will sit on the floor on a mat and have rice and water, no silverware, and that's it. Just like the majority of people in the world.

A nice idea in principle, but it looked a little silly when the guests arrived in limousines. More absurd was the fighting that went on to get a ticket to it. With that many stars going it became a competition to get a seat—even if it was just a seat on a mat with some rice and water.[18]

And so the networks of influence grew and grew. Attending a fund-raiser for Bill Clinton could now get you an agent, a director, or a star for your movie. And, happily, Bill Clinton threw a lot of fund-raisers.

The Clinton Craze

It's impossible to overstate Bill Clinton's impact on Hollywood politics. During the 1988 Bush versus Dukakis race it had been the Republicans who did the best job of using light entertainment to sell their candidate. They were running George H. W. Bush, a wealthy vice president with few connections to the common man. To humanize him, his campaign director, Lee Atwater, made sure he was seen as often as possible with country-and-western singers— Chet Atkins, Loretta Lynn, and Crystal Gale—and übermacho stars such as Chuck Norris and Arnold Schwarzenegger. The plaid shirts and bulging muscles helped Bush win the hearts of blue-collar voters. Meanwhile, Democratic candidate Mike Dukakis was rolling in contributions from the Hollywood Women's Political Committee and various other moviemaker donors, but he failed to exploit their endorsements on the campaign trail. Nirvana manager Danny Goldberg offered to set Dukakis up with a Nashville country-and-western gala, but the Democrats—to his shock—said no. Goldberg:

> I think the people around Michael Dukakis . . . are not listening to talk radio, are not watching prime-time television, are not going to see the top movies, and someone around [Bush] is. Democrats had 90 percent of the [celebrity] fish this year and [the Republicans] did better with 10 percent.[19]

Bill Clinton never made that mistake; Clinton was Hollywood through and through. He had a great story (the boy from Hope), looked good, was charming, had the right liberal views, and—crucially—enjoyed a party. While Dukakis had reportedly loathed flying out to Los Angeles to be lectured by celebrities about things they claimed he didn't understand, Clinton basked in the company of passionate, beautiful people. In return for big bucks donations he gave them a patient ear and a warm smile. He was perfectly in tune with Hollywood etiquette, with that dislike of saying no.

Bill also came along at just the right moment. By 1992 the Republicans had controlled the White House for twelve years, and Democrats were hungry for a win. The moviemakers were particularly keen to kick the social conservatives out of power. At the 1992 Republican convention, speaker after speaker tore into Hollywood values. Pat Buchanan spoke of a "cultural war" for the heart and soul of America. Vice presidential candidate Dan Quayle had recently blamed a sitcom, *Murphy Brown*, for riots in Los Angeles—and his wife told the convention audience, "Not everyone joined the counterculture. Not everyone demonstrated, dropped out, took drugs, joined in the sexual revolution or dodged the draft." The Republicans were attacking everything the moviemakers held dear.[20]

The economic circumstances were also right for a rally behind Bill Clinton. The entire country was feeling the pinch of recession, while in Hollywood the creeping corporatization of the industry was fostering anxiety among both talent and production. Howard Rosenman, a producer, told *The New York Times*:

> Politics is going to be more intense now than ever before in the history of Hollywood. The motion picture industry is in chaos and turbulent. The inability of studio heads to guess what's viable and salable is creating a tremendous insecurity, which relates to the economy. A lot of people with cushy $200,000-a-year jobs will be out of work. People are scared. They're freaking out. And people are coming to their bottom line. And, somehow, it's manifesting itself in support of their political beliefs, whatever they are.[21]

So the moviemakers contacted their political agents and told them to "buy, buy, buy" shares in the Clinton campaign. And this, in turn, fueled the microeconomy of fund-raising events—where folks could network and pitch to each other. The pitching went on all the way to the Democratic convention in New York, where stars, producers, directors, and writers came not only to cheer on the future prez but also to catch a chance encounter with Michael J. Fox, Warren Beatty, Paul Newman, or Laura Dern. From a *New York Times* piece on the rise of Hollywood fund-raisers:

> Each of the week's gatherings offered a shimmy up the political power tree, an opportunity to exchange private telephone numbers, political agendas, and sidelong glances. Invitations indicated whether a party offered a real opportunity for political, social or financial climbing—or merely a palliative for sociopolitical ambition. And the "honored guests" that invitations invoked were used like patron saints or graven images. They represented what a particular group wanted to be, or wanted to be close to.
>
> "Warren and Annette are coming!" was the siren from the week's hottest society tickets. It beckoned the bold-faced, bi-coastal set, those who apologize for their multimillion-dollar real-estate, book and movie deals by their social activism.

> Hollywood activism at its zenith was like a party at Gatsby's place: champagne, beautiful people, power, money. It was possible to spend a vast amount of cash advancing the career of a presidential candidate and a "close personal friend" and have a ball.

> There were moments when the unflappably optimistic rah-rah that is now de rigueur among Democrats at play gave way to real spirit and hope. It happened when Senator Bob Kerrey of Nebraska forgot the world and danced the night away at [East Side nightclub] Live Psychic on Tuesday night. And throughout the week, full-throttle celebration erupted whenever Texas's Governor, Ann W. Richards, partied.

> There was only one person Ann never got to meet, and that was Warren Beatty. "I kept hearing he would be at this party and that, but

I never did see the guy," she complained. And it was exactly that kind of celebrity chasing that would get her beaten by George W. Bush in the 1994 Texas governor's race—when his supporters called her "an East Hollywood Democrat." Ann should've taken note of the lesson from chapter 3: A Hollywood endorsement can be a poisoned chalice.[22]

Clinton Disappoints

Clinton won the 1992 general election by a landslide, and during his first year in office, his administration offered a genuine synergy between Hollywood and Washington. It wasn't just that George Stephanopoulos, the White House communications director, was dating *Dirty Dancing* star Jennifer Grey—or that actors like Michael Douglas began showing up for star turns at the White House Correspondents' Association dinner (so many celebrities visited the West Wing that presidential adviser Paul Begala is supposed to have kept a camcorder in his desk to capture them). No, it genuinely was the case that moviemakers moved from being campaign props to consultants, image shapers, and even policy wonks. Harry Thomason and Linda Bloodworth-Thomason, sitcom czars and creators of the show *Designing Women*, choreographed the inauguration. *Night Court* star Markie Post served as a White House health care adviser.[23] Marge Tabankin told journalists that her clients were helping to plan PR for forthcoming White House initiatives. Barbra Streisand got to enjoy a night as a guest in the White House. And access to the president gave Barbra a little bump in her public profile. "Sleek, chic and so powerful amongst the Hollywood elite, she can tell film moguls: Don't call me, I'll call you," wrote the British *Sun* newspaper in breathless admiration. "Even President Bill Clinton is under her spell."[24] The White House was the new center of

Hollywood's social universe, and there was a stampede to get there. Using a movie metaphor, Peter Guber, chairman of Sony Pictures Entertainment, explained, "The herding mentality is so strong here that when a script is hot, everyone goes after it, whether they've read it or not."[25]

It became a problem. The press called Bill Clinton Elvis, in part because his obsession with stardom was beginning to eclipse the image he'd carefully constructed as an ordinary Joe. At a fund-raising dinner in New York, the president found himself sitting next to an empty seat. Who should fill it? Bill scanned the room, spotted Sharon Stone, and invited her over—to raised eyebrows from all the other guests. Nobody could question Clinton's taste, but it was hardly appropriate behavior for the head of the First Family.

There was worse to come. In May 1993, Air Force One touched down at LAX and sat there for ninety minutes, hogging the runway and forcing ordinary passenger planes to circle the air above. Clinton wasn't in town on business; he was getting his hair cut by the Beverly Hills hairdresser Cristophe (his client list included Barbra Streisand, Goldie Hawn, Ted Danson, and Sally Field). Bill also invited Quincy Jones, the music producer, and Dawn Steel, the movie producer, to come aboard and take a tour of the plane. When the story broke, the press was outraged. Clinton was giving the impression of using the White House as an opportunity to meet people he'd always wanted to meet.[26] His groupie behavior encouraged journalists to treat the president like another celebrity ripe for gossip and ridicule. The editor of the muckraking *Enquirer* explained, "Clinton drew the magic dust of Hollywood, brushing up against Barbra Streisand, Kevin Costner, Ted Danson. He became more than president of the U.S. He became a personality and celebrity." All this unpresidential nonsense influenced the way that both the press and the public responded to the Lewinsky scandal.[27]

Some within the administration got an allergic reaction to all the stardust floating around. About the time of Hairgate the White House invited some Hollywood power brokers to the White House for a summit on Clinton's signature health care reform—including Tristar Pictures chief Mike Medavoy and MCA president Stanley Sheinberg. Halfway through the meeting, Clinton strategist James Carville lost his cool. Sick and tired of pandering to movie people, he shouted and swore and accused the assembled of being spoiled Richie Riches who had no idea what it meant to be middle-class and scrambling to get by on the minimum wage. *Family Ties* producer Gary David Goldberg threw down his notes and cried, "How dare you speak to us this way?!" After all, they had flown out on their own dollar just to offer their help to the administration. Carville was acting like "Anthony Perkins playing Fidel Castro on acid," Goldberg later said—displaying the common Hollywood habit of interpreting everything through movie metaphor.

Officially, the White House said that Carville was in trouble for his behavior. Unofficially, the press speculated that it was far from spontaneous. Pols like Carville sensed that the administration was alienating itself from ordinary folks by becoming too close to Hollywood; it was time to create some distance. But the prez himself just couldn't stay away for long. In December 1993, he showed up at the headquarters of the Creative Artists Agency for a fund-raiser, and Barbra Streisand sang, "Can't Help Lovin' That Man." He walked away with $250,000 in soft money donations.[28]

Actually, there were plenty of reasons for Hollywood not to love that man.

Everyone who meets Clinton attests to his wonderful gifts as a listener: He really seems to understand and care about what is being said to him. But that doesn't mean he necessarily delivers on everything he's promised, as Hollywood quickly discovered. The president failed to produce on his pledge of significant health care reform or to end discrimination against gays serving in the military, compromising with a bizarre policy nicknamed Don't Ask, Don't Tell that expected gays and lesbians effectively to lie to their comrades. His fudging didn't work: In 1994 the Republicans swept Congress and took control of the legislative agenda—in part because Clinton's low public approval harmed his party. For Hollywood types who were convinced that they knew how to craft a narrative and sell it to the public, Clinton's defeat was not inevitable but the consequence of his failure to listen to their advice. They convinced themselves that the Democrats were doing badly because the party was insufficiently liberal. Moviemakers worried that they'd poured money into a man who wasn't quite as brilliant or committed to the cause as they hoped.

The fate of the Hollywood Women's Political Caucus is a case in point. In 1995 they met with Clinton and urged him to veto the Republican Congress's proposals for welfare reform. He did. During the 1996 presidential election, they repaid him with an extraordinary fund-raising effort. They ran a gala in a high-class hotel for which the price of a ticket was a minimum of $2,500 per person, rising to $25,000 for a separate function with the president himself. The Democratic Party took in $4 million in one night. Much of the 1996 election season was like this: Clinton jetting westward to reconnect with his people. In September, Barbra Streisand sang for him again, and Maya Angelou read poetry, all at a Mediterranean-style estate overlooking Beverly Hills that had once been home to the silent-screen star Harold Lloyd. Tom Hanks spoke, the Eagles played. As always, business was done: The suits were out in force to remind the president of Hollywood's case on intellectual property issues. Clinton had cause to listen. That event got him $3.5 million—added to the $18 million Hollywood was estimated to have given him since 1992.[29] In November, Bill won reelection easily. So easily that he might have judged that he didn't really need the help of the movie business at all.

Shortly after the election, Clinton finally signed the welfare bill that Marge Tabankin, Barbra Streisand, and the HWPC thought was hard on the poor and had lobbied so earnestly for him to veto again. The HWPC had an existential crisis. Months later, it disbanded. "The welfare bill was the turning point," said Barbara Corday. Failure to stop it had forced these liberals to reassess why they were engaged in presidential-level politics at all. "Money had become the driving force, rather than politics," concluded Corday. "The richest people are getting to office, and we didn't want to be part of it." Here was an example of moviemakers displaying the quality they are too often accused of lacking: self-awareness and high principle.[30] Michael Medavoy, one of the people Carville shouted at in the White House, told me that his relationship with Clinton was essentially business: "There is a difference between 'close friends' and [genuinely] 'close friends.' I don't think Bill Clinton was my friend." Once they were done assisting each other's ambitions, the partnership was concluded.[31]

One person who was overcome with a very public political malaise even before Clinton became president was Warren Beatty. In 1991 he conducted a magazine interview with Norman Mailer in which Norman teased Warren about running for the presidency. The interview was not a chance encounter between two variants of hypermasculinity (a Beatty biographer said he had slept with 12,775 women; Mailer stabbed his own wife) but was timed by press agents to coincide with the release of a movie (Beatty) and a book (Mailer). Another case of the happy Hollywood collision of art, politics, and profit. Norman began his account of the interview—in the third person—by asking who was the more brilliant of the two of them. He concluded, "If it came down to who respected the other's mind a little more, Warren might hold the door for Norman." Nevertheless, Beatty still had some things to teach him about the state of liberalism. "The Democratic Party practically doesn't exist with its own set of principles now," he said, but is interested only in doing "junior-Republican silliness." What the left needed was a new leader, "someone who will come along and truly speak to the people, . . . a citizen willing to confront public opinion and enlighten it." A citizen like . . . Warren Beatty? Mailer pushed Warren to declare an interest in the presidency, but Beatty demurred.[32]

What he was prepared to do was make a movie laying out his ideas. By his own admission, Beatty got the film *Bulworth* made by stealth. Fox was committed to letting him make a $32 million picture as part of an agreement for withdrawing financial support from his earlier *Dick Tracy*—only the star didn't tell Fox that the movie he wanted to make was an anguished cry for a return to the liberal idealism of the 1960s. It stars Beatty as Senator Jay Bulworth, a Democrat who may once have been worth something to the world but was now just running on bull. In the opening scenes he sits weeping in his office, contemplating his various U-turns on welfare and crime—the office being studded with images of past glories: Jack Kennedy, Martin Luther King Jr., et cetera. Tearfully, he makes some calls and organizes a hit man to have himself rubbed out. Satisfied that his miserable life is now at an end, he goes on a prescription medicine binge and decides to spend his last moments on the campaign trail telling the truth.

What follows is outrageously funny. Bulworth visits a black church and is asked why he's done nothing to rebuild South Central after the Rodney King riots. Well, he says, it's because politicians promised the Earth and then, after the election, "we pretty much forgot about you." Another woman asks why he won't back a health insurance bill. Bulworth's answer: "Because you really haven't contributed any money to my campaign, have you?" Asked directly if Democratic politicians don't care about black people, he replies,

"Isn't that obvious? You've got half your kids out of work and the other half of them are in jail. Do you see any Democrat doing anything about it? Certainly not me! So what are you gonna do? Vote Republican?"

The movie's politics are bracing, even dangerous. Fantastical, too. Bulworth's truth telling starts to gain him new fans, and by the end of his campaign, he's the most popular man in America. Bulworth tries to call off the hit and succeeds—only to have a private health insurance dealer shoot him instead.[33]

Made in 1997, at the height of the Lewinsky affair, Beatty's movie gives us an alternative view of the 1990s. For many it was a golden age of economic stability. But for Hollywood's liberals it was a time of frustration and missed opportunity. Interestingly, some of Beatty's anger is aimed at the moviemakers—at the very networking culture that this chapter is all about. In another scene he visits Hollywood to raise some cash. (Why Hollywood? Because "[w]e got more money from these jokers than the Chinese.") Addressing a crowd in a beautiful Santa Monica mansion, he turns his thoughts to the quality of the moviemakers' output:

Ya know, the funny thing is how lousy most of your stuff is. Ya know, you make violent films, and you make dirty films, and you make, ya know, family films. But just most of them are not very good, are they? It's funny. So many smart people could work so hard on 'em, and spend all that money on 'em. . . . What do you think it is? It must be the money, huh? It must be the money. It just turns everything to crap. Ya know? But, Jesus Christ, how much money do you really need?

Jeremy Pikser, Beatty's scriptwriter, told me, "This was definitely Warren talking about the movie business. Oh yeah, this was him letting them know what he thinks about it—both the movies and the politics of it all."[34]

Those feelings are supported by others. I spoke with a director who attended a movie exec meeting with Joe Lieberman during the 2000 election. Lieberman had just launched a tirade against Hollywood violence, essentially blaming it for all of society's ills. The mood of the meeting before he arrived at the meeting was angry: They were determined to challenge him on his authoritarianism. But as soon as he walked in the room, the atmosphere changed. Lieberman didn't really want to talk about censorship and the execs were happy to be charmed into talking about other, lighter things. My source told me that "the discussion was suddenly birthdays, holidays, frivolities; Lieberman promised to come to everyone's bar mitzvah." What should've been a serious confrontation about ideas dissolved into empty chatter of the kind that could be heard in any cocktail party in Beverly Hills.[35]

Perhaps the alternative to this flakery was to run Jay Bulworth for president. In 1999, socialite Arianna Huffington wrote a column for the *Los Angeles Times* asking if it was time to "Put 'Bulworth' in the White House?" and she nominated Warren Beatty for the job. Beatty was intrigued and put together a circle of friends capable of running a national campaign. Of course, it was an absurd proposition—but there were enough egotists involved for a little while to give it legs. Norman Mailer wanted his buddy to run for something: "So I called Warren up and I said, Will you settle for vice president? And he answered, All right, all right, what do you want? Head of intelligence, I told him. You've got it, he said. How we laughed. Ah, if only Warren Beatty had been president."[36] But Beatty never came through. The reason might well be what is generally recognized by Hollywood folk as a flaw in his life outside movies: "He's so fucking lazy," Pikser told me.

Living with Bill

Bulworth set the tone for a reaction against the ideas-lite networking aspect of Hollywood politics and a renaissance of serious, soul-searching liberalism in its place. On the artistic front it would find expression in *The West Wing*. Politically, it would be articulated in the presidential campaigns of Howard Dean and Barack Obama. But until Clinton left office, Hollywood activism conformed to a depressing logic: Bill had the keys to the White House, so if you want to get a night in the Lincoln bedroom you're going to have to be nice to him. The only alternatives were the Puritan Republicans. So, for a few more years, the Clinton party rolled on.

The Lewinsky scandal helped revive the link between Hollywood and the White House. It may have damaged Clinton's reputation in the rest of the country that he had sexual relations with an intern, lied to his family, and was accused of perjuring himself about it, but Hollywood could sympathize. "The scandal is really a referendum on sexual morality in the country," said Marshall Herskovitz, a Democrat and the producer of *Thirtysomething*. "Those people whose sexual morality accepts the possibility of complexity and ambivalence in a marital relationship have not judged Clinton as badly as those who see marriage as a monolithic, simple entity. And in Hollywood, marriage is often not seen as a monolithic simple entity." The producer Sean Daniel was blunter: "Hollywood has seen worse. When it comes to private matters, Hollywood has made its peace with far more scandalous behavior. And there's an understanding here that you can have a messed-up private life and still do good work." With regret, Charlton Heston agreed: "Hollywood is a fairly active town sexually. The community has been overwhelmingly left-liberal for a long time. They'd be disinclined to turn away from Clinton or take this sex issue very seriously."

Clinton flew out to Los Angeles in the middle of the scandal and retreated into the beautiful people and their money. He attended a fund-raiser at the house of Haim Saban in September 1998. Madonna dropped by; the Democratic Party netted $1.5 million. The fun continued, the network prospered.[37]

And that brings us up to the Hollywood Gala Salute to President William Jefferson Clinton—an event that epitomized the relationship between Hollywood and Washington, D.C. The stars that Peter Paul and Aaron Tonken gathered to say good-bye to Bill and Hillary were drawn by a combination of everything discussed in these last three chapters: to raise money for a politician; to advance their liberal ideas; and to network among the powerful. That two admitted fraudsters could run such a high-profile event in celebration of the president of the United States is perhaps the most damning indictment that could ever be produced of the negative effects of the synergy of Washington and Hollywood. It also feels like an appropriate ending for the Clinton years, which gave the United States comfort and entertainment but also charges of corruption and an aimless drift from principle to moral compromise. Critical questions about the country's future went unaddressed.

As for Hollywood's political network, much of it continues along those same lines of empty partying today. The former Green Party presidential nominee Ralph Nader calls it "a kind of luminous decadence." He took his antinuclear environmental crusade to Hollywood and was unimpressed with what he found:

> Most of it's hot air, how aggressive Hollywood people act when it comes to politics. But I found that you go out there and it's nearly impossible even to raise any money. I think they'd rather you raised money for them. If they don't see any quid pro quo in a campaign—you know, like getting to meet a president or a senator—then they're not really interested.

They put on a good show—lots of great food and drink—but it leads nowhere. I thought it was funny. . . . I knew I was being entertained.

As for their famed courage and radicalism, Ralph said:

Try asking them to make a movie about Yasser Arafat. See how far you get.[38]

Nader makes a point that I've often heard expressed by Hollywood liberals: The corporatization of the studios has left them politically timid. Paul Haggis, the director of the antiwar movie *In the Valley of Elah* (2007) about a father's search for the killers of a son who died in Iraq, told me all about its troubled production:

So we had interest from Warner at first because Clint Eastwood was interested in it, and he really championed it. But then he dropped out, and they lost interest. . . . I think there was some nervousness about doing an antiwar movie, because it's obviously a controversial thing. . . . But we got Tommy Jones onboard, and so we were able to attract more money, and the movie got made. But even when you've done that, you've still got to find a distributor.

And at that point, Haggis sensed that he ran into political opposition.

If you believe in something more, then you promote it more. And the distributors, I think, didn't believe in this antiwar movie. So the promotion wasn't great, and the movie didn't do as well as it should. . . . You see, as the studios were acquired by corporations, and they became corporations themselves . . .

decisions became corporate, and so their decisions were right-wing.[39]

Haggis infers a conscious bias against *In the Valley of Elah*, but it is also possible that the studio judged that there wasn't an audience for it—after all, the antiwar movies of the noughties tended to do badly at the box office.[40] Hollywood is indeed corporate, so its motivator in all business decisions is money. Sometimes the outcome is conservative. Sometimes the decisions they make are liberal—it all depends on what kind of movie they think will make the most money. One scriptwriter told me that he was asked to write a romance about a soldier fighting in Iraq who comes home and falls in love with a girl. A committed liberal, he decided to make the girl an antiwar protester who wins her brute of a lover around with logic and compassion—in the last ten minutes he quits the army to marry her. The writer submitted his script and the studio turned it down. He demanded a meeting and stormed in, all guns blazing. "I guess this studio's too right-wing to make a movie about what's really happening in Iraq?" he said.

"Not at all," the suits replied. "We turned down your script because we've already got an antiwar movie in production. What we're really looking for at the moment is a prowar movie. If you want to write that, we'd be happy to consider it."[41]

It's an anecdote that communicates perfectly Hollywood's obsession with the bottom line. No wonder that the small nucleus of genuine, committed liberals who lived in Los Angeles in the 1990s and early 2000s found themselves so repelled by their own industry. Luckily for them there was first George W. Bush's war in Iraq to oppose and then Barack Obama to fight the good fight for.

5

THE WEST WING

How Hollywood Created a New Kind of Liberal Hero

Here's a story of art imitating life, and then life imitating art back again.

In 2004, the producers of the TV show *The West Wing* decided that it was time for President Jed Bartlet to retire. Bartlet, played by real-life liberal Martin Sheen, had served as fictional president of the show's alternative universe for eight years—a white, Catholic, liberal Democrat who governed the country with a mix of professorial wit and homespun wisdom. When choosing who would be the next Democratic presidential nominee, scriptwriter Eli Attie decided to mix things up a bit. Attie was tired of seeing the same kinds of men from the same kinds of backgrounds serve in the White House, be it in reality or on TV. So he chose to run Matthew Santos, a liberal Latino played by Jimmy Smits, as an underdog in *The West Wing*'s Democratic primaries. Attie wanted to make him, in the writer's own words, a "post-Oprah" candidate—someone who was neither white nor obsessed with race. It was a fascinating televisual experiment.

Attie was a consummate Washington insider who once worked as a special assistant to Bill Clinton and chief speechwriter to Al Gore. But he didn't even know how to begin to write the character of Matthew Santos, because no one like this had ever run before. "Faced with the task of fleshing out a historical first-ever and actually viable Latino candidate," he said, "I had no precedent, no way to research a real-life version." Looking around for someone who at least approximated to Santos, Attie stumbled upon a young Illinois politician—not even yet a senator—called Barack Obama. Years later Attie recalled, "When I had to write, Obama was just appearing on the national scene. He had done a great speech at the [2004] convention, and people were beginning to talk about him." So he put a call through to Obama's aide, David Axelrod, and said, "Tell me about this guy." Attie wanted to know how he dealt with the issue of color, and Axelrod's answers informed his writing: "Some of Santos's insistence on not being defined by his race, his pride in it even as he rises above it, came from that." They also talked about how Obama became an overnight political superstar. "After that convention speech," said Attie, "Obama's life changed. He was mobbed wherever he went. He was more than a candidate seeking votes: people were seeking him. Some of Santos's celebrity aura came from that."[1]

The plot that Attie ended up writing for Santos proved eerily prescient. Santos was an outsider candidate for the Democratic nomination who was accused of inexperience because he'd only served a few years in Congress. He was up against a much better known, much better financed rival who seemed destined to win. And, to make things worse, the leaders of his own ethnic community regarded him with suspicion, because he didn't seem to spend enough time with his own community.

Santos overcame the odds with a mix of luck and soaring rhetoric. His appeal was his difference: a postracial American who wasn't ashamed to call himself a liberal.[2] After capturing the Democratic nomination, Santos squared off against Republican Arnold Vinick (played by Alan Alda) in the presidential debate. *The West Wing* was so determined to capture the authentic drama of an election campaign that they aired the debate live on two coasts on the same set used by John Kerry and George W. Bush. At one point Vinick accused Santos of being a liberal, and Santos gave a reply that many Democrats have memorized word for word:

What did liberals do that was so offensive to the Republican Party? I'll tell you what they did. Liberals got women the right to vote. Liberals got African-Americans the right to vote. Liberals created social security and lifted millions of elderly people out of poverty. Liberals ended segregation. Liberals passed the Civil Rights Act, the Voting Rights Act, Liberals created Medicare. Liberals passed the Clean Air Act, and the Clean Water Act. What did conservatives do? They opposed every one of those programs. Every one. So when you try to hurl the word "liberal" at my feet, as if it were dirty, something to run away from, something that I should be ashamed of, it won't work, Senator, because I will pick up that label and wear it as a badge of honor.

Santos beat Vinick in the general election. *The West Wing* had created a principled, charismatic ethnic minority presidential candidate who, against the odds, captured the White House. When Obama won his party's nomination three years later in spookily similar circumstances, Axelrod wrote Attie, "We're living your scripts!"[3]

The whole story might seem like the product of pure coincidence.

Attie happened to model his character on Obama, the character happened to win the presidency, and a little while later, Obama happened to do the same in real life.

But if you dismiss the similarities as luck, you'll overlook the symbiotic relationship between Democratic politics and Hollywood. Santos and Obama were almost identical because both are telegenic idealists with images consciously constructed to appeal to liberals—either as voters or TV viewers. They are examples of Hollywood's "liberal hero" archetype. Liberals like to imagine that it's only conservatives who engage in fantasy politics—that the Right is trapped in a Clint Eastwood world of cowboys and Indians, evil empires, and sweaty eighties action heroes. But the Left does exactly the same thing. Its imagination has been shaped by idealized liberal characters created by Hollywood scriptwriters.

As we shall see in this chapter, liberals are also fans of the Great Man (or Woman) theory of history—a belief that progress is made possible by the efforts of exceptional individuals. Conservatives often accuse liberals of being borderline socialists, of valuing the community over the individual. In fact, American liberalism has a strong tradition of individualism that teaches that change only comes because certain charismatic, brave people are prepared to defy the spirit of their era and fight for it. In cinematic terms, think of Malcolm X, Harvey Milk, or Erin Brockovich—individuals glorified by Hollywood in biopics that made them seem even larger than the movements they represented. The liberal hero is someone who is rational and informed and who elevates politics with their presence—wonks willing to confront the ignorance of the mob head-on. Sometimes that means taking on the moderate, do-nothing establishment of their own party, too.

There's more than a hint of arrogance in this worldview. It's a given that the liberal hero is intellectually and morally superior to all those John Wayne–loving conservatives. Martin Sheen, the actor behind *The West Wing*'s Jed Bartlet, called George W. Bush "a moron." Of course, that's a moron who beat Martin Sheen's preferred candidates twice in a row.[4]

The Liberal Cowboy

Hollywood's mythologizing of the liberal hero goes back decades, and a fine early example is *High Noon*, directed by Fred Zinnemann in 1952.

High Noon is a "mature," pessimistic Western about a sheriff who saves a town from its own moral cowardice. Gary Cooper stars as Will Kane, an aging, craggy-faced lawman who marries a Quaker pacifist and wants to settle down. But he learns that Frank Miller—a violent thug who Kane brought to trial—has escaped justice on a technicality and will arrive in town on the noon train to exact his revenge. Kane decides to stay and fight and asks his friends to help him. One by one they each find their own pathetic reason to turn him down (drink, fear, careerism). Kane has to face his nemesis alone. While his victory is guaranteed by sheer dint of being played by Gary Cooper—and boy, he wins in style—the final scene of him throwing his marshal's star away sends a message of rugged individualism. If you want a bad guy shot, you've gotta do it yourself.

Reading that synopsis, you might take Cooper's character for a classic conservative who takes the law into his own hands. In fact, screenwriter Carl Foreman had been a victim of the McCarthyite purge in the 1940s and said that he wrote the script as a cry of rage against the Hollywood executives who allowed their own town to be invaded by the right-wing mob. Conservatives got the message. Director Howard Hawks complained that it was an unthinking presentation of how a real lawman would work, that he wouldn't be "running around town like a chicken with his head off asking for help."[5] John Wayne was blunter. He told *Playboy* that it was "the most un-American thing I ever saw in my whole life. The last thing in the picture is ole Coop putting the United States marshal's badge under his foot and stepping on it." The Duke's memory was off (Coop doesn't step on the badge at all), but it's interesting how much offense this Western caused. Conservatives knew a liberal movie when they saw one.[6]

High Noon can be read as either Left or Right or simply enjoyed without ideological content, but Sheriff Kane does conform to the liberal ideal of a political leader. He is a great man who fights the forces of violence and conformity, and he shows smarts when others show stupidity. This is a type of hero who not only has to confront external threats but also the prejudices of his own community. His moral intelligence isolates him from the crowd. He is better than the rest of us.

The movies are full of Sheriff Kanes. Think of Gregory Peck as the small-town lawyer Atticus Finch in *To Kill a Mockingbird* (1962), the only person prepared to defend a black man against the false charge of rape. Suited in pure white, courteous to all men as equals, obsessed with upholding the law, fatherly, scholarly, and willing to be called bad names for his troubles—Finch is a timeless model for liberal leadership. During the 2012 election cycle, President Obama gave a brief, televised introduction to a replay of the movie on the USA Network channel.

To Kill a Mockingbird brought to life an unforgettable tale of courage and conviction, of doing what was right—no matter what the cost. And it gave us one of the great heroes of American cinema, Atticus Finch. . . . Half a century later, the power of this extraordinary film endures. It still speaks to us, it still tells us something about who we are as a people and the common values that we all share.

Film critic Tom Shone argued that Obama was trying to tell the audience that he was

cut from exactly the same liberal oak as Peck's Atticus Finch. [The broadcast] retrenched Obama's status as the defender of the American mainstream, evoking a blissful, pre-Palin era when "small town" and "liberalism" could be spoken in the same sentence, and no problem seemed too big that it couldn't be solved by an afternoon of somber, sun-dappled reflection by decent, reasonable men in horn rims and seersucker suits.

Finch wins the day with rational argument, just as Obama's fans imagined him winning the 2012 election with reason and intelligence.[7]

Sheriff Kane and Atticus Finch are heroes of the black-and-white era and might not be instantly recognizable to the youngsters who worked so hard and so earnestly for Barack Obama. What's had a much more profound impact on their way of seeing politics is *The West Wing*. The story of day-to-day life in a Democratic White House overseen by the clever, witty Jed Bartlet, it imagines how a group of liberal idealists would handle the challenge of real power. The melodrama lies in the attempt to balance dreams and realities; the joy in their successes, regret in their defeats. Conservative critics call it trite, a liberal love-in. But it's a bible for liberal reformers the world over.

In 2011, Hillary Clinton became the first United States leader to visit Burma since the early years of the Cold War. *The New York Times* reported the following:

One senior administration official familiar with the evolving diplomacy said he was convinced that the country's leaders were embarking on a path of profound change, but that they were uncertain of how to proceed after so many years under an isolated, dictatorial military junta. He cited a small but striking scene: Seeking to learn something about legislative and electoral politics, some new parliamentarians were passing around a DVD containing episodes of "The West Wing."

A year later, Mrs. Clinton confirmed the story during a ceremony to honor civil rights leader Aung San Suu Kyi. She recalled that a government official said to her, " 'Help us learn how to be a democratic congress, a parliament.' He went on to tell me that they were trying to teach themselves by watching old segments of *The West Wing*.

"I said, 'I think we can do better than that, Mr. Speaker.' "[8]

The West Wing has become synonymous with the American political process, to the extent that there's a blur in the line between where reality ends and fiction begins. Outside America the show is a textbook on how a democracy functions. Inside America it's often watched as a guide to how it ought to function. The distinction is important: For many U.S. liberals *The West Wing* incorporates everything they think politics should be.

In April 2012, *Vanity Fair* published an article exploring what it called "the Sorkinization of politics." A generation of kids had grown up watching Aaron Sorkin's soap, absorbed its ideals, and entered politics and journalism determined to mimic its ambition and glamour. It quotes a fan of the show named Meredith Shiner,

a personable 24-year-old congressional reporter for *Roll Call*, who describes herself as "the kind of girl who woke up on Sunday morning and watched *Meet the Press* with my dad."

At Duke, from which Shiner graduated in 2009, she would watch old *West Wing* episodes over milk shakes with friends on what she calls "*West Wing* therapy nights." . . . Shiner's enthusiasm for the show is particularly unbridled: "I always say to my friends, 'I wish Aaron Sorkin could script my life.'"

For this generation of novices, *The West Wing* functions like a political encyclopedia by which they can understand and plan their lives.

"I was interested in politics before the show started," journalist Matt Yglesias told *Vanity Fair*. "But a friend of mine from college moved to D.C. at the same time as me, after graduation, and we definitely plotted our proposed domination of the capital in explicitly *West Wing* terms: Who was more like Toby? Who was more like Josh?"

Not "Who was more like James Carville?" or "Who was more like Karl Rove?" These kids took their role models from TV, not reality.[9]

The West Wing actually gets a lot wrong about how politics works. Because it's motivated by the need for drama, the show overlooks the dull minutiae of everyday politics—like jobs numbers or the cost of living. The locus of the White House also excludes the vast patchwork of state and local government that determines much of what gets done. And it has an unhealthy obsession with the role of personality. *The West Wing* assumes that history is made by great and beautiful individuals rather than shaped by ordinary people. For example, in the course of the sixth season, President Bartlet overcomes his multiple sclerosis to win nuclear disarmament talks with North Korea and bring peace in the Middle East. At the end of one half of an episode, the Israelis are seen staking their lives on retaining control of Jerusalem. The show cuts to a commercial break. By the time it returns the Israelis have miraculously agreed to share Jerusalem with the Palestinians. I shouldn't need to spell out that this isn't how global politics works in real life. *The West Wing* is a wishful fantasy of what the Left could accomplish in the White House if only someone would let them try.[10]

The show's creator, Aaron Sorkin, was a New York Democrat and the descendant of one of the founders of the International Ladies' Garment Workers' Union. His early writing work included *A Few Good Men* and *The American President*—the latter a schmaltzy story about a president who rediscovers his idealism through love and fights for green energy and gun control (directed by liberal stalwart Rob Reiner). In 1997, Sorkin went into a meeting with a studio executive, had nothing to push, panicked, and so pitched an idea for a show that celebrated public service in Washington. The exec loved the idea and took it to NBC. The network held off for a year, because they worried that the public wouldn't take an idealistic show about the White House seriously while Bill Clinton was still in it. But they relented, and *The West Wing* was born.

Sorkin wanted his show to contain "heroic" politicians. In 2000, he explained,

> That's unusual in American popular culture, by and large. Our leaders, government people are portrayed either as dolts or as Machiavellian somehow. The characters in this show are neither. They are flawed, to be sure, because you need characters in drama to have flaws. But they, all of them, have set aside probably more lucrative lives for public service. They are dedicated not just to this president, but to doing good, rather than doing well. The show is kind of a valentine to public service. It celebrates our institutions. It celebrates education often. These characters are very well educated, and while sometimes playfully snobby about it,

there is, in all of them, a love of learning and appreciation of education.[11]

The theme of intelligence is critical to understanding the show's appeal to liberals; not because all liberals are intelligent but because writers and fans of *The West Wing* presume that intelligent people are overwhelmingly likely to be liberal. In *The West Wing* universe, the most rational, evidence-driven policy choices are probably liberal ones, while conservative opposition is partisan and emotive. The only sympathetic right-wing figures are centrists, like Arnold Vinick, who is courageous enough to be both Republican and prochoice. A less palatable Republican is Robert Ritchie—a dim-witted frat boy stand-in for George W. Bush. Ritchie tells Bartlet that he's goofed off a play to attend a baseball game because that's how "ordinary Americans" entertain themselves. Bartlet rips in to his philistinism: "No, I don't understand that. The center fielder for the Yankees is an accomplished classical guitarist. People who like baseball can't like books?" You can imagine the college kids watching at home cheering in delight.

Bartlet is a liberal hero because he gets to say things to conservatives that liberals think politicians ought to say but don't have the nerve. But Sorkin makes Bartlet's job easier by turning his conservative opponents into dumb sitting ducks. He was honest about that decision. In a 2001 interview with *The Advocate*, Sorkin was asked if he would allow Republican voices onto the show. He replied, "For the sake of drama, you want two strong arguments. . . . But I don't think it's my responsibility to achieve political balance on the show. I'm not a journalist. My responsibility isn't to the truth, it's the drama."[12]

In one of the fans' favorite scenes (it has over a million views on YouTube), Bartlet encounters a Christian right talk show host and asks her why she calls homosexuality an abomination. She replies that she doesn't; God does, in Leviticus 18:22. Oh, says Bartlet, in that case can I ask your advice?

> I'm interested in selling my youngest daughter into slavery as sanctioned in Exodus 21:7. She's a Georgetown sophomore, speaks fluent Italian, always cleared the table when it was her turn. What would a good price for her be? While thinking about that, can I ask another? My chief of staff, Leo McGarry, insists on working on the Sabbath. Exodus 35:2 clearly says he should be put to death. Am I morally obligated to kill him myself, or is it okay to call the police? Here's one that's really important 'cause we've got a lot of sports fans in this town: Touching the skin of a dead pig makes one unclean. Leviticus 11:7. If they promise to wear gloves, can the Washington Redskins still play football?

It continues like this until the talk show host is reduced to a quivering wreck. To the liberal viewer this is an instance in which someone finally—finally—turns the tables on those dim-witted evangelicals. Never mind that the conservative on this occasion isn't real and doesn't get to answer back. This scene, and the whole show, is therapy for liberals who imagine that they are the underdogs.[13]

When Al Gore lost the 2000 presidential election, *The West Wing* gained a new emotional meaning for its liberal fans. The rest of the country now had President Bush; they had President Bartlet. Sorkin told *The Advocate* that he saw *The West Wing* as the "voice of the loyal opposition" to Bush. But the writer upped the stakes by saying that he wanted to take on the Clinton tendency, too. "Weak-willed Democrats have been the enemy just as much as the Republicans have been the enemy on this show. If there's an enemy on this show, it's a lack of conviction, a lack of compassion."[14]

That quote only captures a scintilla of the fury that many

Hollywood liberals felt toward Bill Clinton as president. Mike Farrell—one of the stars of *M*A*S*H* and a veteran peace campaigner—regarded him as an elephant in donkey's clothing: "He presided over an execution when he was running for office so that he could get elected. He was something between an opportunist and a coward. You couldn't call him principled, that's for sure."[15] Sorkin wrote his show for those liberals inside and outside Hollywood who believed that Democrats lost elections because their leaders were cowardly or inept. So they went looking for a real-life Jed Bartlet.

Howard Dean Goes to Hollywood, Gets Corrupted

In late 2002, Hollywood opened auditions for a Democrat to take on Bush.[16] The mood in the country was ugly—there was a war on terror, joblessness, and fights over homosexuality, abortion, and euthanasia. Some in the movie business decided that the only way to beat George W. Bush was to pick a Democratic candidate who wouldn't scare the voters. They were looking for a charming, affable centrist who preferably looked good on TV. A sort of Bill Clinton mark II.[17]

Step forward Dick Gephardt, John Kerry, and John Edwards— all of whom made Hollywood their second home.[18] One reporter attended a fund-raiser at the house of liberal financier Stanley Sheinbaum and found the movie business at its political zenith. "It's like everyone in Washington has descended on us," said studio chief Casey Wasserman of Los Angeles. "It's wild!"

"You name it, they're all here," confirmed producer Haim Saban. "They're all on top of the other. It's a very, very, very busy season." Warren Beatty took coats at the door while his wife, Annette Bening, talked recyclables with Congressman Dennis Kucinich. (Barbra Streisand didn't show: The cast of *Sex and the City* was doing a gay rights benefit down the street. She knew her fan base.) The liberal network was in full swing.

Stanley Sheinbaum wallowed in the attention while simultaneously ridiculing the system with all the wisdom of a *West Wing* fan. "Right now I'm in a fight with John Kerry. I love John Kerry," he said. "But Kerry wants me to do a fund-raiser, and it turns out I'm doing one the same day for Robert Reich." (Reich was the Democratic candidate for governor in Massachusetts.) Stanley flipped through a typed list of events he was invited to, trying to locate the date when he was due to present John Kerry his check. How do politicians find time to meet their constituents, he asked the reporter? When he was a kid, they shook your hand at picnics. "Now, they don't even go to kaffeeklatsches anymore," he sighed. "On a face-to-face basis, who do they see? Haim Saban, Jeffrey Katzenberg, Lew Wasserman. That's one of the reasons Democrats have become increasingly conservative. It's why people have developed an aversion to politicians—and not without some reason."[19]

There were plenty of disaffected liberals living in Hollywood who felt the same way. They argued that there was no point in nominating another faceless centrist, either because the electorate would reject a Republican-lite candidate or else—if he/she actually got elected—they'd probably prove ineffectual in office. While the major-league Hollywood power brokers were casting around for another Bill Clinton, the Left was looking for a Jed Bartlet. And they thought they'd found one in Vermont governor Howard Dean.

Dean was a big man with a big voice—his sleeves often rolled up, a tie askew, and a piggy grin that was somewhere between mischievous and evil, depending on your political persuasion. A Yale graduate and a doctor of medicine, in his own state Howard Dean was known as a moderate. He had balanced Vermont's budget and was occasionally endorsed by the National Rifle Association. But he came out against the Iraq War in 2002, and that bought him national attention as a liberal.[20] Dean's pitch was that Democrats lost elections because they failed to provide a clear alternative to Republicans. "I'm on the Democratic wing of the Democratic Party," he liked to say.[21]

As Dean's supporters remember 2004, the governor initially wanted nothing to do with Hollywood—his values were those of small-town America not the metropolitan fleshpots of Los Angeles. But this narrative is a myth. The man who Dean hired to run his campaign, and who later became associated with the grassroots revolution in Internet politics, was a consummate Hollywood insider—Joe Trippi. Trippi began his career working for Tom Bradley's reelection as mayor of Los Angeles in 1982.[22] "It was an unusual experience for a twenty-four-year-old," Joe told me. "I found myself going to parties with Christopher Reeve and Margot Kidder. You took their money, and you didn't take everything too seriously, but I did quickly learn the ability of Hollywood people to get you money. Wow. So much money, they had. A night with the celebrities was worth weeks of knocking on doors."

So Howard Dean did fly to Los Angeles in 2002 and did try to get an audience with Hollywood's great and good. The problem was that they didn't like him.

"Hollywood loves a winner," explained Trippi, "and Dean just didn't look like a winner. Even his mother told him, 'You don't stand a chance of becoming president.'" Dean was awkward around Hollywood people, unwilling to burnish their egos or even unable to remember their names. He won an early endorsement from Rob Reiner, but little else.[23] However, his outsider status turned out to be a good thing; unable to rely on traditional sources of money, he was forced to innovate. In early 2003, Dean reluctantly agreed to attend a fund-raiser organized independently through a Web site called Meetup.com.[24] He expected to meet half a dozen online freaks—Dungeons and Dragons enthusiasts and forty-year-old bachelors. Instead, he found more than three hundred enthusiastic, perfectly sane supporters waiting to greet him. Excited, Dean ordered Zephyr Teachout, his Internet coordinator, to spend more time building his fan base on Meetup. The largest group on the site was a club for witches. Teachout recalled sitting at her desk all afternoon hitting refresh on her Web browser: "I was obsessed with beating Witches. Witches had fifteen thousand members, and we had three thousand. I wanted first place."

Three thousand sounds small, but 3,000 people talking to each other over the Internet has much more power than 3,000 unconnected names on an ordinary mailing list. They threw parties to which each invitee brought two or three friends; by November 2003, the Dean Meetup group had 140,000 members. Dean was a magnet for *West Wing* fans who thought the Democratic Party had lost its guts. Their angry online manifestos electrified a generation. As the money started rolling in, and the site became overloaded with traffic, the governor began to think that he was more popular than he really was.[25]

In June 2003, the liberal Web site MoveOn.org held an online primary. The 317,647 participants broke 44 percent for Dean, 25 percent for Dennis Kucinich, and just 14 percent for Kerry.[26] Overnight Dean became the unofficial Internet candidate. When the fundraising totals for the second quarter of 2003 were released, he had raised $7.6 million to Kerry's $5.9 million. The vast majority of it had come from small donors.[27]

Dean's success convinced many that he was a genuine maverick—someone who operated outside the Democratic machine.[28] The media started to analyze the phenomenon, to try to understand where his support was coming from.[29] The campaign dropped them a few clues. One of those was the endorsement Dean got from Martin Sheen. Joe Trippi:

Getting Martin Sheen was a really big deal for us. Young people watched this show he was in called *West Wing* and they connected with him. In it he played this plainspoken liberal president—Jed Bartlet—and many of the younger voters kind of understood his presence as an endorsement of Dean by Bartlet.[30]

Then *Newsday* columnist Sheryl McCarthy said that Dean's press releases begged a comparison with Bartlet, calling him:

a muscular Democrat; pugnacious and a little prickly; doesn't back down from a fight; willing to play political hardball if that's what it takes to get what he wants.

McCarthy also noted:

Bartlet and Dean are both married to doctors, women more in the Hillary Clinton than Laura Bush mode. Both are mavericks who seem to have appeared out of nowhere, although they really didn't. They're also pretty liberal, understanding that the little men and women are the ones who need the government most.[31]

Martin Sheen agreed. "There are a lot of similarities," he told journalists, noting that they were both blunt in their personality and politics. But, "President Bartlet is a fictional character. Howard Dean is a reality. And that's all the difference in the world."[32]

For Hollywood's power players, the Dean insurgency finally made sense. Now that it was explained to them that he was Bartlet incarnate they could understand his message and reconcile themselves to his difficult personality. Almost overnight, Dean became the unofficial Hollywood candidate.[33] "We were suddenly the coolest campaign around," said Trippi. "Joan Jett was with us at every stop."[34] Norman Lear, who once called Dean "unelectable," was now a top donor—and he was soon joined by Alec Baldwin, Mel Brooks, Paul Newman, and Barbra Streisand.[35] On September 30, 2003, Dean arrived in Union Station at the end of a whistle-stop tour of America. Martin Sheen greeted him: one Bartlet to another. "Let my country awake!" cried Sheen. Rob Reiner hugged the governor. The whistle blew. A journalist asked Dean which entertainers and artists supported him. He replied that there were so many, he'd lost count. The journalist asked, "What is the role of Hollywood progressives in 2004?"

Dean shouted, "The bigger, the better!"[36]

That was a mistake.

Suddenly, it mattered to be seen with celebrities and everything that once defined the campaign as homespun and maverick seemed to have been a launchpad to turning it back into a standard, Hollywood-centric campaign driven by big money. At a fund-raiser at the House of Blues, political consultant Chad Griffin explained the sudden interest that donors had to *Variety*. "Everyone wants to be with the winner and no one wants to be with a loser." Here was Paul Reiser, Drew Barrymore, and Jason Alexander. The Bangles and Big Bad Voodoo Daddy performed. Dean hit the stage like a revival preacher. "We can't beat Bush by being Bush lite!" he cried. "The way to beat George Bush is to stop apologizing for being Democrats and say what you mean!" And the crowd chanted his name.[37]

While Dean's personality type was technically anti-Hollywood—the image of being an outsider/Bartlet figure was pure Hollywood—and so Hollywood was drawn inexorably to the man who had once seemed alien.

Like the ugly duckling in a teen comedy who gets a makeover and—surprise!—is now beautiful and popular, Howard Dean was the prettiest girl at the Hollywood ball. By the end of 2003 he was tipped to be the Democratic front-runner. With the endorsements of Al Gore and Senate leader Tom Daschle, he looked more like the establishment candidate—albeit a definitively liberal one.[38]

But Dean was still Dean, and he didn't have the ability to self-censor that such a role required. Trying to broaden his appeal, he said, "I still want to be the candidate for guys with Confederate flags in their pickup trucks." Trying to sound smart, he said that the Iowa caucus was "dominated by special interests . . . that tend to represent the extremes." The other candidates took the bait and launched an attack. Dean's numbers started to flag.[39] He was looking less like a populist liberal and more like a Hollywood liberal—less like Jed Bartlet and more like Sean Penn. The conservative Club for Growth ran an ad that featured a husband and wife sounding off about the governor. The husband said, "I think Howard Dean should take his tax-hiking, government-expanding, latte-drinking, sushi-eating, Volvo-driving, *New York Times*–reading . . ." His wife jumped in: "Body-piercing, Hollywood-loving, left-wing freak show back to Vermont, where it belongs!"[40]

The problem with the Dean campaign was that it was built on a fantasy. In *The West Wing* universe, President Bartlet is elected because he's a gutsy liberal. Many Deaniacs looked at Bartlet and thought, "If Jed can get elected, our guy can, too." And so a TV show became a political blueprint. But the reality was that Dean was a flawed candidate, probably a little too liberal for 2004, who performed poorly on TV. He was overflattered by Hollywood, whose support wound up doing him far more harm than good. Most important, his campaign only really flourished within a small bubble of support on the Internet—in the age before the widespread use of social media such as YouTube and Twitter. In other words, Dean was akin to a cult hit TV show. Loved by his fans but unknown or weird to casual viewers.

After a bump in the polls in late 2003, Dean was suddenly slipping by the New Year. Iowa voted on January 19, 2004.[41] Dean flew into the state with his wife, a rare campaign appearance for a lady who ran a busy medical practice in Vermont. It was seven degrees above zero when their Gulfstream jet touched down. There was a big crowd waiting for Dean, and he made his way to a "People-Powered Post-Caucus Party." The atmosphere was tense. Everybody sensed that Dean was slipping. Nobody had yet guessed by how much.[42]

That night, Iowans voted 38 percent for Kerry, 32 percent for Edwards, and just 18 percent for Dean. Iowans told pollsters that they thought Dean was too liberal and unelectable. The Deaniacs were stunned but unbowed. When their man addressed them at the after-show party, they went wild. "You know something?" he shouted.

If you had told us one year ago that we were going to come in third in Iowa, we would have given anything for that. Not only are we going to New Hampshire, we're going to South Carolina and Oklahoma and Arizona and North Dakota and New Mexico, and we're going to California and Texas and New York. And we're going to South Dakota and Oregon and Washington and Michigan. And then we're going to Washington, D.C. to take back the White House!

And then he let rip a primal scream that was heard all across America: "Yeeeargh!"[43]

In the crowded hall, it sounded like an enthusiastic whoop. On TV, it was a psychotic howl. The media leaped on it. "Did you see Dean's speech last night?" Jay Leno asked his audience. "Oh my God! Now I hear the cows in Iowa are afraid of getting mad Dean disease." David Letterman said, "Here's what happened: The people of Iowa realized they didn't want a president with the personality of a hockey dad."

A week later, New Hampshire chose Kerry over Dean by 38 percent to 26 percent. The Bartlet dream was over.[44]

Obama as President Jed Lincoln

Howard Dean's candidacy might have been a failure, but it was also a trailblazer. He demonstrated the power of the Internet as a campaign tool, as a way of raising money without going begging to the Democratic Party bosses. It was a lesson that Barack Obama's team would learn when they developed their own hugely successful social media strategy for the 2008 presidential primaries—a campaign in which Facebook and YouTube achieved a remarkable degree of significance.

Dean opened up a space on the antiwar Left that Obama was able to exploit with greater panache. The liberal hero strategy failed for Dean because he failed to live up to it, but Obama was a smoother operator. He was cooler on TV and never came off as a radical—and he had the benefit of running against the Iraq War at the point when it was at its most unpopular (in 2004 it was divisive but not yet universally regarded as a failure).[45] Moreover, Obama's relationship with Hollywood was more nuanced than Dean's had been. He never allowed himself to get swept up in the excitement of meeting the stars. In fact, he didn't meet very many at all to begin with. In the early stages of the 2008 Democratic primaries, most actor endorsements had been sewn up by Hillary Clinton, and the vast majority of Obama's support was from behind-the-scenes professionals. Will Smith's manager, James Lassiter, the Sony head's wife, Jamie Lynton, and several Harvard law alumni who happened to live in Los Angeles, including Nancy McCullough, Hill Harper, and Crystal Nix Hines.[46]

It was a similar scenario to that faced by Dean in 2004—the

stars stayed away at first, and then came running when Obama took off in the polls. But the difference was that Obama never allowed Hollywood cool to define him, and was even prepared to say things that the stars might not like to hear. At a fund-raiser just before the election, Obama took to the microphone before an audience that included Will Ferrell, Leonardo DiCaprio, Jamie Lee Curtis, and Jodie Foster and delivered a somber verdict on the election that reflected Obama's no-nonsense approach to Hollywood:

> This is not a game. This is not a reality show—no offense to any of you. This is not a sitcom. This is for all the marbles. There is a high stake to this election. If we can cut through the nonsense and . . . the silliness, then I'm absolutely convinced that we're going to win.[47]

Just because Obama didn't have a personal relationship with Hollywood doesn't mean that his candidacy wasn't influenced in some way by movie mythology. On the contrary, Obama inherited Dean's legion of *West Wing* fans. Many of them also found similarities between Obama and Bartlet—intelligence, charisma, an ability to lead. Some commentators spoke as if Bartlet was a real historical figure and used him as a benchmark by which to judge Obama's performance. Aaron Sorkin wrote a piece for *The New York Times* in which he imagined Bartlet giving some advice on how to win the 2008 election (one choice zinger from Bartlet to Obama was on the subject of race: "Brains made me look arrogant, but they make you look uppity.")[48] Lawrence O'Donnell, the executive producer of *The West Wing* and, later, MSNBC host, stated that Obama was actually far better in the White House than Bartlet because O'Donnell personally never rated the latter as a reliable liberal: "It used to drive me nuts when people would simply and offhandedly refer to him as a liberal president. . . . It would just be, 'Oh he told off the religious right.' Who gives a fuck? Tell me, what was the bill? What was the law?"[49]

O'Donnell makes an interesting point: It's unhealthy for people to judge politicians by the high or low standards set by TV. Indeed, the Hollywood liberal hero has proved to be every bit as flawed as an archetype for Democrats as the Wild West cowboy is for conservatives. An example of that is the comparison that Hollywood made between Obama and Abraham Lincoln.

The first movie that Obama screened at the White House after his 2012 reelection victory was Steven Spielberg's *Lincoln*. It was a clever choice. That the anniversary of the passage of the Thirteenth Amendment freeing the slaves should coincide with the reelection of America's first black president illustrated how much the republic had changed for the better in 150 years. Alas, in other ways, it was business as usual.

Lincoln tells the story of a country at war with itself and a president at war with the Congress—a Congress that Honest Abe had to charm, bully, bribe, and blackmail into doing the right thing. There were no Bull Runs or Gettysburgs in 2012, but there was still an ugly culture war to fight. Obama invited most of the Republican congressional leadership to his *Lincoln* party—and none of them showed. It wasn't the first time that they had said they were washing their hair that night. When Obama threw a barbecue for newly elected House Republicans, only one third of them came. House majority leader John Boehner set a record by not turning up to six state dinners in two years. The GOP blamed the president's social skills; he blamed their partisanship. Either way, the empty seats at the *Lincoln* screening told their own story. Politics was gridlocked.[50]

The big political debate at the beginning of Obama's second term was whether or not the president could overcome that divide. His fans looked upon him as a latter-day Lincoln—although Obama pretended to be coy about the comparison. "I never compared myself to Lincoln," Obama told David Gregory on *Meet the Press*.[51] But he did quote Lincoln in his debates against Mitt Romney, he did choose to be sworn in on Lincoln's Bible at both of his inaugurations, and he did choose to deliver his 2013 State of the Union address on Lincoln's birthday. And in case anyone missed the point, the prez did film a metajoke movie for the White House Correspondents' Dinner in which Obama played Daniel Day-Lewis preparing himself to play Obama in a biopic spoof of *Lincoln*.[52]

So Obama never invited any comparisons with Lincoln at all. No, sir. Not once.

What lessons did Spielberg's *Lincoln* have for Obama—a quietly aspirant Honest Abe? It was classic Hollywood liberal hero stuff: be idealistic, be smarter than your opponents, and bridge divides with soaring rhetoric. Be like Bartlet and speak truth to power.

The plot hinges on Lincoln's heroic efforts to squeeze the Thirteen Amendment through the last weeks of a hostile, lame-duck Congress. Opponents underestimate the man from Illinois, with his terrible jokes and eccentric wife; supporters come to know him as the greatest politician of his generation. But Lincoln shuffles toward victory with the hollow cheer of a doomed man. He is shot offscreen and, in the final moments, laid out on his deathbed. Here Spielberg bends history to serve a political purpose. In 1865, Lincoln was laid out naked beneath a sheet and, being too tall for a stranger's bed, had to be stretched diagonally. In 2012, he is in a nightgown, curved in the fetal position. The director wanted his audience to leave the theater thinking of Lincoln as a sacrificial lamb, not a nude giant.

Spielberg tweaks history throughout the movie—all to promote Lincoln as a liberal hero. Consider the opening scene, in which Lincoln meets his exhausted troops. One of them, a young African-American, demands to know why there are no commissioned black officers in the Union army. How can men who are fighting slave owners tolerate racial injustice in their own ranks? Lincoln doesn't answer. His awkward silence reflects the big moral question that plagues the president and is the premise of this entire movie—should Lincoln seek an easy peace that won't trouble America's racist social order or should the North's victory end slavery once and forever? How far is Lincoln prepared to go?

But just as the movie gropes toward historical truth in the vein of Spielberg's *The Color Purple*, it takes a detour into the kind of sentimentalism better associated with *ET*. A white soldier begins to recite the words of the Gettysburg Address with tears in his eyes. To Lincoln's astonishment, the African-American soldier joins in. This would not, could not, have happened. After the movie's release, its historical consultant—Harold Holzer—wrote an article disassociating himself from all its errors. He said of this scene, "It is almost inconceivable that any uniformed soldier of the day . . . would have memorized a speech that, however ingrained in modern memory, did not achieve any semblance of a national reputation until the 20th century." That's a polite way of saying "It's hokum."[53]

Why did Spielberg and his screenwriter invent this moment? It's to communicate the singular greatness of Lincoln, to show us that his unique personality had the potential to unite the nation. Likewise, consider how Spielberg depicts the passage of the Thirteenth Amendment outlawing slavery. We are told that the president has only a few weeks to slip the amendment through Congress before the war ends. Why? Because a lot of Northern support for abolition rests on the belief that ending slavery would demoralize the South and end the war sooner. Should peace come, as it threatens to do, that support would vanish. And so Lincoln forces the amendment through the last days of an outgoing Congress with a mix of high-minded rhetoric and low politics.

Again, this scenario is written with poetic license. Lincoln could have waited for the next Congress to sit before pushing for the abolition of slavery—it contained far more antislavery representatives from his own party. More troubling, this Great Man approach to the historical record gives too much responsibility for the abolition of slavery to one man alone. After seeing the movie the historian Eric Foner wrote an irritated letter to *The New York Times* that noted the following:

> Emancipation . . . resulted from events at all levels of society, including the efforts of social movements to change public sentiment and of slaves themselves to acquire freedom. . . . Moreover, from the beginning of the Civil War, by escaping to Union lines, blacks forced the fate of slavery onto the national political agenda.[54]

Foner is spot-on. By failing to include a single major black character, *Lincoln* oddly cuts African-Americans out of their own history; this would be akin to making a movie about women winning the vote without including a suffragette. Of course, the film also sidesteps Lincoln's own racism—his belief that whites were superior to blacks or his suggestion that African-Americans resettle in Africa. But the most important point is that Spielberg's movie exhibits a preference for telling stories about political leaders over political movements.

If progressives are waiting for a Hollywood-style liberal hero to lead them to the Promised Land, then they're going to be perpetually disappointed. First, few political leaders are that idealistic or that perfect. Howard Dean might have been idealistic, but he was a very poor candidate. Obama might have been the perfect candidate but he turned out to be less idealistic than his supporters wished for. Obama let liberals down when he failed to push hard enough for a public option for mandated health care coverage, when he failed to close Guantánamo, when he oversaw a massive encroachment on civil liberties by the National Security Agency, and when he authorized a troop surge in Afghanistan and the use of drones to kill terrorists (along with thousands of innocent people living nearby). As actor Mike Farrell told me, "Obama is a hideous disappointment. . . . You name it, he'll screw it up."[55] To be fair to the president, even if he had wished to govern like a socialist, the American political system is designed to prevent an individual from wielding the necessary amount of power. For much of his time in office, Obama was constrained by a Republican House. The long wait for Bartlet yielded little.

Eric Foner is absolutely right to assert that progress is usually made by movements rather than men. We tend to forget that truth because the human mind is drawn to the exciting narratives and powerful biographies of individuals. But it was the activism of thousands of ordinary women that won them the vote, the agitation of thousands of ordinary African-Americans that ended segregation, and the courage of thousands of ordinary gays and lesbians that made same-sex marriage a possibility. Likewise, Obama might be one of America's great political success stories—but he wouldn't be where he is without the slaves who fought for their freedom in the 1860s, the men and women who marched in the 1960s, or the multiracial coalition that put him in office in 2008. Liberals claim to speak for the little people, but they all too often get hooked on the Hollywood mythologies of big names.

Then again, conservatives are just as bad.

6

TRUE GRIT

How the Republicans Came to Love the Cowboy

Democrats might have the closest relationship with Hollywood, but Republicans can be suckers for movie myths, too. On June 27, 2011, the Tea Party heroine Michele Bachmann launched her presidential candidacy in Waterloo, Iowa—Bachmann's hometown. In an interview with Fox News, she reminded us that it was also someone else's hometown. Standing in front of a small wooden porch, she said, "I want [voters] to know just like John Wayne is from Waterloo, Iowa, that's the spirit I have, too. It's about loving America, embracing America. It's about sacrificing for America." John Wayne was prepared to give his all for the country he loved, and so, too, was Michele Bachmann.

One small problem: Bachmann got the wrong John Wayne. Movie star John Wayne was actually born 150 miles away in Winterset, Iowa. The only famous Wayne from Waterloo was John Wayne Gacy, a gay serial killer known as the Killer Clown who murdered teenage boys and buried their bodies beneath the crawl space under his house. Gacy's "spirit" was not something voters wanted to see channeled anywhere, least of all in a presidential candidate. Bachmann's eccentric candidacy slipped a few more points in the polls.[1]

This Tea Party favorite wasn't the only cowboy fan in the contest. When Newt Gingrich rebounded after a bad start to his campaign, the press corps scrambled to find some fresh insights into his unlovable character. One thing they unearthed was his obsession with the movie *The Magnificent Seven*, which he often quotes as a fine example of conservative ideals. The younger Newt also went to see *Sands of Iwo Jima* (starring the Duke) four times. One biographer wrote, "There was one place this lonely boy could find stories as big as his own ambitious imagination: at the movies." Another surmised, "These movies almost became a metaphor for life and an extension of life's reality."[2] Likewise, Texas governor Rick Perry did his best to promote an image of himself as a latter-day John Wayne. He received an endorsement by singer and satirist Kinky Friedman, who wrote, "As a Jewish cowboy, I know Rick Perry to be a true friend of Israel. . . . There exists a visceral John Wayne kinship between Israelis and Texans, and Rick Perry gets it." Nothing speaks louder about the eternal appeal of the Christian Duke than his ability to cross ethnic boundaries and become a figurehead for Jewish cattle rustlers.[3]

Perhaps the ideal mascot for the modern Republican Party would be John Wayne riding an elephant. For conservatives, the cowboy represents everything they think they represent: honor, masculinity, faith in God, resistance to authority, guns, self-reliance, the common man made heroic. The man who set the standard for Republican cowboy lore was Ronald Reagan. As candidate and president, Reagan was often photographed riding a horse or working at his ranch— usually wearing a cowboy hat and jeans. His rhetoric was full of "straight talk" and "shoot from the hip" bravado. And his policies embodied the Western dream of uninhibited freedom.

Of course there is a vast difference between the reality of nineteenth-century cowboy life and the lives of contemporary Republicans. The cowboys lived precariously off the land, in an age of violence, ethnic conflict, and often spirit-crushing poverty. During the 2012 Republican presidential primaries, the voting pool was dominated by older rich men living in comparatively luxurious comfort. Likewise, Reagan might have used populist rhetoric, but—to borrow some cowboy imagery—his administration's sympathies lay with the cattle and mining barons, not the poor panhandler or the family ranch. Reagan used his own cattle ranch as a tax shelter. In 1979, it saved him forty-five hundred dollars in federal income taxes.[4]

The Republican cowboy image is a clever construct, a political fabrication. It originates in the early 1970s and was pioneered by two men from very different backgrounds who embraced it for subtly different reasons—although both were inspired by Hollywood. Richard Nixon was the first Republican president to fully exploit movie cowboy lore and to make John Wayne an unofficial member of his administration. As with so much that he did in office, it's reasonable to conclude that Nixon's strategy was largely cynical. By contrast, Ronald Reagan did on some fundamental level believe that he really was a cowboy. As a former actor, the way he dressed, spoke, and thought were constructed by the old studio system. Indeed, his conversion from a young liberal in the 1930s to a mature conservative in the 1960s was a good example of how Hollywood shaped the thought processes of an entire generation of romantic, even naïve, Republicans. Reagan's conversion to conservatism happened not just while he was in Hollywood but because he was in Hollywood.

What we'll see in this chapter is how Hollywood ideals slowly came to shape American conservatism in much the same way that they have liberalism. We'll also see that this has become a problem for the Republicans and for the American people as a whole. For the United States isn't some wilderness waiting to be tamed by a Western hero. It's a complicated republic that requires compromise and intellectual dexterity to govern. The cowboy costume has become the Republican Party's straitjacket.

Nixon Throws a Party

You might recall from chapter 3 that 1972 was a renaissance year in liberal Hollywood activism. The radicals in the film community gave their all to George McGovern and, unwittingly, helped get him defeated. What's less well-known is that McGovern's rival, President Richard Nixon, made just as big an effort to court Hollywood votes—albeit among older, less zeitgeisty stars. Why? Because he was a brilliant political tactician who understood that film excites conservative, nostalgic emotions as well as revolutionary, progressive ones.

On August 27, 1972, four hundred limousines snaked their way along the coast road toward the town of San Clemente, California. They were headed to La Casa Pacifica—a ten-room house balanced on a seventy-five-foot cliff edge overlooking the Pacific Ocean. The cars stopped at the gates and out stepped some of the biggest names in Hollywood: Sammy Davis Jr., Frank Sinatra, Charlton Heston, Glen Campbell, Clint Eastwood, Jack Benny, Jimmy Durante, George Hamilton. They wound their way on foot up a narrow road under eucalyptus trees. Waiting for them at the end of the avenue was Richard Nixon. One of the least glamorous men to ever be elected president had attracted the largest gathering of Hollywood talent in political history.

Inside the stars hung around the swimming pool and drank cocktails. The Freddy Martin Band played foxtrots in the shade of the royal palms. Nixon had thrown around a lot of money for this party. The White House staff was told that it should be "a very high-level, spirited occasion," with food ordered in from Chasen's (the famous Hollywood eatery). The president asked that they provide the "very best brands of Scotch and Bourbon, not the ordinary stuff we've used in the past." Composing the guest list, he wrote, "We must, of course, go for all the new stars." Nixon's idea of "new stars" showed his age: "Ruby Keeler, Gloria Swanson, Joan Crawford, Ginger Rogers, Bette Davis." *The New York Times* described the crowd at La Casa as "vintage Hollywood." One guest called it, "a cocktail party at the Hollywood Wax Museum."

Even if the guests were a little arthritic, Nixon deserved credit for drawing in almost every Golden Age star still living. And they came regardless of party affiliation. Frank Sinatra had stumped for Nixon's nemesis Jack Kennedy in 1960. George Hamilton had dated Lyndon Johnson's daughter. Quarterback-turned-actor Jim Brown had campaigned for Democrat Hubert Humphrey in 1968. Headlining the official "Democrats for Nixon" group was Charlton Heston, who had changed a lot since he marched for civil rights in 1963. "I didn't vote for President Nixon in 1960 or '68," he told reporters. "But I'm going to vote for him this fall."[5] Perhaps the unlikeliest convert was the black entertainer Sammy Davis Jr. Sammy had marched for civil rights in Birmingham, Alabama, and campaigned for the Kennedys. But when he arrived at La Casa Pacifica, he had just returned from a week's vacation with Elvis Presley and Donald Rumsfeld (imagine that party). "I dig Nixon," Sammy explained, and was there a greater vindication of the civil rights movement than a black guy drinking a martini with a Republican president? "I bought the bus," he laughed. "There's nothing wrong with making money. . . . I'll give mine away when John Wayne gives his away."[6]

After ninety minutes the president mounted the bandstand and gave a little speech. He told the crowd that while he enjoyed foreign films, "I like my movies made in the United States." These are the best, he said, because they are made by men and women who understand why people go to the cinema. "Movies can educate—have a lesson—but don't knock entertainment. People need to laugh, to cry, to dream, to be taken away from the dull lives they lead."

Those words, "don't knock entertainment," contained a subtle political message. Many of the veteran stars in the audience thought that contemporary Hollywood had been hijacked by left-wing amateurs, radicals who made poorly crafted movies attacking the American way. The party and the speech were calculated to draw the Golden Age stars into the court of Nixon, and to use their endorsement to shape the president's image.

Richard Nixon was the movie buff in chief. In the sixty-seven months that he was president, he spent over five hundred nights at the movies—either at the White House theater, in the family room at Camp David, or in the living room at the Casa Pacifica. Able to watch anything to order, Nixon was a very lucky man; these were the days before VCRs or Netflix. His daughter Tricia recalled that he was a disciplined viewer. "My father is patient and loyal to a movie," she said. "The rest of us keep saying let's go, come on, this is lousy, but he says no, let's wait a bit, and maybe it will get better." Nixon confirmed, "I've never gone to sleep in a movie, or a play. Even as dull as they can be."[7]

President Nixon's viewing tastes betrayed his nostalgia for the past. In 1973, he wrote Jane Wyman (an Academy Award–winning actress and Ronald Reagan's first wife) to complain, "So many of the movies coming out of Hollywood, not to mention those that come out of Europe, are so inferior that we just don't enjoy them." This wasn't an artistic judgment: Nixon meant that he was disgusted by the sex, violence, and bad language of what Hollywood was producing in the 1970s. Even a saccharine hit like *Love Story* (1970) offended him. The family saw it on Christmas Eve, and he told reporters afterward that his daughters were horrified by its smattering of foul language. "I wasn't shocked," he confided. "I know these words, I know they use them [nowadays]. It's the 'in' thing to do." He concluded that swearing "has its place, but if it's used it should be to punctuate." Those remarks would seem ironic four years later, when the Watergate tapes revealed that Nixon had the vocabulary of a sailor.[8]

Nixon liked musicals, epic dramas, and action movies. His favorite movie was *Patton*, which starred George C. Scott as the eponymous war hero. The president saw *Patton* five times before he ordered the bombing of Cambodia in 1970. He avoided most of what is now considered the classic canon of 1970s movies (he never saw anything with Dustin Hoffman in it) and sat through just fifteen R-rated features. Reportedly, Nixon had been to see *West Side Story* in 1961 and walked out halfway through in disgust. An aide later said, "He just couldn't stand all the propaganda."

Nixon gravitated toward movies that recalled the simplicity of the America of his youth. He was born in 1913 in Yorba Linda, California, in a house that his father built. Life was innocent but also precarious and cruel; two of Nixon's brothers died young of tuberculosis. Cinema was a welcome distraction, and Nixon later said that going to the movies was a rare and marvelous luxury for his family. His father was a movie fan, and when he acquired three cows, he named them Dorothy Lamour, Loretta Young, and Gary Cooper. After he won a place at Duke University, young Richard was delighted to gain access to the student union's Saturday night screenings, which only cost a nickel. Movies were the backdrop to his courting of Patricia Ryan, his future wife, who had financed her studies at the University of Southern California by working as an extra. The summer before they were married, Nixon wrote Pat a list of the movies he wanted to take her to: *Daughters Courageous*, "Sonja Henie's latest," *Beau Geste*, and *On Borrowed Time*. During the war the two swapped letters describing the films they had seen. When he returned home and threw himself into politics, he remarked to a supporter that he often dreamed of slipping anonymously into a theater and watching a good movie.[9]

For the next twenty years, Nixon developed a strong understanding for how visual propaganda works. In 1952, after he had been picked to be the Republican vice presidential candidate, Nixon was accused of misusing his expense account. On September 23, he flew to Los Angeles and delivered a thirty-minute televised address in which he defended himself and detailed his family's finances. He closed the speech by admitting that he hadn't declared one gift from a Texas supporter: a black-and-white cocker spaniel called Checkers. "And you know," Nixon finished, "the kids, like all kids, love the dog, and I just want to say this right now, that regardless of what they say about it, we're gonna keep it." That bravura performance kept Nixon on the ticket and rescued his career.[10]

But Nixon's screen image failed to move with the times. In 1960, he ran for the presidency against the telegenic Jack Kennedy. He refused to wear makeup during a televised debate, in part because he thought to do so would be "effeminate." He looked so unbecoming that his mother rang to ask if he was ill. Nixon lost the election by a wafer-thin margin, and it's possible that his shabby appearance made a difference.

In 1968 he put himself into the hands of new handlers, who better understood the medium. He hired TV producer (and future president of Fox News) Roger Ailes to create a "New Nixon." Ailes was scathing about his product: "Nixon's a funny looking guy. He looks like someone hung him up in a closet overnight and he jumps out in the morning with his suit all bunched up and starts running around saying, 'I want to be president.' I mean, this is how he strikes some people." That's why it was important to smarten him up—"To make them forget all that."[11] Nixon got it. He told his people, "We're going to build this whole campaign around television. You fellows just tell me what you want me to do and I'll do it."[12]

The power of words was eclipsed by the power of image. To quote his media adviser William Gavin, "Reason requires a high degree of discipline, of concentration; impression is easier." On TV, that impression could be controlled, because the image "can be edited so only the best moments are shown." Nixon was filmed doing question-and-answer sessions with audiences that had been fed both the questions and the right moment to applaud.[13] His team created ads that were a collage of images set against tone poems. Assistant producer James Sage described them as "rosy sunsets . . . bustling factories and . . . little kids playing in the sun." Over all of this the candidate read out a spiel about peace and prosperity replacing chaos and poverty. "Nixon says such pap!" laughed Sage. "In fact the radicalness of the approach is in the fact of creating an image without saying anything."[14]

So when Nixon won the office in 1968 he did so in defiance of many popular expectations. It was the Democrats who were regarded as the party of Hollywood, glamour, and modernity; the Republicans were the conservative squares who wore shabby suits. Yet in '68, Nixon was the one who used television the best. His critics complained that he ran a campaign that was too controlled, almost unreal. But it was exactly this kind of calm that the public wanted to see from a president. Vietnam was still raging, claiming thousands of American lives. At home major cities burned, as antiwar and civil rights protesters tore up the streets. It seemed like America was on the brink of civil war. From September 1969 to May 1970, there was at least one bomb threat in America every day.[15]

Nixon believed that one way to get reelected was to appeal to the "silent majority" of Americans who yearned for a return to law and order. He was advised by political scientist Kevin Phillips to emulate the style of John Wayne, an actor who communicated both firmness and nostalgia. "John Wayne might sound bad to people in New York," Phillips said, "but he sounds great to the schmucks down there along the Yahoo Belt."[16] Phillips only thought it was necessary to echo Wayne's language, but Nixon went further. He courted the man himself. Dick invited the actor to the White House for awkwardly formal one-on-one dinners; Nixon called him "Duke" and Wayne called him "Mr. President." Nixon needed no encouragement to indulge in these ultrapolite evenings: He had been a fan for thirty years. Even as president he sent Wayne fan mail about his movies (of which he saw twenty-five while in office). When Wayne won an Oscar for *True Grit* in 1969, Nixon wrote him, "Dear Duke: I have been delighted to read the rave reviews. . . . I saw it in the W.H. with my family and for once we agree with the critics—you were great!"[17]

In 1970 Nixon gave a speech in Denver about law and order. After a few lines, he wandered from his notes and started talking about Wayne's latest movie—*Chisum* (1970). Thinking aloud, Nixon noted that a modern president was sort of like a cowboy. "There was a time when there was no law," he said of the Wild West. "But the law eventually came, and the law was important from the standpoint of not only prosecuting the guilty but also seeing that those who were guilty had a proper trial." The message couldn't be clearer: Vote Nixon, get Wayne.[18] Even Nixon's purchasing of a house in San Clemente was an effort to capitalize upon his California upbringing and portray himself as a man of the West. Wayne was an occasional guest.[19]

It was a time of panic about lawlessness and disorder, of rape in Central Park and riots on the Berkeley campus. The journalist Gary Wills understood what the president was doing when he wrote, "Nixon had policies, but beneath those positions were the values Wayne exemplified."[20] The Duke spoke at the 1968 and 1972 Republican conventions and voiced ads for Nixon. He recorded an LP called

America: Why I Love Her. It featured Wayne reeling off some geographic marvels ("a Kansas sunset, Arizona rain, San Francisco fog, snowflakes in the Rockies"), accompanied by the Billy Liebert & Orchestra and a chorus singing "Aaaa-mer-iiii-caaa!"[21] Desperate not to be left out, Henry Kissinger told an Italian interviewer that he saw himself as being just like the Duke, as a "lone cowboy."[22] The Wayne myth's appeal crossed borders and oceans. The leader of the Soviet Union, Leonid Brezhnev was a cowboy fan, and when he visited the United States, his hosts laid out a Stetson with a Western belt and a toy revolver in his cabin on Air Force One. Brezhnev ignored the hat but was unable to resist wearing the belt. He appeared from his cabin and announced that he was going to do an impression of his favorite cowboy, John Wayne. The leader of the Communist world drew his toy gun over the Grand Canyon and went *bang-bang-bang.*[23]

The Nixon-Wayne partnership was built on a series of myths. John Wayne was not a war hero: He had deferred his way out of service in World War II. The characters he played often had total disregard for the law (in *Chisum*, he reclaims his land through violence, not the courts). And Nixon's campaign to be regarded as cowboy in chief was built on a false premise: Crime had just started to go down, not up. Despite all the bomb threats. In 1972, drug arrests doubled, the national crime rate dipped for the first time in over a decade, and violent crime in some inner cities had been reduced by half.[24] But conservative politicians had a stake in convincing voters that they needed cowboys. And the moviemakers had a stake in that, too. The early 1970s saw a series of box office hits about vigilantes (*Death Wish*, 1974) and hard-boiled cops (*The French Connection*, 1971). Clint Eastwood's *Dirty Harry* (1972) defined the way many people saw the crime problem: out of control and tolerated by a police force hamstrung by bureaucracy. Only a tight-lipped cowboy with a gun could protect them. Many liberals hated Dirty Harry—a handful demonstrated outside the Academy Awards with signs that read: "Dirty

Harry Is a Rotten Pig." But Nixon really, really loved it. He chased Eastwood's endorsement all year and eventually convinced him to attend his renomination. Forty years before his star turn as Mitt Romney's warm-up act Eastwood joined thousands of Republicans at their national convention to watch John Wayne narrate a fourteen-minute documentary called *Nixon the Man*.[25]

In his effort to carve out a conservative message by appropriating movie stars, Nixon changed the nature of Hollywood politics for good. He invited old Hollywood and new Hollywood to pick sides in America's culture war. By reaching out to the stars of the Golden Age, he encouraged them to define themselves as conservatives—even to imagine that they had always been conservatives, and that the movies they made when they were younger and more beautiful had a timeless conservative message. It set off a culture war within Hollywood itself.

On January 4, 1970, reporters gathered to watch one of the most painful sights in American politics: Richard Nixon playing golf. His companions were Bob Hope, Fred MacMurray, and James Stewart. The president's press secretary, Ronald Ziegler, briefed the press that his boss hadn't played in a long time, so they shouldn't expect much. Journalist Robert Semple described the scene:

Bob Hope teed off first, lacing the ball 225 yards down the fairway. Now the president addresses his ball. . . . Mr. Ziegler lit another cigarette, and his boss swung. Lifting his shoulder at the last minute, Mr. Nixon topped the ball, which rolled to a point about 90 yards down the fairway. "At least 200 yards," Mr. Ziegler estimated.

The bystanders politely applauded. "That's a Republican crowd," said Bob Hope.

Nixon was there to congratulate Hope, MacMurray, and Stewart on their work with Vietnam veterans.[26] Bob Hope had long been doing tours for American troops overseas, but under Nixon he evolved from an impartial entertainer to an outspoken hawk. One Pentagon official even referred to Vietnam as "Hope's War." Hope was a committed believer in the Vietnam project, and he was disgusted by what he saw as the reckless hedonism of the antiwar movement. He told reporters that stories of American soldiers taking drugs were lies, and denied that the My Lai massacre ever happened. He took a tour of the United States to drum up support for the conflict, backed by Jack Benny and Glen Campbell. Hope closed his 1970 Christmas special by asking his viewers to "support these men who lay their lives on the line every day." In return, he said, "they ask for one thing:. . . time to do a job. For us to be patient, to believe in them so they can bring us an honorable peace."

As with Wayne's cowboy theatrics, Hope's vision of himself as the voice of ordinary soldiers was pure fantasy. *The New York Times* reported that the Special Services entertainment division had actually considered dropping Hope from its lineup because his gags were "20 years" out of date. More important, his views were "out of tune" with the boys on the front line. Hope was booed when he told some soldiers in Vietnam that the president had a "solid plan" for getting them home. He proudly showed the press letters he received from the parents of men killed in action, thanking him for his support. But it seems less likely that the deceased themselves would have appreciated Hope's aggressive shilling for an unwinnable war.[27]

Jimmy Stewart was just as myopic. After years of silence on political matters, he felt drawn into the arena to defend his "friend" Richard Nixon against the attacks of the antiwar kids. He told a reporter, "The whole attitude toward the military concerns me very much. There are forces today, and where they come from I don't know— probably both from within and without—that are trying to soil the image of the military." Stewart had met soldiers in Vietnam, and he was convinced that they backed the president 1,000 percent. "All you have to do is go to Vietnam to see that the kids are still patriotic," he said. Stewart complained about the nudity and violence in seventies movies, but most of all about the strange, quiet anger of the actors. "The young people I've worked with just don't seem to have any fun in their craft," he sighed. He guessed that they were eaten up with bitterness at Nixon's popularity.[28]

As Hollywood split into conservative and liberal, past and present, old and young, it seemed to personify the choice that voters in 1972 faced between Nixon and McGovern. The party at San Clemente—so peaceful and warm beneath the swaying royal palms—suggested that a vote for Nixon was a vote for a return to the days of the "Chattanooga Choo Choo" and the "Cow Cow Boogie." A vote for McGovern was an endorsement of the grim world of seventies cinema, with its amoral violence and casual sex. Nixon's landslide victory said that the majority wanted a Dirty Harry not an Easy Rider.

On May 24, 1973, Nixon threw a gala at the White House for returning Vietnam prisoners of war. John Wayne (who it is worth remembering never served in uniform) gave the keynote speech. Of the veterans and the president, he said:

> I'm glad y'all got a chance to meet, because y'all have a lot in common. You hung in there when the going was rough, so did he. You stuck by your guns, so did he. You love this blessed country, and so does he, and so does all of us. You men, I wanna say thanks for showing the whole world the kind of men a free country can put up when the going gets rough. You're the best we have, and I'll ride off into the sunset with you anytime.

With tears in his eyes, the Duke said, "I want to thank you, Mr. President, not for any one thing, just for everything."[29]

That image of Richard Nixon as a lone cowboy who defied liberal opinion and "stuck to his guns" created a bond between him and the silent majority. Alas, it also justified in his mind the unethical things he did to stay in office. The people's champion had a duty to do everything within his power to keep the liberals out of the White House.

The Watergate scandal brought an end to Nixon's Hollywood project. There was nothing in the annals of the Golden Age that could justify what he did, and no star wanted to be associated with his increasingly toxic brand. The congressional investigation into White House involvement in the burglary of Democratic headquarters at the Watergate Hotel crippled his presidency. Nixon retreated into alcohol and movies: During 1973 he averaged seeing two and a half features per week.[30] At first, John Wayne stood by him and said that the scandal was a "frame-up" by "those bastards" in the press. But as the story drew out, his confidence shrank. The two men met for the last time over dinner at San Clemente in 1974. The Duke asked the president straight up if he was guilty. The president said no. The Duke believed him.

When the smoking-gun tape was released in August 1974, Wayne cried, "Damn, he lied to me!"[31]

Reagan, the "Authentic" Cowboy

Lies were Nixon's big problem. Yes, he was a first-rate strategist who understood exactly what he needed to say and do to get elected. But the very low cunning this involved always undid him—for he seemed as inauthentic as his mirthless smile (in the 1968 election, Nixon had his smile retouched and widened on his posters—the teeth bleached—and his tan deepened).[32] What conservatism needed to flourish was a populism that came from the heart. John Wayne was convinced that the best man to lend it that air of truth was the governor of California, Ronald Reagan. Reagan was a cowboy by training—a training given to him by Hollywood.

Ronald Reagan grew up in small-town Illinois, with a shoe sales-man father and a deeply religious mother. His second home was the movie house. For thirty-five cents he could sit in his local segregated cinema and watch cowboys shoot injuns.[33] Reagan later wrote that he learned "all the important social skills" from Tom Mix and William S. Hart, elegant gunslingers who knew how to treat women right.[34] They offered a much needed distraction from the nightmare of the Great Depression, which cost Reagan's father his job and drove him to drink. Like millions of others, the family looked for answers in the Democrat, Franklin Roosevelt. "A few months after my twenty-first birthday in 1932," Reagan recalled, "I cast my first vote for Roosevelt and the full Democratic ticket. And, like [my father]—and millions of other Americans—I soon idolized FDR." He was, in his own words, "a near hemophiliac liberal."[35]

Reagan dreamed of escaping drudgery by becoming an actor, but Hollywood and Broadway were too far away.[36] So in 1932 he settled in Des Moines, Iowa, to work as a sportscaster. Reagan was a hit. Incredibly, he didn't see most of the games he narrated—he was prompted from reports relayed to him by a telegraph operator. Yet he built a reputation as a confident, imaginative speaker, capable of dramatizing a football game with his mellifluous voice.[37] In 1936, Reagan convinced the station to send him to Catalina Island in California to watch the Chicago Cubs train. While there he auditioned for Warner and landed a two-hundred-dollar-a-week contract. Overnight, Ronald Reagan became studio property. The studio system controlled him now, from who he dated to the clothes he wore.[38]

Warner polled cinema patrons to ask what audiences thought of their new boy. The pollsters found that he was more liked by women than men, and more favored in towns than cities. This was the rural conservative heartland, the folks who voted Republican even as Roosevelt's Democrats were sweeping the country.[39] So Warner pitched Reagan to the squares. In advertising, they said that their man was

> both in appearance and personality, the representative of all that is admirable in young American manhood. While he is tall and handsome, there is nothing of the pretty boy about him, for virility is his outstanding characteristic.[40]

Reagan evolved from a gangly kid into something between a stud and a missionary.[41] It is remarkable to consider that the image Reagan carried around with him for life—even into the White House—was the product of polling done in the 1940s.[42] His nickname, the Gipper, was lifted from a part he played in *Knute Rockne, All American* (1940): George "the Gipper" Gipp, a football player who falls ill and dies before a big game. The last thing he tells his teammates to do is "win just one for the Gipper."[43] On-screen and off, Reagan believed that any problem could be overcome with willpower.

And yet life is never that straightforward. In Hollywood it might have seemed that all it took to make it was greasepaint and sweat, but elsewhere the American Dream was beyond reach. In 1940, America's unemployment level hovered around 15 percent. Overwhelmed with poverty, the state government of California announced that it was seeking $4.5 million in loans to cover unemployment benefits. In downtown Los Angeles, thousands queued for soup.[44] Meanwhile, Reagan wrote some articles (yes, he was the real author) for the *Des Moines Register* about his new life in Hollywood. He told of restaurants with "more varieties of appetizers than I ever imagined existed . . . bits of ham, pickled fish, spiced meats and goodness knows what else." When finished "you feel so comfortable that you purr like a cat and don't give a whoop." He was particularly impressed with Santa Barbara, which had attracted "more wealthy people from the east than any other community in America . . . more millionaires to the square mile," than anywhere else. "There are scores of magnificent estates with elaborate stables and armies of retainers." From all this, Reagan concluded that California was good, California was beautiful. "And boy, when [the sun] comes up over the rise of the mountains that hedge in Hollywood in the east, with the misty clouds radiating all the colors of the rainbow, it's something to write home about."[45]

If Reagan's journalism reads like a real estate ad, it's no coincidence. Studio pollsters had found that the public's yearning for a return to normality after the nightmare of the Great Depression was expressed in a new taste for marriage and suburbia.[46] So actors became salespeople for the American way.[47] On January 26, 1940, Reagan married the starlet Jane Wyman.[48] Warner Bros. marked the birth of their first child with a press release that listed the objects in their house in the manner of a catalog: sofas, beds, ovens, barbecue, white-marble bath tiles. Reagan's gimmick was his "normality," so his bland personality was used to sell the idea that his privileged lifestyle was well within the reader's reach (when, for most, it patently was not). The happy husband said, "The Reagans' home life is probably just like yours, or yours, or yours. We do the same foolish things that other couples do, have the same scraps, about as much fun, typical problems and the most wonderful baby in the world." Living in such a cocoon of good taste, it's understandable that Reagan lost touch with the world of small-town Illinois.[49]

World War II broke out at the peak of Reagan's career. He was too shortsighted to serve, so instead he was conscripted into making and narrating propaganda movies.[50] Technically, he was in service, so he wore a uniform and was stationed on an air force base. He spent hours in editing suites narrating footage of other men shooting and bombing the enemy. Ed Meese, who later served as

Reagan's attorney general, told me, "Reagan's image of America as a good country was largely shaped by what he saw when he was on that base editing movies. It gave him almost a religious view of America—something holy and worth dying for."[51]

In *Beyond the Line of Duty*, Reagan ran through how to conduct a successful mission over Japan. Hollywood special effects guys built miniature models of Tokyo to represent the terrain. So realistic were the matchstick palaces and Styrofoam forests that even the Washington officers were fooled. "Only an outfit like ours could have accomplished this task," said Reagan, proudly. "Here was the true magic of motion picture making." During the war, Reagan was often called upon to dress as a soldier: The Gipper was seen more often in uniform than any other president barring Dwight Eisenhower.[52] He evolved from an entertainer into a national symbol.

The war brought Reagan some borrowed glory, but it also slowed down his career. Warner offered him few new parts, and those he got he didn't like. Reagan became fixated on playing a cowboy, because he was convinced that he photographed better on a horse than standing up. After much lobbying, he landed a role in the big-budget Western *Stallion Road* (1947)—but he was cast as a vet rather than a gunslinger. Nevertheless, Reagan said that appearing in the movie "opened the door to finding another part of me." He bought the horse he rode in the film and named it Stallion Road. He also purchased a horse ranch.[53] Meanwhile, his salary dwindled. It's at this time that Reagan first privately floated a conservative idea: He complained to friends that the government should introduce a depreciation allowance for actors in recognition of the fact that their income fell over time.[54]

Bored, Ronnie tried his hand at union politics. In 1941, Reagan was elected to the board of directors of the Screen Actors Guild; by 1947, he had become its president. Ronnie was a natural at politics. He was a good debater and could easily charm other people over to his point of view. He also went about remaking SAG in the studios' best interests. He created two categories of member: A Class, to represent stars, and B Class, to represent the unknowns. The As got more votes than the Bs.[55] Sadly, the time Reagan devoted to giving speeches and breaking strikes contributed to the decline of his marriage. Wyman was getting better parts, and she was "bored" with her husband's politics. After she suffered a miscarriage, the couple drifted apart and divorced in 1948.[56]

By the late 1940s, Reagan was obsessed with the creeping influence of Marxism in American life.[57] He happily testified to the House Committee on Un-American Activities on the role of Communists in Hollywood unions. As head of SAG, Reagan insisted that he wouldn't cooperate with any effort to censor the movie industry or hound any of his members just because of their politics. Privately, he gave the FBI the name of every potential red he knew.[58] In 1949, Reagan received a letter from a twenty-six-year-old actress who had been added to an employment blacklist by clerical error. Nancy Davis had been mistaken for another, more liberal Nancy Davis. Ronnie called her to apologize. The two hit it off and went on a date. In 1952, they married.[59]

Hollywood Rides the Backlash

Reagan was a product of the studio system, both as an actor and a politician. Hollywood realized that his skills as a communicator made him a perfect ambassador for their industry, someone who would promote their ideals and their business interests. In the same way that they "handled" his evolution from poor boy to matinee idol, they stage-managed his evolution from faded actor to global statesman.

In 1954, Reagan was approached by Taft Schreiber, head of the

Music Corporation of America's Revue Productions, to host a new drama anthology TV series funded by General Electric. The huge salary of $125,000 a year would allow Ronnie and Nancy to build a new house, but what really appealed was the part of the contract that asked Reagan to tour the country visiting GE employees.[60] GE encouraged him to test out speeches that were overtly conservative. His favorite theme was taxes, and it was in the 1950s that Reagan wrote some of his best zingers about big government: "If it moves, tax it. If it keeps moving, regulate it. And if it stops moving, subsidize it."[61] By the end of his eight-year contract, Reagan was established as a national right-wing personality.[62] In 1962, he reregistered as a Republican in order to vote for Richard Nixon for governor of California. In 1964, he came to the attention of conservatives nationwide when the Barry Goldwater presidential campaign broadcasted a version of his most celebrated General Electric speech.[63]

Reagan's growing public profile benefited the studios in two regards. First, he promoted the increasingly conservative ideology of an aging establishment who still saw Communists everywhere. Second, he validated their claim to being serious political players. To have one of their own in the national spotlight gave Hollywood a sense of significance that it had never had before. Rather than just attractive adornments on other people's campaigns, movie stars were now statesmen in their own right.

In 1966, Reagan ran for governor of California with financial support from MCA executives.[64] Hollywood also lent the campaign some impressive visuals. John Wayne cut an ad for Reagan that featured the Duke dressed as a cowboy, swaggering across the plains. "So what's this empty nonsense about Ronald Reagan being just an actor?" Wayne asked. "I watched Ron work his entire life preparing for public service!" Reagan put on cowboy clothes for a horse ride through the streets of San Jose. Californians loved it: Reagan won by a landslide.[65] He told his campaign manager, Stu

Spencer, "Politics is just like show business. You have a hell of an opening, coast for a while, and then have a hell of a close."[66]

Reagan's conservative image was far removed from reality.[67] As governor he cut spending, but he also hiked taxes. He reduced the number of people eligible for welfare but raised the payments to those who were. He signed a law legalizing abortions and supported the Equal Rights Amendment. Reagan wasn't a fraud; it's just that there was a big gulf between the semantics of a campaign and the day-to-day work of government—much of which Reagan left to others to do. Most politicians are happy to inhabit a paradox. But what frustrated Democrats was that Reagan was rarely called out on it. "I can't find the real man," one Democrat moaned. "Reagan is always playing a part. He's an actor and he's acting out the role of Governor. He says all the clichés but he doesn't do anything. And that, I guess is what the people want—a guy who looks good and sounds sincere and competent, but doesn't actually do anything."[68]

That's not quite true. Just like Nixon, Reagan was tapping into the early 1970s taste for vigilante fight back. He didn't cave to protesting students but confronted them head-on—the Gipper pushed himself as a cowboy going against the outlaws, bringing justice and peace with wisecracks like gunshot. And when Nixon was destroyed by Watergate, Reagan was there as an alternative. John Wayne certainly liked him. The two were friends from the Golden Age of Hollywood, and the Duke was more than happy to campaign for the Gipper when he announced that he was running for the presidency in 1976. Jimmy Stewart joined them. By coincidence, Stewart and Wayne were starring in Wayne's very last movie that year, *The Shootist*. "It's a pure movie about the old West," Stewart told journalists. "We're not trying to be psychological; we're simply showing the good guys and the bad guys." Whereas modern politics and movies seemed complex to the point of morally confused, Reagan, Wayne, and Stewart liked to keep things simple. A vote for

Reagan was a vote for the good ol' days. The Gipper lost in 1976, but when he ran again in 1980, the people voted for that by 51 percent to 41 percent.[69]

Hollywood Takes Over the White House

Ronald Reagan's inaugural gala announced the arrival of old Hollywood into the White House. Johnny Carson told some zingers ("We ought to thank George Bush, who gave up political life to become vice president"). Ethel Merman, looking veritably embalmed, sang "Everything's Coming Up Roses!"—pointing straight at Reagan and shrieking, "Baaaa-byyyy!" Dean Martin and Debby Boone crooned their greatest hits. Charlton Heston read excerpts from American literature. Jimmy Stewart brought the only living five-star general onstage to pay an emotional tribute to "our new commander in chief." No one seemed to find it odd when black dancer Ben Vereen came on to sing a minstrel tribute. Reagan's election had brought Hollywood into the corridors of power. From now on his image would set a powerful standard in Republican politics. It never quite matched the realities of governing, but his mix of Hollywood polish and Western swagger created a new ideal in conservatism: the cowboy president.[70]

Pat Buchanan, who served as Reagan's director of communications in his second administration, was mightily impressed with his boss.

Reagan's televised addresses were incredibly smooth and well timed. They called him the Great Communicator for a reason. . . . He read very little of his briefing materials and never got stuck into detail. The emphasis was always on the art of the performance: the right angle, the right phrasing, the right look. . . . He could turn that magic on and off, just like that.[71]

The Hollywood magic seemed more often turned on than off. The Reagans were frequent participants in the endless rounds of moviemaker fund-raisers and variety shows, marking birthdays, anniversaries, and dinners with a cheerful glamour that could make the casual viewer struggle to tell where the actor ended and the president began. In 1985, the Reagans attended a black-tie charity event in Los Angeles where the performers called him Dutch, and Ronnie even reenacted one of his Iowa sports broadcasts. Frank Sinatra sang "Have Yourself a Merry Little Christmas," Burt Reynolds joked about some of Dutch's movie flops, Ben Vereen and the diminutive Emmanuel Lewis danced to "Hooray for Hollywood," Charlton Heston rehearsed a long and convoluted speech about the terrors of nuclear war ("To the world, you are America"), and still playing the alcoholic, Dean Martin joked: "In 1988, you'll be out of work, but I'll still be drunk." This was a presidency designed for the TV age, with gags and musical numbers thrown in.[72]

The dress was far more ostentatious than it had been at Nixon's San Clemente party a little over a decade earlier. In the eighties the White House men wore black bow ties and the women wore diamonds. Hair was big, shoulder pads were aerodynamic, dresses bounced with ribbons. Leaders led by example, and the Reagans seemed to believe that they could will the country out of the recession they inherited by living an opulent lifestyle. Recall those studio press releases about the luxurious lifestyle of Ronnie and Jane Wyman? Ronnie and Nancy lived an ideal home life in the White House, too. "We do not wear pants. We do not wear clogs. We represent our country," Nancy's social secretary told journalists. The First Lady returned the congressional allowance for refurbishments, fifty thousand dollars, and acquired private financing instead: $1 million. She filled the White House with gaudy antiques and eighties bling. She covered the personal interiors in California colors—pink, salmon, and yellow. The Oval Office was stuffed with yellow sofas and marble-topped tables. In 1982, she scandalized Washington by spending $209,508 on a new set of china.[73]

Style matched some of the substance of Reagan's policies. The new president tore up the postwar consensus of big government at home and accommodation with communism overseas. He cut all income taxes by at least 25 percent, simplified the tax code, and deregulated business. During his time in office the top income tax rate fell from 70 percent to 28 percent. After a harsh recession in the early 1980s, the country rebounded spectacularly. By 1988, America had gained sixteen million new jobs, and inflation stood at just 3.4 percent.[74]

Reagan's policies were equated with his cowboy image: Many critics accused him of having a "shoot from the hip" style. Certainly he often eschewed equivocation or negotiation. When the air traffic controllers went on strike, Reagan sacked them all.[75] Overseas, his administration supported anticommunist groups, including the Contras in Nicaragua and the mujahideen in Afghanistan. In October 1983, U.S. troops invaded Grenada to oust a Marxist dictatorship.[76] Only sixty-nine days into the new administration a deranged gunman tried to assassinate President Reagan. His survival broke a cycle of political killings that had haunted America since 1963, giving hope that the United States was headed in a different, better direction.[77]

Hollywood worked in concert with the White House to affirm a new spirit of national self-confidence. They made movies like *Rambo: First Blood* (1982), which told the story of a Vietnam vet (played by Sylvester Stallone) who takes revenge on a corrupt sheriff, effectively refighting the Vietnam War on American soil. The exorcising of America's post-Vietnam tensions was more obvious in *Rambo: First*

Blood Part II (1985), when the eponymous hero is invited to return to Vietnam to rescue some POWs. Rambo asks his employer in his near-incomprehensible drawl, "Do we get to win this time?"[78]

The Rambo aesthetic (lashings of blood and sweat you can almost smell) was replicated in movies like *Terminator* (1984), *Delta Force* (1986), and *Die Hard* (1988), which helped make screen legends of Arnold Schwarzenegger, Chuck Norris, and Bruce Willis. The producer Mario Kassar, who was responsible for *Rambo, Total Recall* (1990), and *Terminator 2* (1991), called these his "muscle movies." He insists that they weren't designed to promote any particular ideology but rather were created because he realized that there was money to be made in foreign-language markets—so he needed to make movies that were visual and not too talkative. Actors like Arnie spoke with their fists, which meant there was little dialogue to dub. As a result, foreign distributors loved them.[79] The director of *Total Recall*, Paul Verhoeven, confirms that the intent behind the muscle movies was purely commercial (if a little ironic). After a successful art house career in Holland, he arrived in the United States and understood that he needed to make something very different. What he produced were "parodies" of American movies, with a deliberate—almost mocking—emphasis upon cheap thrills and violence.[80]

Reagan took these muscle men movies far more seriously than their makers did. He often quoted Rambo in his speeches, and the neck-snapping, gun-blasting Vietnam vet became shorthand for his foreign policy style. Following the premier of *Rambo II*, Reagan told reporters, "After seeing *Rambo* last night, I know what to do next time [a terrorist attack] happens." When he sent U.S. warplanes to force down an Egyptian airliner carrying the Palestinian hijackers of an Italian cruise ship, the British front pages screamed "Rambo Reagan!"[81] The president once interrupted a cabinet meeting on nuclear weapons to discuss the plot of the movie *WarGames* (1983), in which a teenage boy accidentally hacks into the Western defense system. Reagan quoted the *Star Wars* franchise a great deal, too. He named the Strategic Defense Initiative (a missile system designed to shoot down Soviet nukes) "Star Wars" and referred to the USSR as the "evil empire." When he made an "exoatmospheric" phone call to a U.S. space shuttle, the president told the astronauts: "May the force be with you."[82]

For Ronald Reagan, cinematic myth and reality blurred. Once, at a diplomatic exchange at the White House, Reagan impressed the prime minister of Israel by telling him that he would never betray his Jewish ally, because he had been present at the liberation of Dachau. In fact, he never set foot in Germany at any time during the war. He had been privy to secret footage of the liberation while he was working for the war effort in a California movie studio, and that's probably what he remembered. Over the years he apparently convinced himself that he had personally liberated the death camps.[83]

If Reagan was just reciting the lines that Warner Bros. wrote for him back in the 1940s, it's important to stress that his act wouldn't have lasted had the public not played along. The American voter wasn't just a passive spectator but an active participant in his Western drama. In 1981, a few months after his inauguration, President Reagan gave the commencement address at Notre Dame, in Indiana, the setting for his 1940 turn as George "the Gipper" Gipp, Notre Dame's legendary sportsman. Reagan was greeted by eight thousand students singing "The Fighting Song"—the anthem of the university football team. In an extraordinary layering of emotions and images, Reagan became the Gipper once more. He said:

> As Americans, as free people, you must stand firm, even when it is uncomfortable for you to do so. There will be moments of joy, of triumph. There will also be times of despair. Times when all of those around you are ready to give up. It is then I want you to remember our meeting today, and sometimes

when the team is up against it and the breaks are beating the boys, tell them to go out and win one for the Gipper!

Reagan channeled not just the character of the Gipper but the values associated with that character, too: self-reliance and determination. One BBC commentator observed, "Here is the president of the United States playing his younger self, playing a long-dead football hero, and leaving scarcely a dry eye in an audience of eight thousand." We might ask, Who was the audience cheering? The president, the actor, or the football player? And by playing along with Reagan's fantasy, did the audience not get the performance it deserved? Did America perhaps consciously choose to be governed by an archetype rather than someone who could have reflected the realities of her many problems? Apparently so, for in 1984 they reelected the Gipper by a 59–41 percent margin.[84]

The Cowboy Fetish Endures

Despite his electoral success in the 1980s, Ronald Reagan's myth has become an albatross around the Republican Party's neck. In the 2012 GOP primaries, the candidates competed to be crowned his heir. Mitt Romney said, "America entered the Reagan era as one kind of country and exited it another. His mixture of extraordinary personal and political qualities made it possible. . . . The Gipper's irrepressible high spirits tapped into something deeply rooted in the country: optimism, faith in America itself." Ron Paul ran an ad called "Trust" that touted the fact that he backed Reagan in the 1976 and 1980 primaries. Michele Bachmann promised a "Reagan economic miracle," and Rick Perry pledged to win the war on terror the same way Reagan "won" the Cold War. The media encouraged the nostalgia. During a September 2011 debate, held at the

Reagan library, the candidates were asked, in a question about the economy, "What would Reagan do?"[85]

The problem is that the Reagan image of uncompromising conservatism doesn't match the reality of his time in office. For all his antigovernment rhetoric, government spending actually increased under Reagan, and the deficit tripled. Reagan accumulated more debt than every president between 1900 and 1980 combined. He refused to push for a federal ban on abortion. Reagan's famous resolve in foreign affairs is also an exaggeration. When a U.S. army base in Lebanon was bombed in 1983, Reagan withdrew troops from the country. He offered to scrap America's entire nuclear stockpile in talks with the Soviet Union in 1986, and the administration's illegal policy of selling arms to Iran in exchange for the country's assistance in releasing American hostages smacked of compromise.[86]

The contemporary Republican Party models itself not on the realities of government but on a false memory informed by Hollywood. Ronald Reagan set a standard for how a conservative should look, sound, and behave. In their effort to match that standard, the Republicans have often suspended their critical faculties and surrendered themselves to the myth. Not only has it opened them up to the charge of conservative fundamentalism, it has also had some terrible consequences for policy making.

For example, Reagan's foreign policy philosophy (as contrasted with what he really did when in office) was drawn partly from his Hollywood experience—narrating newsreels on the fight against fascism, tackling communism in the movie unions, playing a cowboy veterinarian. His belief that the world was divided between good and evil was derived from movie lore. At the funeral of John Wayne in 1979, he recalled:

"There's right and there's wrong," Duke said in *The Alamo*. "You gotta do one or the other. You do the one and you're living. You do the other and you may be walking around, but in reality you're dead." Duke Wayne symbolized this, the force of the American will to do what is right in the world. He could have left no greater legacy.[87]

Indeed he could not, for it lived on in Reagan and the Republican Party. George W. Bush modeled himself on a similar, constructed-cowboy archetype.[88] In the days after 9/11, Bush said of Osama bin Laden, "There's an old poster out West that I recall that said 'wanted, dead or alive.'" At a National Cattlemen's Beef Association meeting in February 2002, Bush told the crowd, "Either you're with us, or you're against us." After the Senate approved the War Powers Resolution in October 2002, Bush thanked members of Congress and said, "The days of Iraq acting as an outlaw state are coming to an end." In November 2002 at the NATO summit in Prague Castle, where Bush was generating international support for a war with Iraq, he said, "Contrary to my image as a Texan with two guns at my side, I'm more comfortable with a posse."[89] (Bush wasn't the only one in the administration who used movie language. Dick Cheney referred to himself as a "gun for hire," and the neoconservatives, who self-identified as hard-core policy wonks, were "the Vulcans.")[90]

Public and press played along with Bush's cowboy theatrics. A common theme in editorials was Bush's similarity to Clint Eastwood's Man with No Name. *Slate*'s William Saletan wrote, "[A]nother cowboy is riding into town, less crazy but with much bigger guns: the president of the United States." The *All-American Post*, published by the Vietnam Veterans and Airborne Press, argued that Bush was torn between being like the liberal Gary Cooper in *High Noon* and the conservative Clint Eastwood in *Unforgiven*. The article claimed Bush resembled the Gary Cooper style cowboy after 9/11 in his deliberate approach, and had thus gained much political capital; however, in his dealings with Iraq, Bush emulated East-wood in *Unforgiven* and became a sadistic bully. Piers Morgan, in the UK's *Daily Mirror,* wrote, "I think people look at [Bush] and think John Wayne. We in Europe like John Wayne, we liked him in cow-boy films. We don't like him running the world."[91]

There are good things about the Hollywood cowboy: He means what he says and is kind to his horse. But the myth is built upon too many fallacies to be a good model for government. The world isn't divided between good and evil, and few problems can be solved out-right by violence. Even a cowboy's honesty is hard to imitate, as the Watergate and Iran-Contra scandals showed.

But the image of the cowboy as perpetuated by Hollywood casts a long shadow over the Republican Party.[92] And it is not the only Hol-lywood myth to do so. Reagan's beloved muscleman movies have entered right-wing folklore as well. Their stars have become deluded incarnations of the cinematic gods they played. In 2003, Bruce Wil-lis telephoned the White House and asked President Bush if he could volunteer to serve in Iraq.[93] In 2008, Chuck Norris revived his kung-fu skills for a series of ads promoting Governor Mike Huckabee for president. "There is no chin behind Chuck Norris's beard," said Mike, with a straight face. "Only another fist."[94]

No one has been more caught in the spell of his on-screen char-acter than Arnold Schwarzenegger. In the 1980s he played unstop-pable heroes who would overcome absurd obstacles to defeat their opponents. In 2003, he ran to become "The Governator" of Califor-nia on an equally superhuman platform. On October 7, 2003, he arranged a demonstration for the media of his determination to turn California around through sheer strength of will. The press boarded the *Total Recall* bus and followed Arnie's coach (nick-named "The Predator") to the Orange County fairgrounds. The candidate delivered his address in front of a huge steel wrecking ball. "In the movies," he said in his strong Austrian accent, "if I played a character and I didn't like something, you know what I did? I destroyed it." He didn't like the state car tax, he said, so, to the crowd's delight, the wrecking ball was dropped onto a car. Kaboom! Above the cheers, he cried, *"Hasta la vista, car tax!"*[95]

Arnie repealed the car tax, and California lost $5 billion each year in revenue. The Governator was forced to persuade the legislature to borrow $15 billion to cover the missing cash. Today California is still paying off the interest on the bonds it took out, and it struggles to pay its teachers and policemen.

If only life was more like the movies.[96]

7

MAN OF STEEL

How Hollywood Turned the President
into a Leading Man

Hollywood has influenced the philosophy of conservatives and liberals, but how has it changed the way we think about politicians in general? Well, it's helped to turn them into celebrities—into stars in their own right. Consider the importance politicians place on having a good head of hair.

In 2012, Will Ferrell starred in a movie about a spoof election called *The Campaign*. His character, Cam Brady, is an airhead Democrat from North Carolina with few principles but bags of sexual magnetism who spins out slogans that sound good but really mean nothing: "Schools is this nation's backbone!" Ferrell told journalists that he based the character on the philandering John Edwards, the former senator who could sell ice cream to a snowman: "He can kinda take command of a room, but then you leave realizing he literally didn't say anything that was of any value, or anything with any substance. He just knows he's got great bedside manner and is superpolished, but he's not really of any substance."[1]

An important part of getting the character right was his hair. Edwards's hair is something of a political legend, so rich and powerful that it probably stood a better chance of being elected president than Edwards himself. During his 2004 presidential primary race he hired a Hollywood hairstyling legend, Joseph Torrenueva, to cut it. Torrenueva charged three hundred to five hundred dollars per session, plus air fare. On one occasion he was paid $1,250 by Edwards for two days' work in Atlanta. Why hand over so much money for a haircut? Torrenueva explained, "I try to make the man handsome, strong, more mature and these are the things, as an expert, that's what we do." It's a fascinating lesson in the power of image: a quick trim can give a man of little substance the impression of being "strong" and "mature."[2]

The Campaign satirizes that lesson beautifully. Cam Brady constantly asks his political adviser how he looks, and the answer is, invariably, "Strong, sir." For example:

BRADY: How's the hair?
ADVISER: Strong. So fucking strong.
BRADY: Yeah. My hair could lift a car off a baby if it had to.
ADVISER: Absolutely.

On set, Brady's follicle fetish became a problem for Ferrell: sometimes it held up production. He explained, "I'm focused on my hair throughout the movie, yeah. That's kind of a huge thing. . . . [T]here are moments where we literally reshot something because the wind was blowing and my hair was looking too crazy and it just wouldn't work for Cam. We reshot a whole speech so that I could have more perfect hair."[3]

Another real-life politician who was obsessed with his hair was

John F. Kennedy. When Mimi Alford, a former intern who claimed to have been his lover, published an account of their relationship in 2012, she wrote:

> The president was quite vain, particularly about his hair. . . . He would frequently invite me to the Oval Office and ask me to administer a hair treatment before one of his televised press conferences. The hair treatments were apparently a daily ritual. . . . He insisted on using products only from Frances Fox, a company in upstate New York. He liked to lean back in his rocking chair and close his eyes while I massaged some tonic and an amber-colored ointment into his scalp.

Sex with the narcissistic Kennedy was hardly magical. Of their first act of congress, Alford wrote, "I wouldn't describe what happened that night as making love. But I wouldn't call it nonconsensual, either." The reader gets the sense that Jack Kennedy's heart was truly set on another: Jack Kennedy. When they broke up, he gave Alford a photo of himself as a good-bye present. The hair was impeccable.[4]

I write so much about hair to make the point that Hollywood and television have transformed the imagery of politics. Of course, plenty of men and women still make it to the top who are far from great beauties. But in the last fifty years a new standard has emerged of an ideal politician who is articulate, intelligent, resolute, and—if possible—good-looking, with powerful hair. The standard was set by John F. Kennedy—and he borrowed that standard from the movies. As we shall see, Kennedy consciously modeled himself on the stars of the day. And since the 1960s politicians have modeled themselves on Kennedy. In other words, the Obama mystique is as much an inheritance of Gary Cooper as it is of JFK.

In politics in the television age, style and message are as one.

The image of a politician affects the way that we understand their character and what we expect them to do in office. This glamorization of U.S. politics—the growth in tailoring, oils, and treatments—has had an unhealthy effect upon the way that the republic works. It has helped turn the office of the presidency from an executive with limited powers into an imperial court with a movie star—a leading man—at its center. This has been great news for Beverly Hills hairdressers but bad news for the Constitution.

The Kennedys Come to Hollywood

Joe Kennedy was the first Kennedy to conquer Hollywood. After making a small fortune in banking, he formed a production company in 1919 to bring the blackface star Fred Stone out of vaudeville and into the movies. After a few years working in distribution, he purchased a studio outright in 1926 and turned himself into a minimogul—"the Napoleon of the movies," in the words of one critic.[5]

Kennedy proved himself as brilliant as he was megalomaniacal: He assisted in the talkie revolution and helped pioneer the vertical studio system that would make Hollywood the home to so many millionaires. But he also destroyed several studios, slashed hundreds of jobs, and involved himself in the lives of his stars in a manner that could be politely called predatory. When Joe took an interest in Gloria Swanson, he first paid off her enormous tax bill and took control of her accounts. Then, having effectively made a down payment on her body, he leaped on her in a Palm Beach hotel. Gloria was relaxing in a kimono and silk slippers when Joe arrived unannounced. "He entered the room and closed the door behind him. He moved so quickly that his mouth was on mine before we could speak." Swanson did not struggle. "I knew perfectly well that, whatever adjustments or deceits must inevitably follow, the strange man beside me, more than my husband, owned me." Joe didn't just date women: He possessed them.[6]

Joe's appeal wasn't just his money—he also lent some Eastern respectability to the Western Babylon. *Photoplay* magazine described him as "exceedingly American" (i.e., not Jewish) and his "background of lofty and conservative financial connections, an atmosphere of much home and family life and all those fireside virtues of which the public never hears in the current news from Hollywood." He arranged for Hollywood friends to go and give lectures at his alma mater, Harvard University—flattering their egos and winning him access to new circles of power and money. But that Eastern charm had a flipside of cruel calculation. While the Hollywood moguls treated their studios like their children, Joe only ever saw his as a financial investment. This not only allowed him to pick, exploit, and dump studios and stars without a flicker of emotion, but it also gave him an academic eye as to how movies worked. He picked up lessons that would be passed onto his sons Jack, Bobby, and Teddy.[7]

One was the correlation between sex and power. The sex lives of the Kennedy men have been detailed more extensively than the military history of World War II—for the simple reason that they are just as fascinating and horrifying. The Kennedys treated women like morsels and delicacies rather than human beings. Something to be enjoyed and experienced; and then the remainders of the affair were brushed off the plate into a trash can. The actress Joan Fontaine recalled that Joe Kennedy invited himself to dinner at her house and, after the final course, beckoned her into the living room. "I like it," he said to her. "I like your guests, your children, your house. Tell you what I'll do. I'll live here whenever I come to California. I'll invest your money for you. You can do what you like when I'm not here, but there's only one thing, I can't marry you."

Of course not: The old scoundrel was already married. Fontaine declined the offer.[8]

Little was kept from the children. He told both the sons and daughters stories of conquests, and he asked them for suggestions of women he could date. Friends invited to the Kennedy home preferred not to sit next to Joe during screenings in the family cinema because he might start to touch and kiss them in the dark. Sleepovers were ill advised. "The Ambassador prowls at night," Jack told one young lady.[9]

Another lesson Joe picked up from Hollywood was the importance of image. Image in the sense that with the right publicity even a dirty love rat could be sold as embodying "home and family life and all those fireside virtues." But also image in the sense that the camera can turn a short nobody into a tall hero. "Image is reality" was one of Joe's favorite aphorisms. He certainly made it so.[10]

Joe was determined that one of his sons would be president someday. He was ruled out of contention himself partly because of his notorious business ventures and his opposition to FDR's foreign policy (influenced, some insisted, by anti-Semitism. He told one reporter, "It is true that I have a low opinion of some Jews in public office and in private life. That does not mean that I . . . believe they should be wiped off the face of the Earth").[11] After his first son, Joe Jr., died, his presidential ambitions shifted to Jack. And Jack was trained in how to present himself by the moviemakers.

In 1945, Jack visited Hollywood with the express intention of learning how to become a star. His friend Charles Spalding was working as an assistant to Gary Cooper and recalled years later that Jack was obsessed with capturing "the blinding magnetism these screen personalities had." Spalding told historian John Hellmann:

Jack would go out to Hollywood and notice the parallels between people out there—like personalities drawing crowds.

Why did Cooper draw a crowd? We'd spend hours talking about it. His magnetism, did he have it or didn't he?[12]

In person, Jack was shocked to discover that Cooper wasn't magnetic at all. They dined together, and Kennedy told Spalding afterward that he had found the actor boring and even unattractive. So why, on-screen and in photos, was he so godlike? "How does he do it?" Kennedy demanded to know. "Do you think I could learn how to do it?"[13]

When Jack ran for Congress in 1946, Joe employed all the tricks of the movie trade to help him win. Polls consistently showed that voters were more interested in Jack's war experience than his stance on the issues. So Joe developed a stump speech that would turn this slight, stammering man into a profile in courage — along with lessons in elocution to iron out the verbal stumbles and a diet to broaden the shoulders. His gimmick was a mix of sincerity and confidence that came off as charisma. *Life* magazine reported, "When women meet him they give off the kind of glow usually reserved for movie stars. In Milwaukee a starry-eyed waitress who got his autograph whispered admiringly, 'He's got a sort of all-American, wholesome face.'" The campaign was "more of a personality display than a crusade." For Joe, this was not an insult. In fact, he told the *Life* journalist that he was proud of his son's sexual magnetism: "Jack is the greatest attraction in this country today. I'll tell you how to sell more copies of a book. Put his picture on the cover. . . . He can draw more people to a fund-raising dinner than Cary Grant or Jimmy Stewart. Why is that? He has more universal appeal."[14] As Tennessee Williams exclaimed when playing golf with Jack, "Get that ass!"[15]

Just like a star, Kennedy's life became an endless photo shoot. In July 1953, *Life* captured "the handsomest young member of the U.S. Senate" courting Miss Jacqueline Bouvier on Cape Cod. The two are tanned and beautiful: Jack in shorts in the sea, Jackie draping her bare legs over a wall.[16] When the two married, *Life* was there again to capture "Washington's best looking young Senator" on camera. Wearing a stunning white dress, Jackie could have passed for a princess and Jack her prince.[17] Of course, these photos told the world nothing of where JFK stood on employment or economics—but we were slowly entering an epoch in which the looks of a politician mattered more than his brains. Adlai Stevenson—the physically modest Democratic nominee in 1952 and 1956—complained that TV packaged politicians in the same way that it did a breakfast cereal. Kennedy tried to become Adlai's running mate in 1956 and was blocked at the convention. One reason was that he was too darn young.[18]

Kennedy was fighting a battle between physical reality and public image. He had been a sickly child, and when he returned from the war he was struck low by Addison's disease, back pain, chronic weight loss (said one friend, "He looked jaundiced—yellow as saffron and as thin as a rake"), and nonspecific urethritis (it burned when he passed water, which may have been a lingering sex disease). By 1954 "Washington's best looking young Senator" was actually moving around on crutches in constant, searing pain. An operation left him with a metal plate in his spine. He got by with steroids (which might explain that slight puffiness in the face) and painkillers. [19]

All of this was kept from the press (some of them duped, some of them pliant) while Kennedy fixated instead on burnishing the image of an Adonis. When he ran for the presidency in 1960, he had a choice between two photos of himself for the posters: one young and one mature. Jack studied both for ages before announcing, "OK, let's go with the young one." Reporters called him Jack the Back for his habit of facing away from the photographers before he was fully made-up and ready to turn around and smile. The gray was treated with hair dye; his shirts and suits were changed several times a day to avoid displaying a crease.[20]

And one critical addition to the image was the presence of other stars. Nothing elevates one's social status like being seen in the company of famous people, so the Kennedy campaign made sure that Jack was constantly in the company of the rich and beautiful. His opponent in the primaries—the balding windbag Hubert Humphrey—later complained that he and his wife were overwhelmed by the other side's star power:

> Muriel and I and our "plain folks" entourage were no match for the glamour of Jackie Kennedy and the other Kennedy women, for Peter Lawford and Sargent Shriver, for Frank Sinatra singing their commercial "High Hopes." Jack Kennedy brought family and Hollywood. . . . The people loved it and the press lapped it up. While we worked hard to get a couple of dozen folks to coffee parties in a farm home, . . . the Kennedys, with engraved invitations, were packing ballrooms in Milwaukee.

Hubert noticed Jackie most of all, with her "fragile beauty [that] beguiled and entranced men and women and children in an almost mystical way." Jack could get jealous; he complained to aides that more folks wanted to meet Jackie than him.[21]

It's hard not to reach Adlai Stevenson's conclusion that politics was being debased. Sinatra's primaries song, "High Hopes," was an ugly, pointless jingle that spoke not of the ambitions of the country but the thrill that a man this good-looking might someday run it. "Kennedy, Kennedy, Kennedy, Kennedy" ran the theme song of the general election campaign against Republican Richard Nixon. While Nixon pledged to visit every single state personally (why, few could fathom), Jack held endless televised press conferences (sixty-four in 1960) to showcase his good looks. His mastery of the medium may well have won him the White House. After all, that first presidential debate came down to tanned Jack versus shifty Dick. Radio listeners called the debate a tie, but television viewers thought Kennedy walked it. And this was very much a TV election.[22]

JFK won the 1960 contest by just 49.7 percent to 49.6 percent—although that translated into a 303 to 219 Electoral College victory. Some called it stolen by big city machines; it could be joked that the average Chicagoan is so civic-minded that even death won't stop him from voting. It has also been rumored that Frank Sinatra himself acted as a go-between for the Kennedys and the mafia, letting the gangsters know that Jack would be good for business and so worth "helping" in the election—an offer that nobody could refuse.[23] Whether or not he did this would prove immaterial for their long-term relationship. The Kennedys used people. Once Frank Sinatra was done helping them to win the presidency, and even to organize the inaugural gala, he was dropped.[24] In 1962, Jack delivered the final insult when he visited Hollywood. The president declined an invitation to stay in Sinatra's house and lodged with Bing Crosby, a Republican, instead. The reason was that the new attorney general, Robert Kennedy, had read a troubling report from the Department of Justice. It read, "Sinatra has had a long and wide association with hoodlums and racketeers, which seems to be continuing."[25]

Not that Jack was exactly an angel. Playing the part of a star meant adopting many of the same tastes and habits. For JFK and his brothers, southern California became a refuge from the cameras—a place to indulge in casual sex protected by the complicit silence of reporters and the police. Jack rated Hollywood women so highly that he chased those well beneath his social status (Jayne Mansfield) and far above his age (Marlene Dietrich).[26] In return, he exuded a quality that many found irresistible and some became obsessed with. By the time he met Marilyn Monroe, he was the brightest and best of his generation and she was the most beautiful. The image of her breathily singing "Happy Birthday, Mr. President" opens the mind to a multitude of fantasies of seduction and domination. Marilyn's appeal was her mix of sexuality and vulnerability; she was a woman who deserved both desire and respect. She got more of the first, less of the latter than she wanted. If the gossip is all true and Marilyn and the president were indeed intimate, it probably wouldn't have been a very satisfactory experience. Jack was a "wham, bam, thank you ma'am" kind of lover, and he didn't appreciate Marilyn's constant attempts to call him at the White House. She was head over heels in love with him and couldn't let go. On August 5, 1962, Marilyn was found dead of an accidental overdose of barbiturates at her home in Brentwood.[27]

It was nothing personal, Marilyn. To the Kennedys, almost everyone was disposable. Unlike Nixon and Clinton—presidents who were genuinely awed by the stars they met—Jack was always a little cynical about Hollywood. A friend recalled touring Hollywood with Jack in the 1940s, shortly after he'd published a bestseller: "The stars would come over and speak to him: 'Oh, Jack darling, I just loved your book.'" Kennedy "put up with these people, but he saw through them. . . . He was fascinated by the stars and the glamour, sure—but not to take too much of his time." His approach to Hollywood was like his father's: Jack took what he could from Hollywood, both in terms of sex and political magic, and then forgot all the promises he'd made to the people he met. They were like so many words of love whispered on the pillow—something said in the moment, of no lasting importance.[28]

Ultimately, the Kennedy presidency would prove just as insubstantial. Cut short by assassination in November 1963, Jack accomplished very little in office. He resisted the threat of Soviet aggression during the Cuban missile crisis of 1962, but his domestic agenda had to be realized by his successor, Lyndon B. Johnson. Civil rights and the great expansion of federal spending came after he was gone.

What JFK did leave the world was the legacy of Joe's Hollywood photoshoot approach to politics. We are still haunted by those images of Camelot. Jack at the inaugural address telling us that America will "pay any price, bear any burden" to save the world from tyranny. Jack with his back to us, walking along the White House veranda with Robert by his side as they plan their next bluff during the missile crisis. Jackie giving us a tour of the White House, with its magnificent chandeliers and historic portraits. Then there are the photos of the final day. Jack in the car, waving. The head jolting from the shot. Jackie climbing over the car in panic. Johnson taking the oath of office aboard Air Force One, Jackie standing next to him in a daze, her coat covered in blood. She didn't want to be there for that photograph—Johnson insisted that she be in the frame so that Kennedy supporters would acknowledge his legitimacy as the new president. LBJ, too, had come to understand the power of a staged image.[29]

These visions would haunt American politics forever, creating a new ideal kind of president. This ideal was young, handsome, vigorous, strong, charming. Bill Clinton did his best to embody it, assisted by a black-and-white photo of his meeting Kennedy at the White House in 1963 (Bill said this was the moment when he decided to go into politics).[30] The idealized image tortured Nixon, because he knew he could never match it. He did his best, though. In a disastrous attempt to recapture the mood of those photos of Jack walking the beach at Hyannis Port, Nixon put together an identical press call at San Clemente. Selected photographers were placed in strategic locations and, after an interval, Dick strode into view in a windbreaker, trousers, and polished black shoes. He grinned uneasily at the surf, obviously not at home on the beach. More pathetic were his efforts to establish a reputation as a sportsman. Once in the White House he sent a memo to his press secretary that read: "[T]ell [reporters] that RN has become a regular bowler at Camp David at weekends. . . . His average is around 130 to 140 and his best game to date is 204." To emphasize his accomplishment, he added, "He has never bowled before except for a couple of occasions at Camp David in 1960."[31]

Nixon shouldn't have tried to live up to the Camelot ideal, for it was a Hollywood-inspired fraud—a series of carefully framed images that disguised the many moral failings of the people in the pictures. When he ran for the presidency in 1968, Bobby Kennedy tried something different. His campaign was not ordered but chaotic: The lasting images are those of him being pulled apart by adoring fans as he moved among his people. Bobby's people were not the stars of Hollywood (although he welcomed plenty into his campaign) but instead the destitute miners of West Virginia and the ghettoized blacks of Los Angeles. What he promised America was charisma, yes, but also moral leadership. The presidency that his own assassination deprived us of would have probably been infinitely more radical and transformative than Jack's.

And for Teddy Kennedy the Camelot image was a burden he was too weak to bear. When his car went off a bridge into a river on Chappaquiddick Island, killing a young lady within, his reputation was tarred forever. Chappaquiddick coincided with a political era in which reporters were less inclined to hide a candidate's faults. Everybody knew about Teddy's hard drinking and affairs, and his constantly trying to be as heroic as Jack or as saintly as Bobby wore him down. After a visit to Alaska in 1968 to try to look concerned about the plight of the local tribes, Ted got a little lit on the plane and started charging up and down throwing pillows at reporters and chanting, "Eskimo power! Eskimo power!"[32] One biographer wrote that accusations that he "lacked character" came down to "a failure to cover up, as though the ability to hide one's past failings were a qualification for the Presidency that his brothers possessed but he did not."[33]

When Teddy visited Hollywood in the 1970s, he found that JFK had paved the way for him. Bob Shrum, his speechwriter, says:

> The 1960 race had left a big impression on Hollywood because Jack Kennedy was such a compelling figure, and he had real, personal relationships with people in Hollywood. . . . So Ted spent a lot of time in Hollywood when he ran for the Democratic nomination in 1980—he knew a lot of the people there already. I remember one time he was supposed to give a speech at the Beverly Hills Hilton, and Robin Williams reached over and grabbed his speech and delivered it himself. Ted said, "He's stolen all my best lines!"[34]

Ted lost the 1980 race, and Hollywood didn't help. The liberals in the movie business were, by then, toxic publicity for a Democrat. It's fair to guess that the endorsement of Barbra Streisand was probably a net vote loser.

Obama as Kennedy

Perhaps the JFK Hollywood ideal didn't suit or fit Robert or Teddy, but it still serves as a standard of what a presidential candidate should look and act like. In 2008, Teddy tried to pass on the Kennedy torch to candidate Barack Obama. While stumping for Obama during the Democratic primaries, he reminded his audience, "Fifty years ago, another young senator changed history. . . . I think my brothers are on a pedestal unto themselves. But Barack is a very inspiring figure to me." Teddy pitched Obama as the fulfillment of his family's crusade for racial equality, and the Kennedy embrace certainly helped.[35] After Hillary Clinton won the big primary in Florida, the Obama camp buried the news beneath Kennedy endorsements: Ted joined his son Representative Patrick Kennedy and his niece Caroline Kennedy to endorse Obama at an American University rally—as well as to make what was fast becoming a ubiquitous link between JFK and BHO.[36]

The link wasn't really about substance but about star power. Running for the presidency in 2008, Obama had just three years of experience of life in Congress, compared to Jack's fourteen. But Obama still approximated JFK's model of the leading man president/candidate. He was good-looking (he walked topless from the sea like James Bond in *Casino Royale*—you're "very sexy," cooed Barbara Walters on *The View*), virile, and happy to be seen in the company of equally beautiful people. He had his own Camelot of brilliant youngsters who helped him to win, and his very own Jackie in the form of the ever-stylish Michelle Obama (*Forbes* called her "Jackie Kennedy with a law degree").[37] "There's no question he's one of the great orators," wrote Irish journalist Jane Graham, "up there with John F. Kennedy and Martin Luther King in terms of passion, intelligence and righteousness. . . . Obama is the movie star of movie stars, his tenure his celluloid."[38]

Ted Sorensen, JFK's chief speechwriter, said this of the two men: "Both Kennedy and Obama have fantastically winning smiles, and I might say both are very relaxed in front of an audience and on television. They don't shout into a microphone, they talk." Hardly good enough reasons to vote for either man, but ours is not an era of great substance. Sex appeal is far more important. Sorensen again:

> I've heard a lot of high-pitched shrieks of approval, which I assume were coming from young women. I'm told the

phenomenon known as leapers has returned. In Kennedy's case, along the motorcade route young women would levitate themselves to be able to see over the heads of taller people as he was driven by. There was excitement and enthusiasm that went into that leap as well as his good looks. It's interesting they report leaper sightings when Obama appears.[39]

The presence of leapers reminds us that a star can only become a star if the public accepts him or her as such. In 2004, the public never really bought that John Kerry shared much in common with Jack Kennedy, except his initials. But in 2008 the public seemed ready to buy into the idea that Obama was a black Kennedy. For *The New York Times*, Matt Bai reported that he overheard one fan say to another:

> "He's Bobby Kennedy reborn, that's what he is." In Salem, N.H., a few days ago, a woman standing behind me, waiting to get into an Obama rally, said, "He's just like Bobby Kennedy." Another journalist at the rally, picking up on this idea, commented to me on the way Mr. Obama's suit fits his wiry frame tightly and squared at the shoulders, so that his silhouette appears Kennedyesque.[40]

Bai found the comparison unhelpful, but other journalists were more than happy to help rebuild Camelot. Reflecting on the grand staging at the Democratic convention that presented Obama less as a presidential candidate than a latter-day Roman emperor, *The New Yorker* gushed:

> Obama's decision to deliver his speech outdoors in the vast, in-season corral of the Denver Broncos was clearly meant to "play big" in theatrical terms as well as lay down, for the

historically minded, mystic chords of memory evoking Kennedy's "New Frontier" acceptance speech, at the L.A. Memorial Coliseum, and Roosevelt's "rendezvous with destiny" speech, at his renomination in 1936, at Franklin Field, in Philadelphia. The Greek columns onstage summoned . . . Demosthenes rallying the Athenians against the Macedonian threat.[41]

Golly.

Many in the press didn't seem to mind being played, didn't mind their own hunger for the Kennedyesque being so blatantly manipulated. For the *Huffington Post*, Kitty Kelley wrote:

Both elusive men, Kennedy and Obama cared mightily about their public image, not an insignificant concern for politicians. Kennedy, who worried about being portrayed as a rich man's dilettante son, would not allow photographs inside Air Force One, saying that it would look like a playboy's luxury. Obama made sure cameras never caught him smoking cigarettes. Each understood the mesmerizing power of appearances and knew, as the actor Melvyn Douglas says in the film *Hud,* that "little by little the look of the country changes just by looking at the men we admire."[42]

There are downsides to packaging a candidate like a movie star. One is the idea that looks count for a lot more than they really ought to. Since 1900, in 75 percent of cases the taller presidential candidate has won the race. It's unlikely that voters consciously based their decision on height, but details like these have sparked a number of bizarre conversations about the right physique for a president. In 2012, Barbara Walters sat down for an interview with New Jersey governor Chris Christie and asked him point-blank if he was too fat to be commander in chief. "That's ridiculous," Christie replied with obvious offense. "I mean, that's ridiculous. I don't know what the basis for that is." The basis, explained Republican operative Ed Rollins, was that "[b]eing obese . . . makes everyone assume he is a heart attack waiting to happen." But it wasn't just a health issue—it was, to some, an example of blatant antifat prejudice. Rushing to Christie's defense, former presidential candidate Mike Huckabee asked, "Was Obama's smoking cigarettes a disqualifier for him to be president?" No, it was not, which Huckabee interpreted as discrimination in favor of the thin and against the rotund: "It's incredibly discriminating to make Christie's weight an issue when it's whether he's healthy enough to do the job that should matter."

But Huckabee himself was guilty of a little vanity. When he ran for the presidency in 2008 he not only shed a ton of weight first but also made his victory over flab a key part of his candidacy. "I'm like you. I've struggled with weight," he said—hoping to appeal to the millions of Americans for whom supersizing is a way of life. Huckabee's pitch and the debate about Christie's girth raised a serious question: Do we prefer hot politicians to plain ones?[43]

The evidence is mixed. In 2012, Harvard University professor of political science Ryan Enos told *Washington Monthly* that a study based upon showing photos of politicians to undergraduates discovered that Mitt Romney was one of the best-looking men in America. "What a face it is! We gathered the ratings of 728 candidates for Senate and Governors' seats and Romney outscored all but four of them." He is indeed a very beautiful man, but did it make any difference in the presidential race? His defeat suggests not, and Enos said:

Very few voters are willing to cast their ballot for a candidate based on looks—we estimate that if a candidate moves from the 25th to the 75th percentile in attractiveness, this is likely to gain that candidate about 3.5 percentage points in votes among independent voters, which was not enough to decide the winner of even a single Senate race out of 99 that we examined.

This is not to say that looks don't matter. As Enos points out, they give a candidate "significant human capital," and might be the very reason why they've made enough money or gained enough attention to be a contender, and why the media is so happy to promote them. The conversations about Obama's sexiness or Christie's weight indicate that looks have come to play a part in the American political discourse.[44]

Another problem with the leading-man model is that it encourages us to think of presidents less as human beings and more as supermen. Abraham Lincoln, Theodore Roosevelt, and Franklin D. Roosevelt all accumulated power in the hands of the U.S. executive—far more power than is either healthy or strictly constitutional. By glamorizing and mythologizing power, Jack Kennedy and the court of Camelot gave the impression that there is a link between personality and policy—that a virile president will govern in a virile manner, throwing money at domestic problems and expanding American power overseas. The leading man cast as Superman.

The superhero metaphor has been a popular one in recent campaigns. In chapter 1 I mentioned that Barack Obama was compared to Batman in 2012. This isn't the caped crusader's first foray into politics. It was a popular theory when the franchise first rebooted that it was an endorsement of George W. Bush's war on terror. And in the 2008 campaign Barack Obama and John McCain were asked by *Entertainment Weekly* which superhero they most identified with. Liberal Obama chose Spider-Man, because he is riddled with inner turmoil: "The guys who have too many powers, like Superman, that always made me think they weren't really earning their super-hero status." Conservative McCain chose Batman, because he's a powerful man who understands the difference between good and evil: "He does justice sometimes against insurmountable odds." A writer for *The American Spectator* naïvely predicted that his fellow countrymen would pick McCain's Batman over Obama's Spider-Man in the November vote, because "Batman is the cinematic (and comic book) personification of the way Americans like to see themselves. He is a rebel against the Establishment. . . . He is unafraid to act. He is willing to take risks." In the end, however, Spider-Man beat Batman; webs beat wings.[45]

When Obama won the 2008 election, Marvel Entertainment published a comic book in which Spider-Man helped foil a plot to ruin Obama's inauguration. Rahm and Ari Emanuel orchestrated the delivery of thirty collectors' editions of Dark Horse comics to the White House featuring Conan the Barbarian, which they hoped might "inspire" the new president to play the superhero (Obama happens to be a big comics collector).[46] It would be bad if it did, for the problem with the superhero model of leadership is that it breaks the bounds of what a republican government of limited and divided power is supposed to be able to do. Superpresidents send men to the Moon and try to build Great Societies. They also send soldiers to Vietnam to rescue it from communism, support secret invasions of Cuba, use money raised illegally from arms sales to Iran to finance the Contras, and declare war on Iraq to save the world from nonexistent weapons of mass destruction. Superheroes overreach in an effort to fulfill what the public expects of them. The aura of their superness can also filter down into the rest of their administration. During Barack Obama's time in office—the president branded as Batman by Hollywood—the Department of Justice snooped on journalists and the IRS held up requests for tax-exempt status by conservative groups. Drone strikes redecorated the Pakistani countryside, killing thousands, including at least four U.S. citizens. The security state expanded just as much as the welfare state—a momentum of power grabbing that grows fast to keep pace with the ego of the hero president.

And superheroes often end their presidencies in disappointment. A year or two more in office and Jack Kennedy might have been tarred by the failures of Vietnam or the Great Society; his assassination preserved his legacy in the golden amber of nostalgia. By contrast, Obama's failure to deliver on things angered his base. Remember that many liberals were as infuriated with Obamacare as conservatives were. They wanted a serious role for government as a provider of health care, and they were rightly furious at the deal that the administration purportedly made with insurance companies to kill the public option.

But the frustration isn't just down to flip-flopping. The American political system of divided government and checks and balances doesn't lend itself well to grand programs of reform. And so anything big that Obama might have wanted to do has been delayed or even stopped by the Republicans. Consider his failure on gun control. After the horror of the 2013 Newtown school shootings, the president backed a bill in the Senate that proposed a very modest expansion of background checks on people purchasing weapons at gun shows and in online sales. Polls suggested that the bill had vast support among the voters, and Obama was in the full flush of his popularity following reelection. Despite all of these advantages, it mustered just fifty-four votes—six short of the number necessary for passage. Following its defeat, Obama called it a "shameful day" for Washington, but it wasn't much better for him. Whatever your view on gun control, this moment was a damning indictment of Obama's presidency: a flash of style, lots of soaring rhetoric, and, when the votes are actually counted, little to show for any of it.[17]

The Kennedy-style leading-man president raises such high expectations and, when they are defeated, what is there left for him to do? Campaign. It is on the campaign trail that he can act out his hopes and frustrations, generating applause and tears and even the odd leaper. Obama's constant resort to campaigning even when already in office has become tiresome. After a few months into his second term, Chris Matthews concluded that the president

> obviously likes giving speeches more than he does running the executive branch. . . . He doesn't like dealing with other politicians—that means his own cabinet, that means members of the Congress, either party. He doesn't particularly like the press. . . . He likes going on the road, campaigning, visiting businesses, like he does every couple days somewhere in Ohio or somewhere.[48]

This, then, is the central paradox of the leading-man president. The glamour brought by Hollywood to the presidency has filled the role with a greater sense of possibility. But it's a possibility that can rarely be fulfilled—leading, always, to disappointment.

And in the age of 24/7 media coverage, it's hard to stay glamorous. John Edwards's pursuit of the perfect haircut was eventually his undoing. During the 2007 primaries, a video went viral of him fussing over his hair; some wit dubbed over it the tune "I Feel Pretty" from *West Side Story*. How the mightiest haircut is fallen.[49]

8

MODERN FAMILY

How Hollywood's Product Is a Lot Less
Liberal Than Conservatives Claim

t is undeniable that Hollywood is dominated by liberals, but how
far do they go in projecting their values onto the American people? Do they really use TV shows and movies to brainwash viewers into voting Democrat? And, if so, how successful are they at
doing it?

Television and movies are certainly on the front line of the culture war. Republicans and Democrats watch very different things.
In 2010, the media-research company Experian Simmons carried
out a survey of viewing habits and found that Republicans prefer
highly rated TV shows, such as *American Idol* and *Dancing with the
Stars,* while Democrats trend toward cable offerings with moderate
ratings such as *Dexter* and *Mad Men.*

Maybe it's predictable to read that American viewing habits cleave
in two along party lines. But the story is a bit more complicated

than that of a straightforward partisan divide—after all, the surveys show that conservatives don't mind a bit of social liberalism in their TV. The third-highest rated show among Republicans (and the highest-rated sitcom overall) was *Modern Family*.[1] On the face of it, *Modern Family* is a traditional sitcom full of plots about marriages, funerals, proms, feckless teenagers, and sibling rivalry. But the characters comprise three different kinds of families: a white, straight couple with three kids; an interracial, intergenerational couple with a son; and a gay couple with an adopted Vietnamese daughter. The show's attitude toward its trangressive characters is natural, casual, and often very witty (when asked if their daughter will have a typical childhood, one of her dads replies, "That gay cruise ship has already sailed"). In one episode the gay couple—Cameron and Mitchell—want to get their toddler into a popular school. They presume that their sexuality and her race will tick so many minority boxes that the interview will be a walkover. But then they catch a glimpse of the couple going in before them: two women, one in a wheelchair, and an African baby. Cameron says, "Disabled interracial lesbians with an African kicker?" Mitchell replies, "Did not see that coming." When it's their turn with the principal, Cameron decides to up their bankability by pretending to be a Native American. His improvised "injun" accent is met with a stony silence. The daughter doesn't get her place.[2]

Modern Family makes the case that black, white, gay, straight, what bonds people together are the ties of family and love. Jay, the patriarch, considers his dumb son-in-law, his gay son, and his nerdish Latino stepson and says, "When you're young and dreaming of your family, you think of this perfect family; perfect wife, perfect kids. Look at me, I got this sorry bunch. But you know I wouldn't trade them for anything." The show's plots and structure are traditionalist, but the message contains elements of liberalism.

Mitt Romney loves it. In an interview during the 2012 election he and his wife, Ann, said *Modern Family* was their favorite TV show. That prompted *Modern Family* cocreator Steve Levitan to invite Ann Romney to officiate at Cameron and Mitchell's gay wedding—should same-sex marriage become legal again in California. At the time of this writing, Ann has neither accepted nor declined the invitation.[3]

There are conservatives who would say that *Modern Family* is a Trojan horse, and that Mitt and Ann are dupes of a grand Hollywood plan to remake America through its culture. The argument goes that back in the 1960s the Left realized they had lost the case for socialist economics. So they tried to take control of America's opinion-forming institutions instead: universities, newspapers, television stations, movie studios. The goal was to convert the United States to liberalism through its culture: a vast left-wing conspiracy to destroy the family and turn the world gay—with scriptwriters as its vanguard and *Sesame Street* their *Das Kapital*. This thesis was best articulated by Ben Shapiro in his book *Primetime Propaganda: The True Hollywood Story of How the Left Took Over Your TV*. A young conservative who "was born in the shadow of the Hollywood sign," Shapiro tells us that his father tried to stop his kids from watching sitcoms for fear that it would undermine their values. Ben only figured out why when watching an episode of *Friends*. This was his road to Damascus moment in the culture war:

> Ross's lesbian ex-wife, Carol, is having his baby. And Ross is understandably perturbed that Carol and her lesbian lover will be bringing up his child. While Ross is going quietly cuckoo, Phoebe approaches him. "When I was growing up," she tells him, "you know my dad left, and my mother died, and my stepfather went to jail, so I barely had enough pieces of parents to make one whole one. And here's this little baby who has, like, three whole parents who care about it so much that

they're fighting over who loves it the most. And it's not even born yet. It's just, it's just the luckiest baby in the whole world."

Pregnant lesbians and three-parent households portrayed not only as normal, but admirable. This wasn't exactly Dick Van Dyke.

Shapiro says that Hollywood is run by liberals who have consciously used movies and TV to sell liberalism and alter the cultural values of the entire nation.

> The overwhelming Leftism of American television was too universal to be merely a coincidence. It had to be part of a concerted effort, a system designed to function as an ideological strainer through which conservatism simply could not pass. . . . Television's best and brightest wanted to set America sliding down the slippery slope away from its Judeo-Christian heritage and toward a more cultivated, refined, Europeanized sensibility.[4]

Of course, Shapiro is quite right to say that Hollywood is dominated by liberals. Where he is wrong, however, is in his assertion that the TV and movies they produce have purposefully revolutionized American society. Instead, I want to make a case for Hollywood's nervousness about being too overtly progressive and the limits of its impact upon the American imagination. In most cases, TV and movies haven't driven social changes but simply reflected them.

For example, the family models presented in *Modern Family* are far more commonplace than they would be if the show was meant to subvert societal norms. Cameron and Mitchell's relationship is neither as unusual nor as socially unacceptable as it once was: Polls conducted in 2012 found that four in ten Americans have a gay friend or relative and one in four gay couples are now raising a child. Within the GOP, there is a sharp generational divide.[5] A 2012 CBS poll on marriage equality found that, overall, 56 percent of Republicans oppose legalizing gay marriage. But among Republicans under fifty years of age there was actually a plurality in favor of it: 49 percent. This is a long-term political problem for the Right, and they know it. That year the Republican National Committee stated, "Already, there is a generational difference within the conservative movement about issues involving the treatment and the rights of gays—and for many younger voters, this issue is a gateway into whether the party is a place they want to be."[6]

Likewise, *Modern Family*'s inclusion of an interracial couple reflects the changing ethnic makeup of America. By 2040, America will no longer be a majority-white country, with the fastest growth rate among Hispanics. Of course, racial discrimination still exists and tensions still flare, but integration is happening. As of 2012, one in seven marriages is interracial.[7]

If *Modern Family* is at all progay or proimmigrant, then it's because its producers have judged that audiences are sufficiently tolerant to engage with its characters. Producers will generally only permit the degree of liberalism that they think the audience will feel comfortable with. Whenever they've crossed the line, they've been pulled sharply back—which is why some aspects of television in particular remain very conservative (teenage pregnancy and abortion are rarely explored in sitcoms). The underlying motive in TV production is profit, and profit is generated by advertising generated by viewership. Given the domination of the TV industry by the same suits who took over the movies in the 1980s, any show that is too controversial and so loses viewers will be quick to be canned. In short: TV seeks to imitate the values of society, not to change them. And what goes for TV goes for movies, too. It has been that way for a very long time, as a brief history of the sitcom will show.

The Sitcom as a Mirror

When as a Brit I first visited the United States, one of the biggest cultural differences I noticed was the sitcoms. UK sitcoms run for no more than six episodes per season, and the humor is often mean and ironic. U.S. sitcoms seem to run forever, and the humor is warm and family-friendly. Compare our two versions of *The Office*. The British original comprised two seasons of six episodes each, capped off by a two-part Christmas special. The U.S. remake ran for nine seasons, totaling 201 episodes. The British original is essentially about the hell that is other people: The boss (David Brent, played by Ricky Gervais) is a vain creep happy to sacrifice his coworkers for a shot at promotion. By contrast, the U.S. remake reimagines the office as an extension of the family home. Michael (played by Steve Carell) is a vain and unfunny but basically well-intentioned man who genuinely loves his peers. While the UK version focused on an unrequited love affair (consummated with a kiss only in the final episode), the U.S. *Office* has featured affairs, marriages, and a birth. The differences between these two shows in content and mood reflect the vast differences between British and American culture. The Brits prefer to laugh at their sitcom heroes; Americans prefer to laugh with them.

The American sitcom has always tried to do things that a) reflect the values of the wider society in order to appeal to as wide an audience as possible and b) anchor itself in the family. Sometimes that's a literal family (*The Cosby Show*, *All in the Family*), other times it's an extended family found in the workplace (*Taxi*, *The Mary Tyler Moore Show*). It's this permanent search for relevance that keeps the genre so fresh. Every decade has produced sitcoms that try to capture the spirit of the time. Those that don't, fail; those that succeed become part of the American identity.[8]

Take CBS's *Leave It to Beaver*—the epitome of 1950s conservative values. Starting in 1957, it starred Jerry Mathers as Theodore "the Beaver" Cleaver, an inquisitive boy who lived with his parents June and Ward in a leafy suburb. Beaver would get in trouble, his parents would tell him off, and our hero would learn something about the realities of life. In one story line Beaver met the son of divorced parents and was jealous of all the presents he got from his estranged dad. But he quickly discovered that divorce also leads to insecurity and depression, so the episode ended with Beaver begging his parents never to part. Spinsters like prim Aunt Martha were sexless harpies; bachelors, like Andy the alcoholic handyman, were layabout bums. It was a world of conservative certainty held together by a terror of nonconformity.

Today, *Leave It to Beaver*'s heavy-handed moralism and simplistic evocation of the good life seem hopelessly anachronistic. Its faith in parental authority feels saccharine, even oppressive. But it really did catch the spirit of its age. The 1950s were characterized by a rising birth rate, a stable divorce rate, and a declining age of marriage. In 1950 most married women walked down the aisle aged just twenty. Only 16 percent of them got a job outside the home, and a majority of brides were pregnant within seven months of their wedding. They didn't stop at one child: From 1940 to 1960 the number of families with three children doubled, and the number of families having a fourth child quadrupled.[9] Contemporary anthropologists dubbed this the "nuclear family." They meant nuclear as in a unit built around the nucleus of the father and mother, but the name also evokes images of the Cold War. The world was split between communism and capitalism, and U.S. leaders portrayed the family as America's best defense against collectivism.[10]

But in the course of the 1960s, everything changed. And the revolution didn't begin with popular culture but with science. In 1960, the U.S. Food and Drug Administration officially licensed the sale of the oral contraceptive that became known as the pill. By 1962, an estimated 1,187,000 women were using it. Politicians supported its wide availability because they thought that it would strengthen the nuclear family by increasing disposable income via reduced pregnancies. In practice, however, it weakened the links between sexual pleasure, childbirth, and marriage. Now sex apparently had no consequences: Hence people had a lot more sex. Sex before and outside of marriage became far more common, while women who had gotten married became more likely to stay in jobs, or to seek work.[11]

The effects of such subtle changes in sexual practice were revolutionary. Between 1960 and 1980 the divorce rate almost doubled, as the states legalized no-fault divorce. In 1962, only half of surveyed Americans disagreed that parents who don't get along should stay together for the children. By 1977, over 80 percent disagreed. In the early 1960s, roughly half of all women said that they had engaged in premarital sex. By the late 1980s, five out of six claimed that they had done so. In the early 1960s, approximately three quarters of Americans said premarital sex was wrong. By the 1980s that view was held by only one third of the nation. The most obvious legacy of shifting attitudes was the skyrocketing rate of births out of wedlock. In 1960, only 5 percent of births were attributed to single mothers. By 1980, the rate was 18 percent, and by 1990 it was 28 percent.[12]

Television responded to all this change with a mix of liberalism and traditionalism. For example, in 1971, CBS premiered *All in the Family*—a show about a working-class bigot and his long-suffering family. Produced by the proudly left-wing Norman Lear, it was another copy of a UK show (*Till Death Us Do Part*), and it dealt with issues such as racism, sexism, gun control, divorce, and free love. Lear also churned out controversial shows such as *Maude* and *Mary Hartman, Mary Hartman* in the 1970s—but for every daring exercise like those, someone else made something more orthodox, such as *Happy Days* or *The Partridge Family*. And even the conservative patriarch at the heart of Lear's *All in the Family*—Archie Bunker—was actually embraced by some viewers as a lovable curmudgeon rather than the reactionary brute his creator intended.[13]

As time went by, TV may well have woven into its plots more of the new norms of the postsixties era (racial integration, working moms) but *Leave It to Beaver* values never really went away. On September 20, 1984, a new sitcom aired on NBC starring Bill Cosby as Heathcliff "Cliff" Huxtable, a middle-class black obstetrician living with his wife and five children in Brooklyn, New York. It kicked off with a situation that millions of parents could identify with: Cliff's son, Theo, had come home with a report card covered in Ds. Theo's mother was deeply upset and Cliff was outraged. But Theo said that his bad grades didn't bother him, because he didn't want to go to college. His goal was to grow up to be like "regular people," and if Cliff loves his son, he's just going to have to accept him for what he is. The audience applauded. This was what liberals like Lear had been teaching them for over a decade, that love and understanding were more important than competition and success.

But, to their shock, Cosby's character didn't agree. "Theo," he said, "that is the dumbest thing I ever heard! No wonder you get Ds in everything! . . . I'm telling you, you are going to try as hard as you can. And you're going to do it because I said so. I am your father. I brought you into this world, and I'll take you out!" The audience's laughter was nervous at first, but by the end of the scene they were clapping wildly. Bill Cosby had just turned the liberal logic of the 1960s on its head.[14]

Throughout the Reagan era sitcoms could not have been more culturally conservative if their scripts had been written by the White House. The classic setting was a nuclear family, the jokes tended to be gentle, and episodes were often based around learning a "life lesson." Writers produced a "very special episode" that would deal with taboo subjects in a manner close to a 1950s public information film (don't take sweets from a stranger, etc.). The show *Diff'rent Strokes* featured very special episodes about pedophilia, hitchhiking, kidnapping, epileptic seizure, bullies, racism, bulimia, drunk driving, and drug abuse. Nancy Reagan even dropped by Gary Coleman's school to warn about the dangers of drugs—a reminder that she once was something of an actress herself. She was paid union rates for the work and donated the money to charity.[15] As is always the case in the entertainment business, the "very special episode" wasn't just an act of public spiritedness: It was a money spinner, too. Promoting the episode as one that "your family can't afford to miss" gave a nice fillip to the ratings. The format became so overused that it started to feel like every episode was "very special." It wasn't always tonally a neat fit, either. *Mr. Belvedere*, the show about a posh butler struggling to serve a kooky family, dedicated an episode to child molestation. It was a worthy cause, but to fill out the thirty minutes they stuffed in a subplot about how terrible Mr. Belvedere was at golf.[16]

Conservative claims that TV drove the breakdown of the family in the 1970s and 1980s couldn't be farther from the truth: *All in the Family* was a minority report from a televisual culture that otherwise played it safe—one willing to engage in the changes that the 1960s wrought but never in a way that might turn off the audience. Arguably, this cozy consensus distorted America's understanding of itself. *The Cosby Show*, for example, did not reflect the reality of life in Reagan's America for millions of poor African-Americans. The Huxtables were a model of racial integration and material success; regular churchgoers governed by a stern father. They were also a museum piece. In the America of the 1980s, incomes more or less stagnated, while divorce and illegitimacy rose fast. When the show started, 46 percent of African-American children were raised by a single mother. By 1992, when the show ended, 68 percent of African-American babies were born out of wedlock. The Huxtables may have been America's most visible black family, but they were also an ideal rather than the reality. That was highlighted by a final, ironic twist: The very last episode of *The Cosby Show* coincided with riots in Los Angeles.[17]

The 1992 LA riots were sparked by the acquittal of police officers tried for beating a black man, Rodney King. They began with looting, climaxed in two days of rioting, and left fifty-three dead—ten of whom were shot by the authorities. There were open gun battles in the streets as African-Americans turned on the Korean community. Reginald Denny was dragged out of his truck at the intersection of Florence and Normandie and beaten to the point of a near fatal seizure. Fidel Lopez was also pulled from his vehicle; the mob broke his head open with a stereo and tried to slice off his ear. Mayor Tom Bradley went on TV to declare a state of emergency. He also urged citizens to stay indoors and watch *The Cosby Show*.[18]

The NBC affiliate, KNBC, faced a dilemma: Should they air the riots or should they air *The Cosby Show* finale? On the one hand, they felt they had a duty to go on broadcasting the horror in the streets. On the other hand, Cosby's last episode was, itself, a piece of history. After much debate, KNBC's warm and reassuring anchor smiled into the camera and said that they would air *Cosby*, because

[w]e need this time, a bit of a cooling-off period. Giving us some breathing space. Maybe a chance to remember what Thursday nights were like before all this madness began in Los Angeles. Here at KNBC we'll use this hour to update the stories, and during this hour, if major events dictate, be assured we'll return to our coverage immediately. Make sure you use this hour to say thanks to a good friend.

They cut away to the show. When it was done airing, Bill Cosby followed with a statement live on camera: "Let us all pray that everyone from the top of government down to the people in the streets, they would all have good sense, and let us pray for a better tomorrow, which starts today."[19]

Political leadership having failed, Los Angeles took its refuge in a sitcom. But it was a sitcom built upon a false vision of America: wealthy and integrated. This kind of TV was comforting, not radical—and so incapable of adequately exploring the realities of life for most African-Americans.

So if the sitcoms have tended to express a conservative spin on middle-class life, why all the conservative anger at Hollywood? The Republican response to the LA riots gives some clues.

When order was restored, Vice President Dan Quayle went to the Commonwealth Club in San Francisco to give a speech on the causes of urban decay. Quayle is probably now more famous for telling a class of schoolchildren to spell potato with an "e" on the end, or else for his long list of verbal gaffes—of which the best is surely, "Republicans understand the importance of bondage between a mother and child." On the subject of the bondage between children and their parents, Quayle told his San Francisco audience that the cause of the Rodney King riots was fatherlessness, and that this fatherlessness was caused by movies and TV. "Bearing babies irresponsibly is simply wrong," the vice president said.

Failing to support children one has fathered is wrong. We must be unequivocal about this. It doesn't help matters when prime-time TV has Murphy Brown, a character who supposedly epitomizes today's intelligent, highly paid professional woman, mocking the importance of fathers by bearing a child alone and calling it just another lifestyle choice.[20]

Murphy Brown, played by Candice Bergen, was the eponymous lead character of a sitcom about a single female news anchor. *Murphy*

Brown invited political comment because it blended fact and fiction; it often covered real-life events and treated real people like characters. In the show's 1991–92 season, Murphy became pregnant, and when the father of her child refused to give up his lifestyle to help, she decided to keep the baby and go it alone. Before giving birth the character listed the folks who didn't want her to have the child: "Pat Robertson; Phyllis Schlafly; half of Utah!" Invitees to the baby shower included real-life journalists Katie Couric, Joan Lunden, Paula Zahn, Mary Alice Williams, and Faith Daniels.[21]

So when Quayle went gunning for *Brown*, it was appropriate that the show reply. In an episode entitled, "You Say Potatoe, I Say Potato," Murphy responded directly to Quayle's comments in an episode of her show-within-a-show celebrating the diversity of the American family. Blending reality and entertainment this way didn't faze the program's creators, who felt that it was a natural extension of the surrealism of national politics. *Murphy Brown*'s director, Barnet Kellman, told me, "There was a tremendous . . . delight in the fact that Dan Quayle [picked a fight with us], who himself to many of us, I think, felt like a fictional character. He felt like a manufactured pretty boy candidate for vice president, one who didn't have any real substance but was kind of like a telegenic running mate in order to find somebody to [appeal to a certain TV demographic]—an adversary to a fictional character."[22]

So the vice president of the United States found himself caught in a shouting match with a manufactured news anchor and, despite himself being flesh and blood, he lost. *Murphy Brown*'s audience figures hit thirty-eight million, and Candice Bergen won an Emmy. Quayle backed down so rapidly and humiliatingly that he even told the media he had sent toys to Murphy's (fictional) child.[23] Quayle's problem was twofold. First, no one bought the idea that sitcoms had caused the rise of fatherlessness: the proportion of single mothers who had a professional job jumped from 3.1 percent in 1980 to 8.2

percent in 1990, suggesting that Murphy Brown reflected a trend and did not start it.[24] Second, if Quayle had watched the show closely enough he'd have noted that Murphy makes what some would see as the very conservative decision to keep her baby rather than abort it. Some Republicans thought the show's message was admirable. "Murphy Brown was right," the right-wing pundit Pat Buchanan told me. "She kept her child. What did Dan want her to do with it?"[25]

But the Republican war on TV rolled on. One of their biggest targets was *The Simpsons*. Here was a cartoon family that seemed to directly attack all things American: Homer was a lazy slob who would sell his soul to the devil for a doughnut (literally); Bart was a foul-mouthed boy who made not having a cow cool; Lisa was overtly liberal (she even played jazz); and the show included dozens of smaller characters who parodied church, police, army, and nation. A Baptist pastor, Dan Burrell, produced an audiotape called "Raising Beaver Cleaver Kids in a Bart Simpson World," offering instruction on how to give kids the kind of "value and character" that Bart lacked. Barbara Bush called the show "dumb" (the producers sent a letter of complaint to her addressed from Marge Simpson, and Barbara replied with a warm apology), and when President Bush's drug czar discovered—to his horror—a poster of Bart at a drug rehabilitation center that read UNDERACHIEVER AND PROUD OF IT, he said to the patients, "You guys aren't watching *The Simpsons*, are you? That's not going to help you any."[26]

Eventually, the president weighed in. In 1992, speaking at the Annual Convention of National Religious Broadcasters, George H. W. Bush said, "We need a nation closer to the Waltons than the Simpsons, an America that rejects the incivility, the tide of incivility, and the tide of intolerance." Just like *Murphy Brown*, *The Simpsons* used its own bully pulpit to reply. During a rerun of an episode they pasted in a new opening in which the family watches Bush's attack. Bart turns to Homer and says, "Hey, we're just like the Waltons. We're praying for an end to the Depression, too."[27]

Once again a Republican picked on a sitcom, and once again, the fictional character won. The problem in both instances was that the politicians obviously hadn't spent enough time watching the shows they were attacking. If George H. W. Bush had sat down to a season of *The Simpsons*, he'd have realized that it's as American as apple pie. Sure, *The Simpsons*'s writers lean Democrat. The Springfield branch of the Republicans resides in Dracula's castle, and when Sideshow Bob runs for mayor on the GOP ticket, he delivers this beautiful pitch to the voters: "Your guilty conscience may force you to vote Democratic, but deep down inside you secretly long for a coldhearted Republican to lower taxes, brutalize criminals, and rule you like a king. That's why I did this: to protect you from yourselves!"[28]

But the show's core values are a lot like those of *Leave It to Beaver*. A powerful example is the episode "Homer the Heretic." Bored with going to church every week, Homer elects to stay at home, eat waffles, and watch TV instead. Marge is upset and confronts him with an astonishing ultimatum that would make Pat Robertson proud. "Don't make me choose between my man and my God," she tells her husband, "because you just can't win." Homer replies, "There you go again, always taking someone else's side. Flanders, the water department, God . . ." The implication is that in turning his back on God, Homer is turning his back on his household—putting his own selfish desires above his family. And for that he is punished. He falls asleep while smoking a cigar, and the flame ignites some magazines. The house burns, and Homer is rescued by the volunteer fire brigade. Homer pleads with God for forgiveness, because he presumes that it was the Big Man who burned down his house. But Reverend Lovejoy convinces him that God's only role was to work through the hearts of his friends to put out the flames. Homer agrees to give church another try and is there next week "front row and center"—snoring like a bear.[29]

When it comes to TV and movies, conservatives all too often confuse style and message. They presume that because a show or film contains sex, violence, or foul language that its message is liberal. But often the contrary can be true. During the culture wars of the 1990s, Republicans would return again and again to attacking Hollywood, and often they were undone by their poor choice of targets. In the summer of 1995, presidential hopeful Bob Dole tried to garner some early publicity by slamming Hollywood's movies as "nightmares of depravity." He named names, calling out *Natural Born Killers* and *True Romance* as "nightmares" while praising the family values of *The Lion King, Forrest Gump,* and *True Lies.* Hollywood responded with fury; Oliver Stone, director of *Natural Born Killers,* accused him of a new form of McCarthyism. But it would've been simpler just to ask Senator Dole if he'd ever actually seen any of these movies. If he had, he'd have discovered that while *Natural Born Killers* is indeed a film about psychotic murderers and features tons of gratuitous violence, it is also an attack upon the media for wallowing in death and its glamorization of depravity. In other words, its message is far from anarchic. By contrast, the "comedy" *True Lies* features gags about spousal abuse and rape. An aide later admitted that Dole hadn't seen either film. So why did he praise *True Lies* without watching it first? Probably because it starred Arnold Schwarzenegger, a prominent Republican donor. It was another example of that old Hollywood/Washington reciprocity principle in action.[30]

What TV Won't Talk About

So Hollywood's liberals hold back from pushing their politics through their product because TV and movies are made to make money, and anything that appears on the screen that does not at least nod toward the values of its audience will flop. Barnet Kellman, the director of *Murphy Brown*, puts it this way:

> One of the jobs of comedy is to patrol moral boundaries, [be] boundary keepers to test the limits, to find out where we are; that's one of the endeavors. That's what we're exploring. We're trying to find the compass. When we go too far we get called back. When we say something that nobody else is saying, when we acknowledge a previously unacknowledged truth, we get rewarded for it. So patrolling that boundary, finding out where the limits are, is what the business of comedy is. And I think we will go forward and constantly be testing and finding out what's next. I don't know what it is. It will present itself. It'll get tested.

"Patrolling moral boundaries" is another way of saying "avoiding offense," and there's plenty of evidence that this is what Hollywood does. One subject that the industry rarely touches is abortion. In 1972 (when *Roe v. Wade* was some way off, but New York had liberalized its abortion laws), the lead character of Norman Lear's sitcom *Maude* fell pregnant in her early forties. To the horror of many viewers, she elected to have the pregnancy terminated. The story line was shocking rather than funny, and letters flooded in complaining that it was inappropriate subject matter for a comedy.[31] Curiosity ensured that the episode was a ratings hit, but there was a wide recognition that it had crossed a line and offended public taste. After all, U.S. sitcoms are essentially about the family, and there's nothing more antifamily than abortion. Since then, no major sitcom has featured abortion at all—a concession to polls that suggest America has actually become more prolife since the 1970s and 1980s rather than less.

The notable exception is in animated series like *South Park* and

Family Guy, although even their crude gags about terminations come with qualifications. *South Park* is, if anything, antiabortion. In one episode the character Eric Cartman tries to persuade a Latino girl to terminate her pregnancy with this cynical argument: "Abortion is the ultimate form of cheating! You're cheating nature itself! Why do rich white girls get ahead in life? Because they get abortions when they're young! They get pregnant, but they still want to go to college, so, whatever, they just cheat! They cheat that little critter in their belly right out of a chance at life."[32] *Family Guy*, by contrast, is staunchly proabortion but was censored by the Fox Network when it devoted an episode to the subject. The episode, titled "Partial Terms of Endearment," was pulled off the air and released on DVD instead.[33]

Movie coverage of abortion tends toward the prolife. Take the movie *The Ides of March* (2011), in which a politician played by George Clooney gets a young staffer pregnant. Without bothering to discuss her options, the girl is driven to an abortion clinic and left on her own to face the procedure. She returns to her hotel room later that night and commits suicide—and Clooney's character doesn't give a damn. *The Ides of March* is not making a comment on the rights and wrongs of abortion per se, but it implies that often the decision to abort is an exercise in peer pressure rather than an example of women controlling their own bodies. That theme of agency is picked up in a more positive way in *Juno* (2007), a wistful comedy about a teenage girl who gets pregnant, weighs up the options, and without any moral pressure placed on her, chooses to have her baby and offer it for adoption. The character's free decision to keep the child is presented as a mature, even liberating, thing to do. Some commentators talked of a *Juno* effect as a way of explaining a surprise fall in abortion rates after 2007.[34]

The influence of soft social conservatism can be found in some very surprising places. When the final installment of the *Twilight* saga, *Breaking Dawn: Part 2*, premiered in Los Angeles in 2012, the streets thronged with its core audience of teenage girls. But as the handsome cast strode up the red carpet, they were also welcomed by a group of religious conservatives waving placards. The head of security rushed over to confront them, assuming they were there to protest against the film's mix of "satanic" vampires and dark eroticism. But he was wrong. The demonstrators had come to cheer the stars and promote the movie. It turns out that some on the religious right had adopted *Twilight* as a tool in the fight against legalized abortion.

The saga is about an everyday girl named Bella who falls in love with a dashing vampire named Edward. After several adventures with a race of hot werewolves, who seem contractually obliged to take their tops off every three minutes, the couple finally marries and produces a baby fang of their very own. Some fundamentalists worried that this mix of sexuality and witchery was a gateway to full-blown Satanic possession, but that paranoia wasn't shared by everyone. Kate Bryan, the young prolife activist who organized the *Breaking Dawn* demonstration, told me that *Twilight* contains "elements of chastity" that encourage more responsible behavior among teens. Vampirism is a metaphor for sex, and at the beginning of their relationship the lovers struggle with an adolescent sexual impulse that could prove fatal—there's always a risk that Edward will lose control in flagrante and suck his woman dry. Bella is keen to run the risk anyway, but Edward insists that they save the magic for their wedding night. "Young girls watching see how well [Edward treats] Bella," says Bryan, "and they make the connection between that and chastity."

After Bella and Edward get married and give in to those primal lusts, Bella falls pregnant—and bearing the half-human, half-vampire fetus almost kills her. Abortion is discussed, but Bella refuses. Although the book and movie are at pains to stress that the decision is hers, the choice that she makes is one that Ryan's prolife activists applaud: "There's a very powerful moment in the movie when one character says that 'it' is a baby . . . and Bella's decision to keep the baby is a strong message about love and life."[35]

Hollywood Changes Biden's Mind

On the whole, then, Hollywood can be cautiously conservative if it suits it. But there is one exceptional issue upon which it has taken a stand and shown remarkable influence upon the American public: gay rights. When Joe Biden told an interviewer in May 2012 that he had changed his mind and now supported gay marriage, he identified a TV show as a major reason why. "I think *Will & Grace* probably did more to educate the American public than almost anything anybody has ever done so far," he said. "This is evolving."[36]

As I argued in chapter 1, a major cause of Obama's switch to supporting same-sex marriage was the influence of Hollywood money—but Biden is probably right that Hollywood's subtle massaging of public opinion on the issue made the switch politically feasible. On this subject, unlike many others, producers have shown genuine courage. There had been several small, generally absurd stereotypes of gay people in TV shows prior to the late 1990s, but it was the sitcom *Ellen* that really changed the rules.

Starring Ellen DeGeneres, *Ellen* started out with its eponymous lead being a regular girl who dates guys and is unlucky in love. But the network sensed that she lacked chemistry with her male love interests, the reason probably being that the real Ellen was a lesbian. Because the show lacked romantic spark and was in danger of losing steam, the network innocently suggested that Ellen get a puppy to liven things up. The writers rejected the idea, but kept the title "The Puppy Episode" to describe an episode of the show that would change history.[37]

In the summer of 1996, Ellen DeGeneres opened negotiations with ABC and Disney to have her character come out. She was tired of portraying a lie. Airing a coming out wasn't just a brave act for DeGeneres. Jonathan Stark, one of the writers of "The Puppy Episode" told me, "The risk in this was beyond any risk I've ever seen in television. I will always give the people in charge at ABC and Disney high, high marks for sticking to their guns. . . . I mean, ABC could have been buried for this, and Disney. And Disney, you know, is known as a family-friendly network. So this was even a larger risk than that for them." He doesn't exaggerate. When the episode was broadcast in April 1997, polls showed that half of Americans thought gay sex should be a crime. While it was being filmed, the set had to be cleared after a bomb threat.

Ellen's coming out worked as a piece of TV partly because it was good drama but also because its lead was so endearing and so "normal." Having watched the show for three seasons, the audience had come to regard Ellen as a friend—which made her the perfect vehicle for exploring a difficult life decision in a way that wouldn't alienate more conservative members of the audience. In "The Puppy Episode," Ellen dates a guy and tries to convince herself that she's into him—at one point she declares, "Men, men, men, men, why do I love men so much?" But when she meets a girl played by Laura Dern, Ellen is smitten. She fights and fights her desire until, eventually, she admits to Dern's character, "I'm gay"—inadvertently broadcasting her announcement over an airport's public address system. The moment was awkward, sweet, and easy to identify with. As Jonathan Stark put it, "The episode of *Ellen* was not an episode about somebody coming out, in my opinion; it was about somebody struggling with who they are, and that's what everybody relates to." Certainly, it was a hit: "The Puppy Episode" drew forty-two million viewers.[38]

If TV patrols moral boundaries, Ellen actually pushed a little too far, too fast. The show's next season became fixated on the gay issue to the extent that even some in the LGBTQ community felt it had become overly serious, and even obsessive. Its fifth season would prove to be its last, and *Ellen* faded away as inauspiciously as it once began.[39] But what followed in the noughties was an extraordinary slew of gay-themed TV, including drama (*Queer as Folk*, *The L Word*), lifestyle shows (*Queer Eye for the Straight Guy*), musical comedies (*Glee*), and sitcoms (*Will & Grace*).[40] What they all had in common was that they treated homosexuality as something normal, or even aspirational—they made it cool to be gay or to have gay friends. They probably didn't change anyone's mind overnight (few Americans would sit down in front of *Queer as Folk* and, by the end of the episode, decide that they now support gay marriage—and those who found it distasteful wouldn't bother to watch it at all), but increased visibility leads to familiarity, which leads to a shift in attitudes.

And the change has been dramatic.[41] In 1996, only 27 percent of Americans thought same-sex marriages "should be valid." By 2013, it was a slim majority at 53 percent, but three quarters of respondents thought legalization was inevitable. The link to familiarity is clearly there. Pew polling found in 2013 that nearly nine in ten people knew someone who was gay, and half said a close friend or relative was gay.[42]

Shifts in popular culture have helped make homosexuality the new normal, and TV and movies have arguably played a much bigger role in this than politicians. It's often forgotten that Barack Obama and Joe Biden were strongly opposed to gay marriage until their sudden conversion in 2012—that they clearly waited for a change in cultural attitudes before switching their positions. Janis

Hirsch, a former writer on *Will & Grace*, summed up the impact of TV to me this way:

> It's a remarkable thing that Joe Biden said that—that *Will & Grace* did more to change attitudes toward gays than a politician. And it was dead on. Because when you . . . can laugh [then] . . . you can identify. You know, a politician doing this to you is like your mother doing this to you, and you know you're going lah-lah-lah-lah, and you're not listening. But when you're laughing, the next day when you see someone who's gay, instead of going *errgh* or whatever your reaction was gonna be, you're—you're interested, you're talking. You know—when you see gay couples now with kids, your first instinct isn't necessarily to say, Where's the mum? You just go, oh, cool, these are your kids.[43]

Learning to Tolerate Through TV

If the one area where Hollywood has made a difference is gay rights, the rule still stands that Hollywood patrols moral boundaries rather than moves them. In American society, the nuclear family unit has declined as a norm, sexuality has become more fluid, racial integration more common, and the social conservatism of the Reagan era less rigid. In 2013, even George W. Bush remarked that straight people should not cast the first stone when it comes to judging gay couples. And it's worth noting that many of the biggest names from his administration—Condoleezza Rice, Dick Cheney, Donald Rumsfeld, John Bolton—have endorsed same-sex marriage rights. The campaign against the anti–gay marriage Proposition 8 in California was given legal assistance by Ted Olson, Bush's former solicitor general.[44]

But in so many other ways American society remains fairly conservative in outlook. Faith still matters, sexual incontinence is generally regarded as bad, and family comes first in everything. This helps to explain why *Modern Family* is so popular among Republicans. The social mix of its characters—gay, Hispanic, straight, old, young—reflects the mixture that most Americans encounter in their daily lives. *Modern Family* isn't an example of a liberal agenda being forced on people but rather of TV pithily capturing the spirit of the moment. Moreover, the show is instinctively conservative in that it's all about the importance of maintaining family unity no matter what differences might be found within it.

In one episode, the gay characters Cameron and Mitchell introduce their adopted Vietnamese baby to the family. At first, Jay—Mitchell's father—looks on with a mix of confusion and horror. It's one thing to finally accept that his son is gay, another to accept that he has found a life partner. But it's a whole new step to find out that they've adopted a child. The audience wonders what Jay will do next. Make a scene? Walk out? Instead, he shrugs, takes a sip of his drink, and says, "What the hell do I know anyway?"—and kisses his new granddaughter. Ken Levine, a writer, director, and producer who worked on *M*A*S*H*, *Cheers*, and *The Simpsons*, explains the scene:

> Jay's there to represent the raised eyebrow at all of this. Yeah. But he's tolerant, and he loves his son, and he loves his granddaughter; it's just a new world for him. But it's not something that he particularly embraces. He accepts; he doesn't embrace it.[45]

And when Mitt Romney watched and fell in love with *Modern Family*, perhaps something in that character appealed to him, too.

9

THE GREAT GATSBY

How Hollywood and Washington
Face the Future and Dance

No book better captures the ambition and the illusion of the American Dream than Scott Fitzgerald's *The Great Gatsby*. Set in the Jazz Age of the early 1920s, it tells the story of the enigmatic Jay Gatsby—a man of mysterious means who buys a grand house, fills it with beautiful strangers, and lives in the style of a king. He has brought his millions to New York with the single goal of winning back his childhood sweetheart, Daisy, now married to a priggish aristocrat. But Gatsby's pink suit and fake pedigree cannot bridge the social divide between them. Daisy retreats back into her "money and vast carelessness," and Gatsby is shot for a crime he did not commit. He dies a martyr to ambition, but the reader is urged not to shed any tears. The narrator, Nick Carraway, feels contempt for his mix of childlike naïveté and outright lies: "I disapproved of him from beginning to end."

The Great Gatsby was written to be a parody of excess. How telling, then, that when Hollywood released a movie version of the novel in 2013 it became a celebration of excess. Filmed in 3-D, its colors are unreal, the dresses shimmer with sequins, its stars are beautiful to the point of beatific. Gatsby's yellow car—awkward and silly in the book—zooms like a bright banana through the streets of New York, leaps out of the screen, and threatens to hit the viewer square between the eyes. When the car strikes a jaywalker, she flies up into the air and is cast against the stars like a new constellation—hanging there just long enough for the audience to get the giggles. Most infuriating of all, director Baz Luhrmann misunderstood the very title of the book. *The Great Gatsby* isn't great—the moniker is a joke. When the narrator, Nick, first meets Gatsby at a party he is so nondescript that Nick thinks he is just another guest. It is Gatsby's purchased reputation that makes him "great" rather than the reality behind his forged personality. Yet when Gatsby makes his entrance into Lurhmann's movie we are in no doubt about who he is: Leonardo DiCaprio turns to the camera, the sky fills with fireworks, and the soundtrack bursts with *Rhapsody in Blue*. Fitzgerald had contempt for Gatsby; Luhrmann is in love with him. And who could blame the Australian director? Played by DiCaprio, Jay Gatsby looks good enough to eat.

Luhrmann's Gatsby is an unintentional indictment of American cinema in the early twenty-first century. It was packed with enough stars and enjoyed enough of an advertising push to generate a handsome return. But critics lamented that it confused bling with beauty and action with art. They were all the more angry for the choice of source material: Luhrmann had traduced America's greatest, most emblematic novel. According to the *Wall Street Journal*, what was, "intractably wrong with the film is that there's no reality to heighten; it's a spectacle in search of a soul."[1] For the

Financial Times of London, it "has the terrible endlessness of films where everything is too short. We are jabbed with effect after effect, in our faces and up our noses in 3D."[2] *Salon* concluded, "It surely belongs to the category of baroque, overblown, megalomaniacal spectacles dubbed 'film follies.'"[3]

The American movie industry has come to place its faith in big budgets, and the same could be said of American politics. *Gatsby*'s budget was $105 million; the cost of the 2012 U.S. election was over $2 billion.[4] In both instances the increasing quantity of money spent has not been matched by increasing quality of product. Critics of both institutions would say that the sums involved only heighten the sense of disappointment. The corporate-think that runs Hollywood struggles to produce great art; the expensive razzmatazz of the two-party system has not created a balanced budget, eliminated poverty, or brought peace to the world. Indeed, the growing emphasis upon "performance" has reduced politics to the level of entertainment. The *New Yorker* wrote of the 2012 conventions:

> Political journalists used to prowl Convention floors in search of scoops about backroom deals. Now they write cultural criticism of a sort that is normally aimed at "American Idol" contenders (who actually performed at both Conventions this year). Whose heartstring-pullers connected? Whose narrative cohered? Whose Twitter feed trended?

In the judgment of *The New Yorker*, the Democrats won the contest. Michelle Obama gave a tear-jerking speech about growing up poor, Bill Clinton descended like Charlton Heston from the mountaintop to give the commandments of liberalism, and the stage was filled with flags and veterans.

The Republicans' allowing Clint Eastwood to improvise like an also-ran at a talent show, on their Convention's most important night, only heightened the contrast.[5]

When viewers were asked to vote for the best performance, the Democrats won: Obama bounced two points after his convention; Romney fell two points. Give it time and the conventions will be broadcast in 3-D.[6]

Hollywood and Washington have both fallen victim to the same tendency to place spectacle above vision. They're motivated by similar concerns: the challenges of marketplace competition, changing technology, declining popular interest, and the fear that boredom will keep viewers/voters at home. Although the amount of money flowing through Hollywood and Washington suggests that they are in rude health, they are actually going through periods of profound intellectual crisis. The money they spend is not a symptom of success but of panic. They sense, like Fitzgerald did of the Roaring Twenties, that the party can't last.

But both industries are also experienced in the art of survival; they have innovated their way out of trouble before, and they will do so again. As we shall see, there's evidence of a new wave of small, independent, socially aware talent coming.

Hollywood in Trouble

In the old days, Hollywood sold movies on the strength of the people in them. A star, so the theory went, could sell a movie no matter how badly it stunk. There were exceptions: Even Elizabeth Taylor swimming in milk couldn't save *Cleopatra* (1963) from losing money. But stars were still the money magnets that Hollywood relied upon to turn a profit.

Today things are very different. At the time of this writing, the highest-grossing movie in history is *Avatar* (2009)—a 3-D extravaganza set on an alien planet populated by blue-skinned aliens that resemble talking fawns. Its two leads were buried beneath special effects, and its only major Hollywood royalty, Sigourney Weaver, was limited to a supporting role. This wasn't a star movie but an "event" movie, and because its success depended upon the promise of visual spectacle, it probably would have done just as well if the lead was played by Mitt Romney. It conformed to a pattern in 2009. Out of the top ten grossing movies of that year only two (*The Blind Side* and *Sherlock Holmes*) contained A-list talent (although both Sandra Bullock and Robert Downey Jr. were a little long in the tooth). The rest featured nobodies or very recent somebodies who had been made famous by the movie franchise they were starring in. The second-highest grosser was the critically panned *Transformers: Revenge of the Fallen*—with a cast headed by Shia LaBeouf, a former Disney Channel favorite who leaves little impression on the screen. Number three was *Harry Potter and the Half-Blood Prince* (something people went to see because they are fans of the books), and number four was *Twilight: New Moon*—another movie that did well because its fan base of adolescents dragged Mum and Dad to see it. *Transformers*, *Harry Potter*, and *Twilight* are all franchises aimed at kids under eighteen. The audience isn't very intellectually or artistically demanding.[7]

The year brought bad news for many established stars. According to *The New York Times*:

Mr. Ferrell bombed in "Land of the Lost," a $100 million comedy that sold only $49 million in tickets in North America. Ms. Roberts missed with "Duplicity," a $60 million thriller that attracted $40.6 million. "Angels & Demons" (Mr. Hanks) was soft. The same for "The Taking of Pelham 1 2 3"

(Mr. Washington and Mr. Travolta). "Imagine That," starring Mr. Murphy, was such a disaster that Paramount Pictures had to take a write-down. Mr. Sandler? His "Funny People" limped out of the gate and then collapsed. Some of these may simply have not been very good, but an A-list star is supposed to overcome that.[8]

But 2009 was not an off-year. In 2013, Hollywood suffered six big-budget summer film flops, including Will Smith's *After Earth* and Johnny Depp's *The Lone Ranger. The Lone Ranger* was the third consecutive movie starring Johnny Depp to fail: *The Rum Diary* only earned $24 million with a budget of $50 million and 2012's *Dark Shadows* barely made back its $150 million budget. The message to the studios is simple: Folks won't go to see a movie just because someone famous is in it. It has to actually be good, and too many nonevent films are being made that are expensive but basically bad.[9]

On the set, economics is undermining the power of stars. Remember that since the 1960s the studios have increasingly become controlled by Wall Street. The suits now in charge of the movie industry are interested only in maximizing profit, and they have little time for the egos of their artists. After Hollywood was hit by the collapse of the DVD market and the rise of Internet piracy in the mid-noughties, it was forced to cut costs. It was still important to invest in visual spectacle (the budgets for the 2009 hits listed above were historically high), but they also went looking for savings elsewhere. One method was to get tough with the unions. When the Writers Guild of America went on strike in 2007 to demand a level of pay for scripts that reflected the enormous profits of the studios, the studios were ready. They stockpiled scripts and cheap reality TV shows in the months running up to the industrial action—in the same way that the British government in the 1980s stockpiled coal in order to break the National Union of Mineworkers. The strategy worked: Although the studios eventually agreed to settle for a pay increase, the strike lasted over a year, cost ordinary scriptwriters their incomes, and probably saved the suits millions of dollars.[10]

It wasn't just writers who got the tough treatment. Stars were told to trim their ambitions and to share unevenly what little gold the studios were prepared to put around. When Marvel made *The Avengers* it gave Robert Downey Jr. a staggering $50 million. But his costars, including significant names like Scarlett Johansson, Chris Evans, Chris Hemsworth, Mark Ruffalo, Jeremy Renner, and Samuel L Jackson, only got a paltry $200,000.[11] And other studios discovered that it was cheaper not to bother with stars at all. *The Hunger Games* (2012) was an absolute joy to make for Lionsgate. They took in $691 million at the box office after an investment of just $78 million—a figure kept low by putting the unknown Jennifer Lawrence in the lead and paying her just $500,000.[12] The same went for *Twilight* (2008). Summit Entertainment raked in $392 million despite spending just $37 million. The stars, Robert Pattinson and Kristen Stewart, were each paid just $2 million to do the movie.[13]

The bottom line is the bottom line. In the twenty-first century movies have become absurdly costly and the returns can be slender—which has made investing in the development of stars something that many studios have decided they can't afford. And they don't even need to bother with stars when the hook for a movie is its special effects or its link to a franchise.

You can find similar trends on TV, where there's been a rise in cheap, tacky program making that turns nobodies into somebodies and generates cash by glorifying the awful. Someone we can all learn a lesson from is the socialite Paris Hilton.

Paris's rise to fame through partying was a family tradition and nothing new to Hollywood. Her great-grandfather, Conrad Hilton, built a hotel empire and forged a glitzy Hilton brand by marrying Zsa Zsa Gabor; her grandfather followed in his footsteps by wedding Elizabeth Taylor.[14] Paris entered Hollywood's social scene in her teens but only really gained national attention when she made *Vanity Fair*. She has always insisted that she plays a public role, and that in private she is gentle and smart, but *Vanity Fair*'s portrait of "Hip Hop Debs" introduced the world to a spoiled alien desperate to become famous by any means: "Paris Hilton alights on the porch. She has sleepy, unnaturally blue eyes, and looks as if she'd be hot to the touch. . . . She's wearing a white T-shirt, jeans, and a pair of four-inch-high Lucite sandals that look as if they would be worn by streetwalkers on the planet Zorg." One of Paris's friends told *Vanity*, "[All she] wants to do is become famous, . . . to wipe out the past, to become somebody else." She achieved that through modeling, party going, and unwittingly starring in a celebrity sex tape that plunged entertainment journalism to new levels of depravity. This was all followed by a part in a reality TV show, *The Simple Life*. Paris was a new kind of star: attractive yet repulsive, covered in bling yet strangely cheap, an heiress with the manners of a trucker.[15] The crooner Joshua Radin posted this account of one of her Las Vegas performances on his MySpace page: "Paris, who had been swilling straight vodka from [a] Grey Goose bottle for hours, . . . has the people in charge throw her 'record' on the house stereo for her to lip sync two of her songs. She gets up on the stage, pukes, leaves. . . . I find the music business charming."[16]

Hilton was the product of an age in which anyone can find themselves surrounded by cameras so long as they misbehave with sufficient color and glamour. One group of teens who wanted to live like stars with almost zero effort entered Hollywood lore as the Bling Ring. In the late noughties this gaggle of largely affluent adolescents stalked the movements of celebrities on the Internet, worked out when they wouldn't be at home, and broke in and stole all their stuff. The Bling Ring gang robbed Paris Hilton several times before she noticed anything was amiss. They found a way into her gated community via Google Earth and knocked on her front door. When there was no answer they found a key beneath the mat—which proved to be unnecessary, as the door was unbolted. On no less than five separate occasions they entered her property and committed theft; they even claimed to have snorted coke there and to have pranced around in Paris's shoes as a kind of "victory dance." It wasn't until nearly $2 million in jewelry went missing that Hilton called the cops.

The Bling Ring gang did not steal for money but as an act of homage to the celebrities that they adored. They were obsessed with Paris Hilton and Lindsey Lohan; they wanted to wear their clothes and take their drugs, to go shopping in their wardrobes. It was a shortcut to the experience of being famous, turning their lives into an episode of *The Simple Life* and photographing and filming it on their iPhones. One of the Bling Ring, Alexis Neiers, had recorded a pilot for a reality TV show about her socialite family when she was arrested for breaking into Orlando Bloom's house. When she was released from prison she announced her plans to write a memoir (at just twenty-one years old). Sofia Coppola was fascinated enough by the story to turn it into a movie, *The Bling Ring* (2013), and so give a kind of artistic benediction to the gang's spree. Paris Hilton, although reportedly still traumatized by the burglaries, allowed Coppola to re-create them in her home.[17] Nobody could ever accuse the heiress of not understanding the meaning of publicity, which is part of the reason why she has developed into a fine businesswoman. Her chain of handbag and accessories stores has grown large enough to open a branch in Mecca.[18]

Politics in Decline

A surfeit of money, the decline of talent, the rise of reality TV—these are all problems that can be found in politics, too. In the same way that Wall Street has come to dominate Hollywood, so corporate money has had a massive influence upon Washington. In 2008, Barack Obama was the corporate choice for president. Wall Street donations accounted for 20 percent of his funds, and five out of his top twenty contributions were from the financial sector. In total, 57 percent of individuals on Wall Street gave to the Democrats rather than to the Republicans.[19] When Obama formed his administration, he gave roles to a small but heavy-hitting team of corporate types—the political equivalent of Hollywood's suits. Prior to becoming chief of staff, Rahm Emanuel had earned a reported $16.2 million working in investment banking for Wasserstein Perella and made $320,000 sitting on the board of Freddie Mac. Rahm's replacement when he quit the administration to become mayor of Chicago, William Daley, had previously worked at Chicago's Amalgamated Bank and JPMorgan Chase (at Chase, he reportedly made about $5 million per year). Jacob Lew, Obama's second head of the Office of Management and Budget, served for a while as an alternative investment adviser at Citigroup—making a reported $1.1 million from betting correctly on the collapse of the housing bubble. And heads of the National Economic Council—first Larry Summers and now Gene Sperling—were old Wall Street hands. Summers worked at the hedge fund D. E. Shaw and raked in $5.2 million in 2008. Sperling made $887,727 from Goldman Sachs for work advising on a nonprofit project that year.[20]

The question of how much Wall Street influences policy making under Obama is a controversial one, although one outstanding test is that there has not been a single arrest or prosecution of any banker for their role in the outright fraud that led to the 2008 financial crash. As a president, Obama has been reluctant to take corporate interests head-on and, in many regards, has proven a good investment. When pushing his signature reform—Obamacare—he failed to make a passionate or consistent case for a public option component, a government-run health agency that would compete with private providers. One theory why was that he had struck a deal with the health care industry to ensure that the legislation didn't threaten to undercut their business. The price was a guarantee of campaign funds in the 2010 midterms and 2012 presidential election.[21] This was seen by some to be part of a K Street strategy invented by Rahm Emanuel in which liberal policy commitments would be compromised in exchange for donations— essentially using the threat of social reform to leverage continued Wall Street support. Indeed, what social reform that has come to pass has proven to be very profitable. On June 24, 2009, during an ABC town hall meeting, Obama told the CEO of the health insurance provider Aetna that his was "a well-managed company, and I am confident that your shareholders are going to do well." If it seems a little odd for a president to give stock tips, consider how right he proved to be. From 2009 to 2012, Aetna's stock value jumped 80 percent. Far from Obamacare threatening to undermine the free market in medicine, compelling all Americans to buy health care has rejuvenated it.[22] Overall, Obama's presidency has been a good one for the corporate world: Stock market performance in his first term ranked in the top third of all presidents who have served since 1900.[23]

When the 2012 presidential election came around, the money race was even bigger. The Supreme Court's decision in *Citizens United v. Federal Election Commission* meant that corporations, associations, and labor unions were no longer limited in how much money they could give to individual candidates.[24] As a result, over three quarters of the spending in the presidential race came from donors who had been liberated from limits on donations—including over $100 million from corporations.[25] In the primaries, rich individuals were able to turn second-tier candidates into serious contenders just by opening their wallet. When Newt Gingrich performed well in debates against Mitt Romney and emerged from an appallingly weak field as a potential conservative standard-bearer, he suddenly gained the attention of Sheldon Adelson, a megabillionaire casino owner who described himself as the "richest Jew in the world." Adelson's two individual donations of $5 million apiece to Gingrich's super PAC represented the largest of their type in U.S. history and helped push a candidate with many disadvantages (two divorces and an obsession with mining the moon) into the top tier of the Republican race. It might also have been the biggest individual waste of money in history: Gingrich took just South Carolina and his native Georgia.[26]

Sadly, what establishes a front-runner candidate nowadays is less talent than money. This is not to say that American politics is devoid of charisma but rather that the qualifications for the presidency have changed. Richard Nixon served as a congressman, a senator, and a vice president before running on the Republican ticket in 1960. Jack Kennedy served in the House for six years and Senate for eight (and was considered a relative political neophyte). By contrast, Mitt Romney served only one term as governor of Massachusetts before getting the Republican nod in 2012, and Obama had only done four years in the Senate before running in 2008. Obama is undoubtedly one of the most gifted politicians of his generation, but he was never a notable legislator. His astonishing rise to the top has come down to his charisma, his rhetoric, and his ability to use his extraordinary personal story to attract the kind of money that would make him a serious contender. "I don't have a typical situation," he said in 2006 on the subject of campaign finance. "One of the virtues of [my] celebrity is—my fund-raising capacity is higher just because I get a lot of attention. So, it's not entirely fair, but I don't have to go and just work the phones now the way I had to do when I was an unknown candidate, for example."[27]

Obama represents the culmination of the politician as celebrity—someone who smart investors can turn into a box office sensation with minimal work. If he stands at the high end of that celebrity scale, Sarah Palin inhabits the lower end. It would be cruel and wrong to dub Mrs. Palin the "Paris Hilton of politics," but her career did exploit a similar dynamic. As in Hilton's case, the media was simultaneously fascinated and repelled by Palin—appalled by her errors of judgment but never quite able to turn off the camera.

Palin was elevated to fame not on the basis of experience but of personality. When she was chosen to be John McCain's running mate in 2008, she was not only the youngest governor in Alaskan history, but hadn't even completed one term in that office (and she never did). Palin was picked because Team McCain saw her as a game changer: a candidate who could appeal to women and outdo Obama for novelty value (such was the comedy and drama of the scenario that HBO even made a movie about it based on the book *Game Change*). Although undeniably talented, it quickly became obvious that she had been poorly vetted and was totally unprepared for a national campaign. Palin's best moment was her convention speech ("What's the difference between a pit bull and a hockey mom? Lipstick!"); her worst was a TV grilling in which she failed to name a single national newspaper that she regularly read.[28]

Sarah Palin was important less for what she thought than for who she was. Within days of being unveiled as McCain's running mate she announced to the national media that her teenage daughter, Bristol, was pregnant by a kid called Levi Johnston. Johnston turned out not to be a keeper, and he dropped Bristol after the campaign ended—only to resurface posing for *Playgirl*. He also claimed that Bristol got pregnant to punish her mother. Some outlets hypothesized that Palin's youngest child was actually Bristol's, a scurrilous rumor fed by old photos of Bristol that showed her with just the hint of a paunch. If all of this reads like the plot of a low-rent reality TV show, it reflects the declining quality of both political discourse and political coverage. And although Palin might have been a victim of the soap opera–style of reporting, it was a role she and her family played with relish.

After the 2008 election Bristol tried to cling onto fame by campaigning for sexual abstinence, appearing on *Dancing with the Stars*, and writing her own memoir. She also made a reality TV show for Lifetime, which—in keeping with the Hollywoodization of politics—was about her relocating to Los Angeles. Bristol wasn't well received by either the critics (the *Chicago Sun-Times* panned it as "the Alaskan Kardashians") or by local Democrats. She was filming a scene in which she was riding a mechanical bull when a liberal Hollywood agent named Stephen Hanks shouted, "Did you ride Levi like that?" A furious Bristol confronted Hanks and demanded to know why he was being rude: "Is it because you're a homosexual?" she asked. "Because I can tell you are." That was about as exciting as the show got. "It's Paris Hilton's 'The Simple Life' but with a real simpleton at the helm," said the *New York Post*.[29]

It didn't work, and now Bristol Palin doesn't even own a handbag shop in Mecca.

Hope for Hollywood

Overfed on money, low on ideas and talent—it's a verdict that suggests both movies and politics have hit a nadir. However, we mustn't surrender entirely to pessimism. Both Hollywood and pol-

itics are creatures of invention, and they survive as institutions because they are so good at adapting to change. Take Hollywood. It's
still capable of serious art on the big screen. In 2012 we got *Margin
Call* (a brilliant analysis of what caused the credit crunch), *Cosmop-
olis* (a movie by David Cronenberg about a millionaire who lives in
his limo), *Prometheus* (an *Alien* prequel that explores the existential
themes of childhood identity and the need for God), *The Descen-
dants* (George Clooney plays a slacker widower trying to get his life
back together), *Moonrise Kingdom* (a beautiful fantasy about a scout
who falls in love), and *Young Adult* (a hilarious tragicomedy about a
teen fiction author who returns to her hometown to stalk her former prom date). Many of these movies involved "risky" story lines
with limited obvious popular appeal that invited audiences to think
as well as to indulge their eyes. And some have even made money:
Prometheus drew $403 million, *The Descendants*, $177 million. Meanwhile, TV has entered a golden age to rival that of the late 1950s and
early 1960s. *Mad Men, The Americans, The Wire, 24, Dexter*—all
these shows boast fine writing, acting, and intricate plots that
stretch the mind. And as technology changes, so new ways of dis-
tributing and watching TV emerge. Netflix has moved from distribution to production, creating shows that the public can download
and watch a whole season of instantly—a new kind of niche television that can be watched and enjoyed in an entirely different way.
The Netflix season of *Arrested Development* premiered a different
kind of sitcom: fifteen interlocking episodes stuffed with self-
referential jokes and a kaleidoscopic plot that can only really be understood through repeated views. It's television made by and for
hard-core fans, and the results have been stunning.[30]

Technological evolution has also made the job of producing a
movie far cheaper, which has opened up a space in the market for
independent filmmakers. The success of *Paranormal Activity* (2007)
is a case in point. Oren Peli, a computer software programmer,

made his superscary movie about a poltergeist home invasion for only fifteen thousand dollars, using a home video camera and a cast that was paid just five hundred dollars each for their work. Scripting was minimal; the action and dialogue were largely improvised. Filming took place over just seven days—recording day and night—editing at the same time, with special effects added as the acting footage was finalized. Peli took it to the Screamfest Horror Film Festival, where an assistant at Creative Artists Agency loved it and recommended it to senior agents. They shopped around a DVD version that eventually won the approval of Steven Spielberg, who bought it with the intention of shooting a remake. The original plan was to make a multimillion-dollar version with the home video camera version added as an extra to a DVD. But they changed their mind after running a test screening of the original. The audience started walking out during the screening, and the execs presumed it was a bomb. Only when they discovered that folks were walking out because it was so scary did they realize they had a hit on their hands. Domestic and international rights were bought for $350,000, and the movie was released in 2009. A movie that was made in a week for $15,000 ended up grossing $193,355,800. Of course, Hollywood then took control of the franchise and milked it for all it was worth: four sequels of rapidly declining quality. But what *Paranormal Activity* shows is that modern independent filmmakers can exercise far greater control over their own product than ever before. And the quality of their product is sometimes much higher than that of the studios.[31]

This technological adaptation applies to the way that Hollywood does politics, too. On February 2, 2008, a video went viral of a song by will.i.am called *Yes We Can*—a video that helped promote Obama's presidential candidacy and give him an edge among young voters. Released on DipDive.com and YouTube, it was produced by Jesse Dylan, son of Bob, who told me that it represented

Internet activism coming of age: "We did this ourselves, we were able to distribute it through the Internet . . . and it helped give a push to Barack Obama's candidacy."[32] The song itself was composed of an Obama speech sung/read by various celebrities. By March 28, it had been viewed over seventeen million times, and in June it won an Emmy. *Yes We Can* set a new trend in celebrity video making: Take twenty stars, get them to read a script, cut it up so that they alternate lines, shoot it in black-and-white to make it look superserious, and maybe add some light hip-hop in the background to make it sound current. Its impact relies upon presumed deference on the part of the viewer: If they stuck twenty ordinary, ugly folks in the ad then, probably, no one would watch. Of course, these videos make some big assumptions about who the public is prepared to take political advice from. When the cast of the sitcom *Parks and Recreation* joined a video campaign for gun control in late 2012, the genre had arguably embraced the ridiculous. And the declaration of the celebrity-fueled "I Am Bradley Manning" campaign that Maggie Gyllenhaal was in fact Bradley Manning led to a mocking response on Twitter: "Wow, she really is a great actress!"[33]

The career of Arianna Huffington is another example of Hollywood's activism embracing the future. There was a time when Arianna was a very conservative Republican: Her first book, *The Female Woman*, was an attack on feminism, and she rose to prominence during the failed GOP Senate bid of her husband, oil man Michael Huffington. Today Arianna and Michael are separated, but she keeps the surname. Their life was good—living in a $4.3 million Italian-style mansion in Montecito, California. Life there was allegedly less good for the poor folks who had to work for them. According to *Vanity Fair*, Arianna "issued orders over a speakerphone from the bathtub, kept a lock on the refrigerator, threw frequent tantrums, and sent the children's bodyguards to the store for her Tampax. Worse still were slurs overheard by the staff about being 'stupid and lazy.' "[34]

Michael came out as gay in the 2000s and now dedicates himself to the campaign for marriage equality. I've never met a man who better embodies the lack of self-awareness so prominent among the elite. I interviewed Michael in the opulent surroundings of the Soho Club, and he told me about his affinity for regular Americans. "I gave up flying everywhere in a private jet," he said, "because it's so much more interesting to share a plane with other people."

"But do you fly first or second class?" I asked.

"First class," he replied. "Because I have very long legs and I need the extra leg room."[35]

As a single woman, kicking her heels and looking for some limelight to grab, Arianna's first foray into Internet campaigning was the Web site Resignation.com, which she used to demand that Bill Clinton quit in the wake of the Lewinsky scandal. She called the president, a man of "staggering narcissism and self-indulgence . . . investing his energies first in gratifying his sexual greeds and then in using his staff, his friends and the Secret Service to cover up the truth."[36] But not long after that she mysteriously converted to liberalism and ran for governor of California on a tax-hiking ticket. Although not a woman of the movies, Arianna embodies Hollywood's culture of reinvention, an ability to adapt to meet the demands of the times with that perverse mix of idealism and self-interest.[37] In the early 2000s she was associated with liberal filmmakers, who exploited the explosion of the direct-to-DVD market to produce documentaries about Iraq and environmental decay.[38] In 2005, she and three other founders (including, surprisingly, the conservative blogger Andrew Breitbart) launched the *Huffington Post*. The immediate success of *HuffPo* puts it in a grand tradition of Hollywood political Internet activism. The influential *Drudge Report* began life as an e-mail circular sharing the latest celebrity gossip. Its founder, Matt Drudge, picked up a lot of the goodies while working as a gift-shop clerk at CBS Studios.[39]

HuffPo's success stemmed from its ability to quickly aggregate and reduce news to bite-size chunks. But it also stood out from its competitors for its aggressive use of Arianna's phonebook—which was filled after years of forcing her exuberant personality upon the rich and famous. Where else could one read Mia Farrow's opinions on Darfur? Alec Baldwin on fracking? Or Sean Penn on the rightful ownership of the Falkland Islands? Here was a new kind of politics that used celebrities to highlight issues and the Internet to disseminate their opinions. In the past those celebs would've had to crawl to *The New York Times* or *The Washington Post* to get a column printed on their favorite cause—now they only had to ring Arianna, and it would be up online and read by millions in a matter of minutes. Andrew Breitbart suggested they install a special voice-mail box for celebrities, so that they could ring a number, dictate a post, and the *HuffPo* staff could write it down and put it up online for them. That way the stars wouldn't even have to go to the trouble of putting their fingers to the keyboard.[40]

But we should not be unduly cynical about what Hollywood or celebrity has the capacity to do for the world. Angelina Jolie might on the surface be a self-obsessed star with airhead politics, numerous past relationships (bisexual, and sometimes involving BDSM), adopted children with silly/ethnic names (Maddox, Pax, Zahara, Shiloh, Knox, Vivienne), and a talent for eccentric scene stealing—she and her one-time husband Billy Bob Thornton demonstrated their love by wearing vials of each other's blood around their necks. And some politicians have been reluctant to be too closely associated with her. A staffer in the Bush White House told me, "We tended to discourage her being seen with the president. She had a weird vibe."[41]

But for all her faults, no one can deny Jolie's dedication to good causes. She has served for over a decade as a goodwill ambassador for the United Nations High Commissioner for Refugees; met with displaced people in more than thirty countries; visited war and earthquake zones, and civil wars; helped establish a day-care center for kids with AIDS in Cambodia; and lobbied extensively in Washington, D.C. All of this was encouraged and facilitated by the politics wing of the Creative Artists Agency, proving that even orchestrated giving can produce great results. And Jolie's remarkable decision to have a double mastectomy to ward off an inherited threat of breast cancer—and to go public about it—was hailed as a radical, brave move that millions of women could take inspiration from. While many celebrities project a shallow, even shambolic image that can do harm to the people who imitate it (just ask the Bling Ring), others can genuinely provide the audience with a mature, intelligent role model to follow. Stardom has changed a lot in one hundred years, and actors have lost a lot of their mystery, industry, clout, and class. But it doesn't mean they can't do good.[42]

And so can the movies. Whatever you think of their politics, it's surely a good thing that Michael Moore has been able to make films about gun control and the Iraq War, that Matt Damon has voiced a documentary about the credit crunch, and that Al Gore has enjoyed a second career as an environmental activist with his movie *An Inconvenient Truth* (2006). Gore might've missed out on his ambition to be president, but he's the only vice president in history to win an Oscar. He's contributed to Hollywood's attempt to offer intelligent fare to mature audiences.

Tea Parties and Occupied Wall Streets

Technological change, independent campaigning, the rise of outsiders—all these things have happened in politics, too. The two most significant political happenings since 2008, the Tea Party and the Occupy movement, were homemade. Their critics might insist that they were started and financed by rich backers, but they were actually embraced by regular people. The Tea Party began on-line, in blogs and social media Web sites, and went national after business news editor Rick Santelli gave an impressive rant on CNBC in which he attacked the government for subsidizing "los-ers' mortgages" and called for a Tea Party to start the fightback. What emerged from that priceless piece of TV (and note that the revolution started on TV and not in Congress or off the back of a regular politician's campaign) was a series of nationwide pro-tests and the emergence of a network of grassroots conservative groups. Their power was tested in the 2010 midterm elections, when around 35 percent of likely voters told pollsters they were Tea Party supporters and 32 percent of Tea Party–identifying candidates won their races, including five out of ten Republican candidates for the Senate.[43]

The Republicans responded to the Tea Party in much the same way that studios did to *Paranormal Activity*: They saw something they knew had potential, bought the rights to it, and profited from its success. This is a familiar pattern in U.S. politics, which has seen the causes of independent populists, Dixiecrats, and supporters of Ross Perot all picked up by one of the mainstream parties and inte-grated into its machine and narrative. In 2012, every major Repub-lican presidential candidate pitched themselves to the Tea Party, and the selection of Paul Ryan as the vice presidential candidate was heralded as a sign that it had really made it. "Mr. Ryan is now unquestionably the face of the Tea Party caucus in Washington," opined *The New York Times*, "and his success is certain to embolden House lawmakers whose proudly unyielding approach to gover-nance has contributed to legislative gridlock. Once considered a fringe of the conservative coalition, Tea Party lawmakers are now indisputably at the core of the modern Republican Party."[44]

Alas, when the Tea Party became part of the GOP regular

machine, it lost some of its independent identity. In the same way that Hollywood cranked out *Paranormal Activity* sequels that lacked the verve of the original, the Tea Party came to look exploited and exhausted. Its fringe rally at the 2012 Republican National Convention was a washout—thanks to Hurricane Isaac, in more ways than one. The banners looked photocopied and the sound cut out during a rendition of the song "I Am America" (which contains the disturbing line, "We're takin' names . . ."). But the Tea Party's influence was still felt elsewhere—either in the hot rhetoric of the convention hall or in its top ten grossing movie—*2016: Obama's America*—that was showing four times a day in Tampa and had already taken $9.2 million nationwide since opening.[45]

The key point is that when the Tea Party emerged, the Republicans had to play catch-up. Increasingly, the terms of politics are dictated by the restless grassroots rather than by the men and women in Washington, D.C. That's a bad thing if it means politicians end up playing to their radicalized bases rather than to the vast majority of Americans who inhabit the political middle. But it's also a state of affairs that simply reflects the failure of mainstream politicians to do their job—to break the deadlock in Congress, to reduce the debt, to reform entitlements, and to get the American Dream back on the road. In June 2013, confidence in Congress fell to an all-time low: just 10 percent. In the same way that big movies have sunk, faith in traditional big politics has declined. People are looking for something different, something more authentic and in touch with their experiences and needs.[46]

What role can celebrity play in this rebellion against Washington? Surprisingly, a lot.

As star power dims in Hollywood, it grows elsewhere. Take the 2011 occupation of Wall Street. Michael Moore and Alec Baldwin tweeted revolutionary screeds from Zuccotti Park, while Zach Galifianakis, Billy Bob Thornton, and Aaron Eckhart videoed messages of support. Roseanne Barr told the crowd to guillotine the guilty bankers. It was, for Roseanne, the beginning of a complex political journey. She declared her candidacy for the Green Party presidential nomination and came in second at its convention, a result that she didn't much like. Barr made a big fuss about losing and ran on the Peace and Freedom Party ticket instead, although she spent much of her time attacking the Green nominee, Jill Stein. Whatever credibility Barr might've had with progressives was damaged when she attacked Stein's support for the right of transsexuals to use the restrooms of the gender they identify as. "Women do not want your penises forced in their faces or in our private bathrooms," Roseanne tweeted. "Respect that FACT." The Peace and Freedom Party took fifty thousand votes in November 2012, less than one tenth of 1 percent of the popular vote.[47]

The *fact* that the celebrities in Zuccotti Park belonged squarely in the 1 percent of rich folks targeted by the demonstrators did not go unnoticed. The record producer Russell Simmons, a man worth an estimated $340 million, was booed when he tried to speak. "You're part of the problem, Russell!" one woman shouted at him. "You're down here selling records!" cried another.[48] Republican New York State senator Dean Skelos chided Alec Baldwin for siding with socialists and anarchists when Baldwin had just spent $11.7 million on a condo in Greenwich Village. This sparked a Twitter war between the two men. Importantly, Baldwin overwhelmed his opponent with superior numbers: Baldwin's 478,000 Twitter followers easily outnumbered Skelos's 1,000. Baldwin wasn't actually just another 1 percenter trying to muscle in on an historic event: He brought a social media clout to the party that few others could beat.[49]

The Internet has quietly expanded the public reach of plugged-in celebrities—often far beyond that of mainstream opinion formers. In 2009, actor Ashton Kutcher and CNN entered an unofficial contest to see who could become the first person to have over 1 million followers on Twitter. Ashton won.[50] By the time of the 2012 election he was being followed by 9.3 million people, far more than Mitt Romney's then 288,000. Likewise, Twitter gave Baldwin a platform from which to tease the press with the threat of a run for the New York City mayoralty, as well as turning a sitcom actor into both a much-sought-after endorsement among national Democrats and a host of his own MSNBC show, *Up Late with Alec Baldwin*. Most of Baldwin's 478,000 followers were apolitical fans of *30 Rock*. But Twitter allows the star to draw their attention to events and ideas that they would otherwise not encounter. It would only take 10 percent of his following to retweet a Baldwin missive about global warming for several million more to end up reading it. According to one 2009 study, Twitter's demographic lends itself to liberal evangelizing: The site's users are more likely to be female than male, under thirty-four, and well educated. Ergo, Baldwin's tweets give him personal access to millions of potential activists and donors. That's why the random thoughts of this TV star matter more than they should. Thanks to social media, the power that stars are losing in Hollywood is still being felt within grassroots politics. They might find themselves reduced in status within their own industry, but the very same forces that are undermining the two parties actually give them an advanced stake in national politics.

The action isn't only limited to the Left. One of the heroes of the Tea Party was Jon Voight, Angelina Jolie's father; he showed up at an anti-Obamacare rally on the Hill in 2010 to tell the cameras that the Founding Fathers envisioned a "very small government."[51] The comedy actor Vince Vaughn backed Ron Paul for president in 2012 and started turning up at Rand Paul fund-raising barbecues in 2013. If anything, conservatives have been even better than liberals at combining the forces of Hollywood, the Internet, and politics to get their messages across.[52]

It was the work of the late conservative blogger Andrew Breitbart that helped to expose the sextual shenanigans of Representative Andrew Weiner, and his Breitbart.com is as much interested in detailing the alleged political bias of Hollywood as it is the evils of the Obama administration. Anger at moviemakers' reflexive liberalism is a common theme in right-wing blogging. Pajamas Media, started in 2004, was cofounded by scriptwriter and reformed liberal Roger Simon as an online video and blogging platform to counteract left-wing bias in the media.[53] One of his cohosts is Lionel Chetwynd, another conservative scriptwriter, and the two make a compelling pair of grouches. Lionel told me, chomping on a cigar in his study, that his career had been constantly stalled by hard-core "liberals." It is his belief—a view shared by Breitbart and Simon—that any kind of right-of-center thinking can be professional death in Hollywood.[54] Although they all seemed to be doing rather well when I met them. Their online presence is a reminder that while the Iraq War fired up the Hollywood Left, it also had a profound effect upon the Hollywood Right. Some moviemakers, often Jewish and with a strong emotional attachment to Israel, felt compelled to come forward and defend George W. Bush. In 2008, David Zucker—one of the geniuses behind the *Naked Gun* movies—made a parody of Michael Moore called *An American Carol*, starring Kelsey Grammer, Jon Voight, Dennis Hopper, Trace Adkins, Gary Coleman, Jillian Murray, and Leslie Nielsen. It was a bomb—not because of critical political bias but because it wasn't funny. It must be possible to produce a conservative hit comedy, but no one seems to have found the magic formula yet.[55]

Were these guys really locked out of Hollywood on the basis of their politics? Most of them have been very successful, but for any conservative who does claim to have hit a brick wall of uninterest, I suspect their problem is personal rather than political. After all, I've repeatedly made the case that Hollywood rarely excludes any people or ideas out of hand. Hollywood is all about business, and that business is driven by ideas. For anyone to exclude any idea on the grounds of ideology would be stupid—it would lose the viewership of at least half the country.

No, the problem that the Hollywood conservative faces isn't intellectual, it's social. Conservatism tends to be raw and unfiltered. In conversation, it punctures the zen equilibrium that sustains everyone else in Los Angeles. The industry works by networks, and anyone who can't sustain a long conversation about the importance of raw carrots and natural fibers to the functioning of yin and the flowing of yang won't fit in. One right-wing writer told me that, following 9/11, he found work had dried up. There was plenty of interest in his output, but when it came to small talk before pitches, or gossiping with the writers in the LA Farm restaurant, he was immediately frozen out. "People would open with, 'Isn't George Bush a moron?' And I would say, 'No, I voted for him.' And I could feel I was losing their respect."[56]

True, this confirms Hollywood's left-wing prejudice. But the real problem with what the writer said wasn't the content but the act of disagreement itself. Hollywood conversations deal in hyperbolic affirmations covering for lies: "You're amazing. That pitch was the best ever. You're the most beautiful woman I've ever met. Adam Sandler is the funniest man alive!" Disagreement and contradiction are like acts of verbal assault.

Why is Hollywood so sensitive to criticism? Because it's a town motored by untested ideas. If they were to tell everyone who came up with a new plot line or idea for a commercial that it sucked (and nine out of ten of them do), then nothing would get done. If you were to tell that idiot on the street corner strumming a one-string guitar that he's actually quite bad, it would spark an industrywide crisis of confidence. Writers, actors, and directors are sensitive people. They need to know that everything they do and say is "fantastic!" The cynical lash of raw conservatism doesn't fit.

Why, if that is true, did Ronald Reagan flourish in Hollywood? Because he was very, very nice. He was, by all accounts, the actor's actor, and in conversation he deflected controversy with quips and anecdotes. Ronald Reagan was the master of right-wing charm, and few national conservative leaders have been able to channel his remarkable spirit.

The Great Obama-Gatsby

When the gaudy *The Great Gatsby* hit cinemas, columnist Suzanne Fields argued that its decadence had something to tell us about American politics. Writing for *The Washington Times*, she said that Obama was the contemporary Jay Gatsby—a man whose wonder and mystery at first entice and then slowly repel. Obama brought a great party to town, we danced and danced, and then the next day we woke up to debt and political scandal.

> Daisy tells Gatsby how he always looks so "cool," just like the man in an advertisement. That sounds like Barack Obama. Whether we like or dislike his message, the man remains cool. We've paid a price for that. Like Nick Carraway, the narrator of *The Great Gatsby,* we watch scandal and shame unfold with an ominous sense of failure and menace, craving moral attention.[57]

Fields is obviously a conservative driven by partisan passions, but she has a point. Throughout this book I've argued that there's a connection between Hollywood fantasy and modern politics, a tendency for both to put style before substance. Both institutions might be heading toward some critical turning point. Hollywood has bashed out one epic too many; politics has become hamstrung by its own rhetoric. Both are polluted by money, both can underestimate the intelligence of the voters, both feel intellectually exhausted.

Yet, there is hope on the fringes. We are seeing the birth of a new kind of cinema and TV, with a greater emphasis upon plot and character. We are also seeing the arrival of a new kind of politics, which is angrier and more innovative than what came before. They have their critics, but the Tea Party and Occupy do articulate the views of millions of people who feel frustrated with the status quo. And they are talking about the kinds of "big questions" that mainstream politicians often dodge—debt, taxes, corporate power, war.

And the link between Hollywood and politics will remain strong. The stars have been the first to latch onto the new movements, injecting themselves into the tumult and using social media to propagandize their participation. This is to be expected. The moviemakers have adapted to suit every new age of political development—giving money to the party machines in the 1930s, door knocking for radicals in the 1970s, running professional lobbies in the 1980s, partying with the Clintons in the 1990s, and, now, tweeting from the front lines of the next revolution. Hollywood still chases the zeitgeist.

MR. SMITH GOES TO WASHINGTON

L ove it or loathe it, Hollywood is a town that fuels our dreams. We go to the movies for entertainment and enlightenment, comedy and violence. From cradle to grave, it's told us what is desirable, what is horrible, what is funny, what is sad, what is right, and what is wrong. It's given us gods and demons to worship and fear. It's where many of us learned how to make a pass and what to do if it succeeds. When I was a boy, *Titanic* was the movie to take your sweetheart to, and all the boys greased their hair to try to look like Leonardo DiCaprio. That kind of cultural power is priceless.

In this book I've detailed some of the ways in which Hollywood has changed political history. Stars have run for office, and even occupied the presidency. They've helped raise billions of dollars over the years, sending thousands of politicians to Capitol Hill, or even the White House. Hollywood has also changed the mechanics of politics, assisting in the development of the Internet as a campaign tool and making the most of relaxed rules on fund-raising to take campaign spending to new levels. It's no exaggeration to say that 2012 was a Hollywood election, given the role that rich liberal stars played in helping Obama win and the eccentric role played by Clint Eastwood in helping Mitt Romney lose. Some dismiss the relationship between Hollywood and Washington, D.C., as vain and insubstantial. On the contrary, the movie industry has become an important component in modern American democracy and will continue to be so for a very long time. In the summer of 2013 the president invited several power players to the White House—including singer Jennifer Hudson, actress Amy Poehler, and representatives for Oprah Winfrey, Alicia Keys, and Bon Jovi—to ask them to become ambassadors for Obamacare.[1] In October, Nina Dobrev, star of *The Vampire Diaries*, posed topless with a sign held up across her breasts that read, "#GETCOVERED."[2]

But Hollywood's influence on the national scene has its limits. As we have seen, many politicians—Obama chief among them— will take all the money and endorsements they can get from Hollywood . . . and then never call back. Moviemakers can buy themselves a place at the table, but that doesn't guarantee that anyone will listen to their demands or ideas. Franklin D. Roosevelt happily took the Warner brothers' dollars, but he eventually let the trust busters get to work on undoing their monopoly. Jack Kennedy might have gone to bed with Marilyn Monroe, but that didn't mean he would take any of her calls in the months that followed. The stars and executives who were invited to Bill Clinton's White House to give advice on improving America's health care were shocked when James Carville shouted that he didn't give a damn about the opinions of spoiled rich people from Beverly Hills. Yes, there are limits to Hollywood's personal influence in the same way that there are limits to any industry's influence.

And there's also a snobbery toward actors that hurts them deeply—maybe more than we can ever tell. When I interviewed Marge Tabankin, Barbra Streisand's political organizer, I put it to her that Ted Kennedy's chances were damaged by being seen with Miss Streisand when he ran for president in 1980. I touched a nerve.

"No!" said Marge. "That's so ridiculous. That's so crazy." After all, Barbra has raised millions of dollars for the Democratic Party, so she can't be all bad—it's so typical, so disappointing, of Democrats to blame all their missteps and mistakes on one Hollywood actor.

I suggested that maybe Barbra was, at the very least, unhelpfully associated with a particular brand of elitist liberalism—"No!" Marge insisted. Barbra was not raised in the refined atmosphere of the Kennedy family. "She grew up poor, I mean really poor, in Brooklyn. She had no dolls. One of the most emotional stories I ever heard about her was that she had a hot water bottle that her neighbor gave clothes for, and that was her doll. . . . No wonder she [now] collects dolls and has dollhouses in her house. . . . Barbra understands poverty." And yet, I said, many people are skeptical about how qualified she is to talk about nuclear power and school vouchers. "I know, I know," Marge said with a sigh.

> I actually sat in a room once where a very prominent journalist said [to Barbra], "Why don't you just shut up and sing?" And [we were] mortified because he was like this elitist, inside Washington guy who thought "Who the hell is she?" And [Barbra proudly replied], "Excuse me, I didn't have to give up my passport just because I happen to have good pipes."[3]

Not that the outside world's snobbery ever seems to stop Hollywood from getting involved. Part of the conviction that the moviemakers matter comes from their idealism, part of it from self-delusion. I encountered that firsthand when I spent a day in the company of a professional Hollywood fund-raiser who—for the sake of hiding his identity—I'll call Stephen. I was introduced to Stephen by a friend who said that he was one of the best connected men in Los Angeles that he'd ever met. It took a little while to track Stephen down (that cell phone was always busy), but eventually he suggested brunch in Culver City. He arrived late, apologized, and said that he had to go to an environmental awards dinner that evening. But I was welcome to tag along with him as he got ready, and he might even be able to get me into the event. "Why not?" I said. We jumped into his beat-up old car (the window winder was missing next to my seat) and sped off to his home nearby. Stephen lightened up the journey with a few anecdotes about his "close personal friend" Al Gore. That's always a bad sign.

The house turned out not to be his; he was sharing with a friend. Stephen took me through to his bedroom, and before entering stopped and said, "Watch out for the floor. The dog's taken a shit on it." Sure enough, sitting in the middle of his bedroom carpet was a large, calcified dog stool. "It's been there for days," said Stephen. "Take a seat."

I sat down on the bed, doing my best to keep my feet away from the turd—a tricky act to pull off because the room was really quite small. Stephen said that he'd write an e-mail for me to the organizer of the environmental awards event asking if they'd let me in. "Then I'd better freshen up and put on my tux." He wrote the e-mail, disrobed, and got into the shower. I sat nervously on the bed—just me and the dog crap—wondering if all of this was a prelude to an attempted seduction. Twenty minutes later Stephen came back in and put on his clothes. "We should wait for the e-mail," he said. So he sat down next to me on the bed, wearing the top half of a tux and a pair of boxer shorts beneath, and we both waited in silence. Finally, he shrugged. "I guess her e-mail isn't coming," he said.

"What do you want to do?" I asked.

"Well, you could still come with me to the party if you want."

"But how will I get in?"

"The same way I'm getting in. There's a guy I know who says he can let me in through the back door."

So that was Stephen's "invite" to the environmental awards. He was going to "gate crash" in.

I said that I was game anyhow, and we got back into Stephen's car and drove downtown. But somewhere near city hall he got cold feet and obviously decided that bringing someone else along might compromise his strategy, so he stopped the car and asked me to get out. I watched him speed off into the distance, and then started my lonely trek to the nearest subway. This sort of experience wasn't unusual during my time in Hollywood. It's a town of hucksters, where people often play a much smaller game than they talk.

But for all its limitations, Hollywood's power as an image maker—shaping America's political imagination—is indisputable. It's helped liberals to define their heroes as wonkish mavericks defying the ignorance of the mob. It's given conservatives the ideal of the cowboy who rides into town and puts all the bad guys in their place. Most important, it's created the narrative that what America needs is a superhero to save it from its problems. Of course, the U.S. government has been expanding in power for decades without Hollywood's help. But the moviemakers have helped to increase popular expectations of what politicians can and should do. Some of those politicians have—consciously or subconsciously—used the superhero narrative to help themselves get elected. Barack Obama has been everything from Batman to Spider-Man, from Atticus Finch to Abraham Lincoln. Other politicians have failed to build a convincing narrative for themselves and so done less well. Politics abhors a bore.

This has encouraged a sense of unreality in American politics.

The compelling stories behind politicians' lives, their looks, their wit, their hair, their ability to speak well in public have all become more important than their wisdom or experience. And politics that sticks to a single narrative (we are conservatives, we don't raise taxes; we are liberals, we don't cut spending) has turned into dogmatism and created political gridlock. Modern American democracy has become like a movie in which people play two-dimensional characters rather than real-life statesmen, all rehearsing lines that are meant to appease their audience rather than tackle the real problems of the world with genuine insight and honesty. And America's problems are very real: debt, lingering unemployment, competition from China, terrorism, immigration reform, poverty, racism. Tackling issues such as these requires qualities that are sadly becoming rarer and rarer. A willingness to reach across the aisle and compromise. A preparedness to work hard on passing unglamorous bills. A readiness to make cuts and sacrifices that might cause pain to special interests. In other words, America has a political culture that fails to reflect the needs of its economy and society. But it rumbles on, partly because that's the way the two parties want it and partly because the public enjoys the show.

Hollywood continues to worm its way into daily politics. Two planned TV projects about the life of Hillary Clinton were nixed in the fall of 2013, after the Republicans threatened not to participate in presidential debates held by their potential sponsors—CNN and NBC. But the idea of a biopic still inches along in Hollywood, where the movie script for *Rodham* (in which a twenty-something Hillary falls in love with a handsome boy from Hope, Arkansas) finally gained a director in October 2013.[4] Iowa senator Tom Harkin said that the shutdown that started that month was "like a scene from the Hollywood western *High Noon*." In his telling, Obama was the good sheriff (natch) and the Republicans were the outlaws (boo, hiss).[5] Tea Party senator Ted Cruz has done his best to establish himself as a tough guy from the West; he even wears a pair of black ostrich-skin cowboy boots that he calls "my argument boots."[6] But the Republican style isn't drawn exclusively from cowboy movies. Conservatives compared Cruz's famous anti-Obamacare faux filibuster to the one delivered by Jimmy Stewart in *Mr. Smith Goes to Washington* (1939); right-wing pundit Mark Levin called him "Mr. Cruz going to Washington."[7] And when libertarian senator Rand Paul held his own thirteen-hour filibuster against the confirmation of John Brennan as the new director of the CIA, Marco Rubio offered some support with a speech peppered with quotes from songs and movies, including *The Godfather* ("I'm going to make him [Rand] an offer he can't refuse").[8]

All this cine fantasy has serious consequences. In September 2013, Tom Moran, a columnist for the Newark *Star-Ledger*, picked up on the oft-made comparison between New Jersey governor Chris Christie and TV's Tony Soprano: both hypermasculine, Catholic, conservative, loudmouthed, and enjoying a reputation built upon bravado. It's that larger-than-life personality, said Moran, that keeps Christie viable both as a governor and a presidential candidate. It certainly isn't his job performance—crime, poverty, and taxes are rising in the Garden State. But polls show that while the voters disapprove of the condition of New Jersey, they love Christie. Moran explained:

> At town hall meetings, Christie is relaxed, funny and persuasive. He usually looks to pick a fight at the end, like an entertainer singing the crowd favorite as an encore. It's compelling stuff. But it's thin gruel, in the end. Because the substance doesn't remotely measure up to the spin.[9]

And that neatly sums up the situation. Politicians act like entertainers, and the substance of their policies rarely match the spin of their rhetoric.

CONCLUSION

The only solution to politics-as-spectacle is to embrace a different kind of politics altogether. A politics in which philosophy is valued more than personality and intellect more than charisma. It would be a politics that expects less of the state, because it would expect less of its politicians. No more Kennedy-style leading men, no more supermen or cowboys, no more exaggerated expectations, and, hopefully, no more unsustainable programs or costly wars. It would have to hark back to an early period in American history—when the guiding principles of politics were not campaign money or cinematic visuals but the Constitution, reason, and compassion.

As Jack Nicholson observes in *Easy Rider*, "This used to be a helluva good country." I'm sure that if it rediscovers its essentials, it can be again.

ACKNOWLEDGMENTS

This book was made possible with the generous support of the Leverhulme Foundation, Royal Holloway College, University of London, and the Rothermere American Institute, University of Oxford. I wrote the bulk of it while at the Rothermere and owe a great deal to the kind support of Nigel Boles, the Director, and Gareth Davies, a fellow at St. Anne's College. Because of all my travel, I didn't get to spend nearly as much time at Oxford as I should or would've liked—and I appreciate everybody's patience.

Critical to making *Citizen Hollywood* happen was my wonderful agent, Fredi Friedman. Much more than just an agent, Fredi kindly worked through the early proposals and drafts and helped turn a massive academic daydream into a readable book. She's a smart, warm woman who knows how to turn the screws on a publisher. And, on that note, I also must thank the marvelous staff at Thomas

ACKNOWLEDGMENTS

Dunne who have been so kind and helpful. Peter Joseph and Thomas Dunne are brilliant publishers whose knowledge base often exceeded my own.

In Los Angeles, I benefited from the friendship of Jamie Ruddy, Stephen Nemeth, Tracey Durning, Lenora Claire, Charles Coulombe, Thomas Watson, Richard Metzger, and the sublime Rupert Russell. In Washington, D.C., my great buddy Carl was on hand to play host and provide beer. Billy Newton is the best conversationalist in D.C. and Thomas Peters an example of Catholicism at its compassionate best. In the UK, I have to thank my mother, Alex, Daniel, Chris, Tom, Andrew, Ed, Will, Pat, Peter, Con, Sue, David, Phil, Thomas, Sally, Sarah, and Nick for all their moral support. Intellectually, I am always indebted to Tony Badger, my supervisor at Cambridge.

Finally, I wrote this book while transitioning from academia to journalism. The *Daily Telegraph* is a fantastic newspaper that has never said "no" to me taking time off to pursue my mad adventures in America. Chris Deerin and Rob Colvile are great bosses who have taught me a lot. But two people deserve special mention. First, Damian Thompson, who has been a fine friend as well as a wise editor. Second, Luke "L-dog" McGee, who might look like a mess at first glance but who is really super smart and maybe the funniest person on the earth. Lord Quakington needs to give him a pay raise.

NOTES

Introduction:
Dirty Harry vs. Harold and Kumar

1. "Clint Eastwood Earns Bad Reviews for 'Weird' RNC Speech," *Boston Globe*, Aug. 31, 2012.
2. "Poll: Romney Trails Empty Chair," *New Yorker*, Aug. 31, 2012.
3. Interview with Stuart Stevens.
4. "Eastwood Says Speech Was Entirely Spontaneous," *New York Times*, Sept. 8, 2012.
5. Interview with Stuart Stevens.
6. "Kal Penn, a Star Turn on Both Coasts," *New York Times*, Nov. 11, 2011.
7. "Kal Penn: Change Well Worth Defending," *USA Today*, Sept. 7, 2012.
8. "A Star Turn," *New York Times*, Nov. 11, 2011, ST10.
9. "Why Did GOP Invite Clint Eastwood?," CNN.com, Aug. 31, 2012.

10. "Carmel-by-the-Sea Journal; Eastwood's Law and (Mostly) Order," *New York Times*, Sept. 1, 1987.

11. "The Curious Friendship of Weiner and Affleck," *New York Times*, May 6, 2009, A26.

12. Interview with Andrew Breitbart.

13. "Weiner's Behavior Prompts a Question: Why Did He Do It?," *New York Times*, July 29, 2013, A16.

1. The Dark Knight Rises

1. "Inside the Secret World of the Data Crunchers Who Helped Obama Win," Nov. 7, 2012.

2. "Showing Their Colors: Anna Wintour's Party for an Obama Reelection Campaign," *New York Times*, Feb. 8, 2012, E15.

3. "Glenn Beck Calls Anna Wintour 'The Devil,'" June 5, 2010.

4. "Obama Fund-Raises $4.5 Million from Celebs in Just 8 Hours in NY," *Daily Mail*, June 14, 2012.

5. "No Longer Your Father's Electorate," *Los Angeles Times*, Nov. 8, 2012.

6. "Obama Hails Deficit Plan on California Stops," *Los Angeles Times*, Sept. 26, 2011, A5.

7. "Matt Damon Disappointed in Obama: 'I No Longer Hope for Audacity,'" *Salon*, March 3, 2011.

8. "Matt Damon Dismisses Barack Obama as a 'One Term President,'" *Daily Mail*, Dec. 21, 2011.

9. "Jane Lynch Not Impressed with Obama's Progress on Gay Rights: 'He's Just Nicely Walking the Middle,'" *Daily Mail*, Dec. 21, 2010.

10. "The Ungrateful President," *New York Times*, Aug. 7, 2012, A19.

11. "Harvey Weinstein on Obama: 'The Paul Newman of American Presidents,'" *Weekly Standard*, Aug. 7, 2012.

12. "Michelle Obama's 'Jealousy' and 'Resentment' Led to Rift with Oprah," *New York Post*, May 13, 2012.

13. "How Oprah Fell from Favour at the Court of the Sun King, Barack Obama," *Daily Telegraph*, May 14, 2012.

14. Interview with Dustin Lance Black.

15. "Hollywood & Politics: Dustin Lance Black Blames Obama and Romney for the Mess of Gay Marriage," *Hollywood Reporter*, April 26, 2012.

16. "How Proposition 8 Passed in California—And Why It Wouldn't Today," *Washington Post*, March 26, 2013.

17. "Hollywood Pays Tribute to a Gay Hero. But 30 Years on His Legacy Is in Peril," *The Guardian*, Oct. 26, 2008.

18. "Dustin Lance Black Debuts Prop. 8 Play in New York," *Hollywood Reporter*, Sept. 20, 2011.

19. "Chuck Todd on Importance of Biden's Gay Marriage Comments: 'Gay Money Has Replaced Wall St. Money,'" *Mediaite*, May 7, 2012.

20. "President Obama Getting Heat on Gay Marriage from Media, Hollywood, Donors," *Hollywood Reporter*, May 8, 2012.

21. "A Scramble as Biden Backs Same-Sex Marriage," *New York Times*, May 7, 2012, A1.

22. Interview with anonymous source.

23. "The Gay Marriage Endorsement Was All About Hollywood's Money and Obama's Ego," *Daily Telegraph*, May 11, 2012.

24. "Joe Biden Cites 'Will & Grace' in Endorsement of Same-Sex Marriage," May 6, 2012.

25. "Obama's New Courting of Hollywood Pays Off," *Daily Telegraph*, May 9, 2012, A18.

26. "The Gay Marriage Endorsement," *Daily Telegraph*, May 11, 2012.

27. "'On My Behalf, Really?," *Weekly Standard*, May 9, 2012.

28. "Obama's New Courting of Hollywood Pays Off," *New York Times*, May 9, 2012, A18.

29. "Michelle Obama on Kimmel: Reveals Her Disguise, President's Advice to Daughters," *Hollywood Reporter*, Oct. 25, 2012.

30. "Will and Jada Pinkett Smith's Malibu Home," *Architectural Digest*, Sept. 2011.

31. "Michelle Obama Is Guest of Honor at Jada Pinkett Smith, Salma Hayek Lunch," *People*, Oct. 26, 2012.

32. "Remarks by the First Lady at a Campaign Event," Whitehouse.gov, Sept. 28, 2013.

33. "Hollywood Cash: Obama 16–1 Over Mitt," *Newsmax*, Oct. 29, 2012.

34. Interview with Andy Spahn.

35. "How Hollywood Helped Obama Win—With Money, Glee and an Empty Chair," *Daily Telegraph*, Nov. 12, 2012.

36. "Obama's Top Fund-Raisers," *New York Times*, Sept. 13, 2012.

37. "Obama's Contraception Trap for the GOP," *The Dish*, Feb. 13, 2012.

38. "Senate Candidate Provokes Ire with 'Legitimate Rape' Comment," *New York Times*, Aug. 19, 2012.

39. "A Nation of Julias," *National Review Online*, May 4, 2012.

40. "Obama Campaign: 'Vote Like Your Lady Parts Depend on It,'" *Weekly Standard*, Oct. 2, 2012.

41. "Priorities: On Eve of Election, Rightbloggers Rage at Slightly Sexy Obama Ad," *Village Voice*, Oct. 28, 2012.

42. "The Obama Generation X Factor," Philly.com, Oct. 27, 2012.

43. "Romney's New Foe: 'Batman Bane,'" *Washington Examiner*, July 16, 2012.

44. "'Star Wars' Icon: 'Snake Oil Salesman' Romney 'Must Be Defeated,'" NewsBusters.com, Oct. 5, 2012.

45. Interview with Stuart Stevens.

46. "Survey Shows Latinos Aligning Themselves with More Liberal Views on Abortion," *Huffington Post*, Jan. 24, 2012.

47. "Survey: One in Five Americans Has No Religion," CNN.com, Oct. 9, 2012.

48. "The Top Ten Celebrity Reactions to Barack Obama's Election—From Donald Trump to Niall Horan," IrishCentral.com, Nov. 8, 2012.

49. "Sighting: Obama's McCormick Place Rally Leaves Celeb Supporters Star-Struck," *Chicago Tribune*, Nov. 12, 2012.

50. "Hollywood Raids Pentagon Files," *Daily Beast*, Aug. 13, 2011.

2. The Color of Money

1. "House of Cards," *Washington Post*, Oct. 9, 2005.

2. Aaron Tonken, *King of Cons: Exposing the Dirty Rotten Secrets of the Washington Elite and Hollywood Celebrities* (New York: Thomas Nelson, 2004), 6.

3. "Celebrities: 'Best Eight Years of Our Lives'; Stars Drive SUVs to Hillary Clinton for Senate Fundraiser," Media Research Center, Aug. 15, 2000.

4. "Movie Folks' Final Farewell to Bill," *New York Post*, Aug. 13, 2000.

5. "First Lady's Family Aids Senate Run," Associated Press, Aug. 13, 2000.

6. "Hillary Returns Bucks to Ex-Felon," *Washington Post*, Aug. 17, 2000, 21.

7. "The Cuban Coffee Caper," *Time* magazine, Feb. 12, 1979.

8. "Money, Politics and the Undoing of Stan Lee Media," *Los Angeles Times*, July 20, 2003, C1.

9. "House of Cards," *Washington Post*, Oct. 9, 2000.

10. "Not Guilty Verdict for Fund-Raiser," *Los Angeles Times*, May 28, 2005.

11. "Political Drama Abounds in Trial Involving Mrs. Clinton's Hollywood Fund-Raiser," *Washington Post*, May 9, 2005.

12. "House of Cards," *Washington Post*, Oct. 9, 2000.

13. Amanda B. Carpenter, *The Vast Right-Wing Conspiracy's Dossier on Hillary Clinton* (New York: Regnery Publishing, 2006), 26–27.

14. "Largess to Clintons Lands CEO in Lawsuit," *Washington Post*, May 26, 2007.

15. "Serta's CEO Optimistic as Company's Sales Rise 7% in 1Q," *Furniture Today*, April 5, 2011.

16. Steven J. Ross, *Hollywood Left and Right: How Movie Stars Shaped American Politics* (New York: Oxford University Press, 2011), 70.

17. Neal Gabler, *An Empire of Their Own: How the Jews Invented Hollywood* (New York: Crown Publishers, 1988), 79–83.

18. Anthony R. Fellow, *American Media History* (Boston: Wadsworth, 2010), 228.

19. Otto Friedrich, *City of Nets: A Portrait of Hollywood in the 1940s* (Berkeley: University of California Press, 1986), 16.

20. Mark A. Vieira, *Irving Thalberg: Boy Wonder to Producer Prince* (Berkeley: University of California Press, 2009), 82.

21. Terry Christensen and Peter J. Haas, *Projecting Politics: Political Messages in American Film* (New York: M. E. Sharpe, 2005), 46–49.

22. Friedrich, *City of Nets*, 356–57.

23. Diana Altman, *Hollywood East: Louis B. Mayer and the Origins of the Studio System* (Tapley Cove, ME: Tapley Cove Press, 2010), 169.

24. Scott Eyman, *Lion of Hollywood: The Life and Legend of Louis B. Mayer* (New York: Simon & Schuster, 2005), 140.

25. Todd Donovan, Daniel A. Smith, Christopher Z. Mooney, *State and Local Politics: Institutions and Reform: The Essentials* (Independence, KY: Cengage Learning, 2009), 254.

26. Paul McDonald, *The Star System: Hollywood and the Production of Popular Identities* (London: Wallflower Press, 2000), 46–50.

27. Lee Server, *Ava Gardner: Love Is Nothing* (New York: Bloomsbury Publishing, 2010), 58.

28. Shirley Temple Black, *Child Star: An Autobiography* (New York: McGraw-Hill, 1988), 319–20.

29. Server, *Ava Gardner*, 58.

30. "Lion of Hollywood: The Life and Legend of Louis B. Mayer," *New York Times*, July 6, 2005.

31. Kevin Brownlow, *The Parade's Gone By . . .* (Berkeley: University of California Press, 1968), 38.

32. "Lion of Hollywood," *New York Times*, July 6, 2005.

33. Ernest D. Giglio, *Here's Looking at You: Hollywood, Film, and Politics* (New York: Peter Lang, 2005), 7.

34. Mark Feeney, *Nixon at the Movies: A Book about Belief* (Chicago: University of Chicago Press, 2004), ix.

35. Eve Golden, *John Gilbert: The Last of the Silent Film Stars* (Lexington, KY: University Press of Kentucky, 2013), 173.

36. Ross, *Hollywood Left and Right*, 64.

37. Scott Eyman, *The Speed of Sound: Hollywood and the Talkie Revolution 1926–1930* (New York: Simon & Schuster, 1997), 250–51.

38. Alex Ben Block and Lucy Autrey Wilson, *George Lucas's Blockbusting: A Decade-by-Decade Survey of Timeless Movies Including Untold Secrets of Their Financial and Cultural Success* (New York: HarperCollins, 2010), 63.

39. Ian Scott, *American Politics in Hollywood Film* (Edinburgh: Edinburgh University Press, 2011), 27–28.

40. "FDR Knew How to Act the Role of President," *Los Angeles Times*, Dec. 10, 2012.

41. E. J. Stephens and Marc Wanamaker, *Early Warner Bros. Studios* (Charleston, SC: Arcadia Publishing, 2010), 7–9.

42. Gabler, *Empire of Their Own*, 324.

43. Linda Civitello, *Cuisine and Culture: A History of Food and People* (New York: John Wiley and Sons, 2011), 308.

44. Gabler, *Empire of Their Own*, 317–18.

45. Cass W. Sperling, Cork Milner, Jack Warner Jr., *Hollywood Be Thy Name: The Warner Brothers Story* (Lexington, KY: University Press of Kentucky, 1998), 161.

46. Colin Shindler, *Hollywood in Crisis: Cinema and American Society, 1929–1939* (London: Routledge, 1996), 161.

47. Michael Szalay, *New Deal Modernism: American Literature and the Invention of the Welfare State* (Durham, NC: Duke University Press, 2000), 234.

48. Nancy Snow, "Confessions of a Hollywood Propagandist: Harry Warner, FDR and Celluloid Persuasion in Martin Kaplan and Johanna Blakeley, eds., *Warners' War: Politics, Pop Culture & Propaganda in Wartime Hollywood* (Los Angeles: Norman Lear Center Press, 2004).

49. James Chapman, *Cinemas of the World: Film and Society from 1895 to the Present* (New York: Reaktion Books, 2004), 106.

50. Stanley Green, *Hollywood Musicals: Year by Year* (New York: Hal Leonard, 1999), 24.

51. Ross, *Hollywood Left and Right*, 96.

52. Ibid., 71–77.

53. Brian Neve, *Film and Politics in America: A Social Tradition* (London: Routledge, 1992), 15.

54. Schindler, *Hollywood in Crisis*, 41.

55. Steve Neale, *Classical Hollywood Reader* (London: Routledge, 2012), 168.

56. Schindler, *Hollywood in Crisis*, 43.

57. Thomas Schatz, *Boom and Bust: American Cinema in the 1940s* (Berkeley, University of California Press, 1999), 14.

58. M. B. B. Biskupski, *Hollywood's War with Poland, 1939–1945* (Lexington, KY: University Press of Kentucky, 2010), 222.

59. William D. Romanowski, *Reforming Hollywood: How American Protestants Fought for Freedom at the Movies* (Oxford: Oxford University Press, 2012), 119.

60. Eyman, *Lion of Hollywood*, 481.

61. "Chris Dodd Warns of Hollywood Backlash Against Obama Over Anti-Piracy Bill," Fox News, Jan. 19, 2012.

3. Easy Riders

1. Emilie Raymond, *From My Cold, Dead Hands: Charlton Heston and American Politics* (Lexington, KY: University Press of Kentucky, 2006), 73.

2. Charles Euchner, *Nobody Turn Me Around: A People's History of the 1963 March on Washington* (Boston: Beacon Press, 2010).

3. Raymond, *From My Cold, Dead Hands*, 78.

4. Sherry L. Smith, *Hippies, Indians, and the Fight for Red Power* (New York: Oxford University Press, 2012), 22.

5. "Scholar Asserts That Hollywood Avidly Aided Nazis," *New York Times*, June 25, 2013, C1.

6. Louis Pizzitola, *Hearst over Hollywood: Power, Passion, and Propaganda in the Movies* (New York: Columbia University Press, 2002), 123.

7. Wheeler W. Dixon, *American Cinema of the 1940s: Themes and Variations* (New Brunswick, NJ: Rutgers University Press, 2006), 61.

8. "Hitler in Hollywood: Did the Studios Collaborate?," *New Yorker*, Sept. 16, 2013.

9. Reynold Humphries, *Hollywood's Blacklists: A Political and Cultural History* (Edinburgh: Edinburgh University Press, 2010), 17.

10. Ibid., 11.

11. Michael E. Birdwell, *Celluloid Soldiers: The Warner Bros. Campaign Against Nazism* (New York: New York University Press, 1999), 78.

12. Thomas Doherty, *Hollywood's Censor: Joseph I. Breen and the Production Code Administration* (New York: Columbia University Press, 2007), 201.

13. Steven Mintz and Randy W. Roberts, *Hollywood's America: Twentieth-Century America Through Film* (Oxford: Wiley and Blackwell, 2010), 171.

14. Ibid., 173.

15. Edward M. Yager, *Ronald Reagan's Journey: Democrat to Republican* (Lanham, MD: Rowman and Littlefield, 2006), 20.

16. Kevin Starr, *Embattled Dreams: California in War and Peace, 1940–1950* (New York: Oxford University Press, 2002), 168.

17. Gregory D. Black and Clayton R. Koppes, *Hollywood Goes to War: How Politics, Profits, and Propaganda Shaped World War Two Movies* (New York: The Free Press, 1987), 48–81.

18. Thomas Schatz, *Boom and Bust: American Cinema in the 1940s* (Berkeley: University of California Press, 1999), 218.

19. "Review: Casablanca," *Variety*, Dec. 1, 1942.

20. Aljean Harmetz, *Round Up the Usual Suspects: The Making of Casablanca: Bogart, Bergman, and World War II* (New York: Hyperion, 1992), 13.

21. "The Most Outrageous Experiment Ever Conducted in the Movie Industry. Do Those Working in the Movies Know the Difference Between John Ford and Henry Ford? Should They?" *TV Week*, Nov. 13, 2013.

22. Brian Neve, *Film and Politics in America: A Social Tradition* (London: Routledge, 1992), 172.

23. Michael Woodiwiss, *Organized Crime and American Power: A History* (Toronto: University of Toronto Press, 2003), 158.

24. Ronald Reagan, *Where's the Rest of Me?* (New York: Duell, Sloan and Pearce, 1965), 162.

25. Robert Dallek, *Ronald Reagan: The Politics of Symbolism* (Cambridge, MA: Harvard University Press, 1999), 23.

26. Donald T. Critchlow and Emilie Raymond, eds. *Hollywood and Politics: A Sourcebook* (New York: Taylor and Francis, 2009), 146.

27. Joel H. Spring, *Images of American Life: A History of Ideological Management in Schools, Movies, Radio, and Television* (Albany: State University of New York Press, 1992), 179.

28. Jennifer Burns, *Goddess of the Market: Ayn Rand and the American Right* (New York: Oxford University Press, 2009), 125.

29. Michael Freedland, *Hollywood on Trial: McCarthyism's War Against the Movies* (New York: Anova Robson Books, 2007), 71.

30. Jon Lewis, *Hollywood v. Hard Core: How the Struggle over Censorship Created the Modern Film Industry* (New York: New York University Press, 2002), 45.

31. Colin Shindler, *Hollywood in Crisis: Cinema and American Society, 1929–1939* (London: Routledge, 1996), 67.

32. Humphries, *Hollywood's Blacklists*, 88.

33. Marty Jezer, *The Dark Ages: Life in the United States, 1945–1960* (Cambridge, MA: South End Press, 1982), 94.

34. "To Name or Not to Name," *New York Times*, March 25, 1973, 34.

35. Ronald Radosh and Allis Radosh, *Red Star over Hollywood: The Film Colony's Long Romance with the Left* (New York: Encounter Books, 2005), 162.

36. "Washington Wire," *New Republic* 120 (1949), 48.

37. Ross, *Hollywood Left and Right*, 128.

38. "Lionel Stander: Who's Afraid of John Wayne?," *New York Times*, May 23, 1971, D15.

39. Interview with Haskell Wexler.

40. Leonard Quart and Albert Auster, *American Film and Society Since 1945* (Westport, CT: Praeger, 1984), 96.

41. Robert Beverley Ray, *A Certain Tendency of the Hollywood Cinema: 1930–1980* (Princeton, NJ: Princeton University Press, 1985), 162.

42. Marian Edelman Borden, *Paul Newman: A Biography* (Westport, CT: Greenwood Biographies, 2010), 92.

43. Ibid., 93.

44. Ronald Brownstein, *The Power and the Glitter: The Hollywood-Washington Connection* (New York: Pantheon Books, 1995), 235.

45. Interview with Curtis Gans.

46. Interview with Robert Vaughn.

47. Francis R. Valeo, *Mike Mansfield, Majority Leader: A Different Kind of Senate, 1961–1976* (New York: M. E. Sharpe, 1999), 214.

48. "The Now Generation Knew Him When," *Life*, Sept. 12, 1969, 64.

49. "Going Beyond Myra and the Valley of the Junk," *New York Times*, June 5, 1970, 49.

50. Bernard F. Dick, *Columbia Pictures: Portrait of a Studio* (Lexington, KY: University Press of Kentucky, 1992), 183.

51. Lester D. Friedman, *Arthur Penn's Bonnie and Clyde* (Cambridge: Cambridge University Press, 2000), 83.

52. Lewis, *Hollywood v. Hard Core*, 155.

53. "The Godfather Wars," *Vanity Fair*, March 2009.

54. "Film and Music Stars Raise $300,000 at a McGovern Concert," *New York Times*, April 17, 1972, 38.

55. "Now the Big One: It May be Winner Takes All," *New York Times*, June 4, 1972, E1.

56. Interview with George McGovern.

NOTES

57. Jonathan Kirshner, *Hollywood's Last Golden Age: Politics, Society, and the Seventies Film in America* (Ithaca, NY: Cornell University Press, 2013), 211.

58. "Film and Music Stars," *New York Times*, April 17, 1972, 38.

59. "Warren Beatty Sexes Up George McGovern," *Village Voice*, April 27, 1972.

60. Interview with Leonard Nimoy.

61. "Politics and Performers," *New York Times*, May 18, 1972, 47.

62. "The Oscar-Extravaganza-Pure Hollywood," *New York Times*, April 12, 1972, 91.

63. "McGovern '72: An Oral History," *Vanity Fair*, Nov. 6, 2012.

64. "Shirley: Let's Tax Diapers!," *New York Times*, Aug. 8, 1971, D9.

65. Jan Bondeson, *Blood on the Snow: The Killing of Olof Palme* (New York: Cornell Press, 2005), 79–80.

66. "Fonda: A Person of Many Parts," *New York Times*, Feb. 3, 1974, 16.

67. Jerry Lembcke, *Hanoi Jane: War, Sex, and Fantasies of Betrayal* (Amherst, MA: University of Massachusetts Press, 2010), 2.

68. "The Truth About My Trip to Hanoi," janefonda.com, June 22, 2011,

69. "It's Not Just Fonda and Company," *New York Times*, March 21, 1971, D1.

70. Patricia Bosworth, *Jane Fonda: The Private Life of a Public Woman* (New York: Houghton Mifflin, 2011), 326.

71. Ibid., 329.

72. "Radical Chic: That Party at Lennys," *New York*, June 8, 1970, 27–56.

73. "'Acid, Amnesty, and Abortion': The Unlikely Source of a Legendary Smear," *New Republic*, Oct. 22, 2012.

74. Jefferson R. Cowie, *Stayin' Alive: The 1970s and the Last Days of the Working Class* (New York: New Press, 2010), 133.

75. "The New Cool," *New York Times*, Feb. 10, 1973, 31.

76. "Shirley MacLaine Back in Her Dancing Shoes," *New York Times*, April 18, 1976, 45.

77. Interview with Michael Laughlin.

78. John King Fairbank, *China Watch* (Cambridge: Harvard University Press, 1987), 73–74.

79. "A Turning Point in the Career of Shirley MacLaine," *New York Times*, Jan. 22, 1978, 40.

80. Humberto Fontova, *Fidel: Hollywood's Favorite Tyrant* (Washington, D.C.: Regnery Publishing, 2005), 11.

81. Interview with Saul Landau.

82. "Cuban Intelligence Defector Reveals: Castro Spies on Celebrities," *Human Events*, June 2, 2005,

83. Fontova, *Hollywood's Favorite Tyrant*, 11.

4. The Social Network

1. Interview with Bob Dowling.

2. Aida A. Hozic, *Hollyworld: Space, Power, and Fantasy in the American Economy* (New York: Cornell University Press, 2001), 104.

3. Sharon Waxman, *Rebels on the Backlot: Six Maverick Directors and How They Conquered the Hollywood Studio System* (New York: HarperCollins, 2013).

4. "Star Wars Director George Lucas to Abandon Blockbusters After Red Tails," *The Guardian*, Jan. 18, 2012.

5. Tom Shone, *Blockbuster: How Hollywood Learned to Stop Worrying and Love the Summer* (New York: Free Press, 2004), 37.

6. "The Real Force Behind 'Star Wars': How George Lucas Built an Empire," Feb. 9, 2012.

7. "Kael on Star Wars," *New Yorker*, May 25, 2012.

8. Noel Brown, *The Hollywood Family Film: A History, from Shirley Temple to Harry Potter* (New York: I. B. Tauris, 2012), 145.

9. Interview with Marge Tabankin.

10. "The Hollywood Campaign," *The Atlantic*, Sept. 2004.

11. "Bill Still Loved, At Least in 90210," *New York*, Feb. 13, 1995, 11.

12. Interview with Candace Block.

13. Robert S. Alley and Irby B. Brown, *Women Television Producers: Transformation of the Male Medium* (New York: University of Rochester Press, 2001), 172.

14. Interview with Andy Spahn.

15. "Hollywood, D.C.," *Los Angeles Magazine*, March 1996, 73.

16. "The Hollywood Campaign," *The Atlantic*, Sept. 2004.

17. "Hollywood and Its Celebrity Charitable Causes," *International Business Times*, July 13, 2011.

18. "The Rich and Famous Clamor to Experience a Taste of Poverty," *New York Times*, Nov. 11, 1991, C11.

19. "Hollywood Hardball," *Mother Jones*, Feb. 1991, 34.

20. " 'Cultural War' of 1992 Moves in from the Fringe," *New York Times*, Aug. 30, 2012, A15.

21. "The Rich and Famous Clamor," *New York Times*, Nov. 11, 1991.

22. "Long Wait for Beatty as Parties Heat Up," *New York Times*, July 17, 1992.

23. "Ready for Your Close-Up, Mr. President?," *New York Times*, Nov. 12, 1995.

24. "Behind the Lines, It's a Hollywood Touch," *New York Times*, July 1, 1993.

25. "Washington Is Star-Struck as Hollywood Gets Serious," *New York Times*, May 9, 1993.

26. "Clinton's Best Friends Find It a Tough Role," *New York Times*, May 27, 1993.

27. "Below the Beltway," *New York Times*, Sept. 22, 1996.

28. Peter C. Rollins and John E. O'Connor, eds., *The West Wing: The American Presidency as Television Drama* (Chicago: University of Illinois Press, 2001), 227–28.

29. "A Hollywood Production: Political Money," *New York Times*, Sept. 12, 1996.

30. "Women's Political Group Disbands in Hollywood," *New York Times*, April 14, 1997.

31. Interview with Mike Medavoy.

32. "Strained Bedfellows," *Spy*, Feb. 1992, 70.

33. Gary C. Woodward, *The Idea of Identification* (Albany: State University of New York Press, 2003), 173.

34. Interview with Jeremy Pikser.

35. Interview with anonymous source.

36. "Norman Mailer, "The Art of Fiction," *The Paris Review*, 93 (Summer, 2007).

37. "Among Hollywood Democrats, President Is Supported as One of Their Own," *New York Times*, Sept. 29, 1998, A19.

38. Interview with Ralph Nader.

39. Interview with Paul Haggis.

40. "Anti-War Movies Faltering at the Box Office," NPR, Nov 16, 2007.

41. Interview with anonymous source.

5. *The West Wing*

1. Jeffrey C. Alexander, *The Performance of Politics: Obama's Victory and the Democratic Struggle for Power* (New York: Oxford University Press, 2010), 309.

2. "Following the Script: Obama, McCain and 'The West Wing,'" *New York Times*, Oct. 29, 2008, C1.

3. "From West Wing to the Real Thing," *The Guardian*, Feb. 21, 2008.

4. "Sheen Slates 'Bad Comic' Bush," BBC News, Feb. 13, 2001.

5. Howard Hawks, *Howard Hawks: Interviews* (Jackson: University Press of Mississippi, 2001), 61.

6. John H. Lenihan, *Showdown: Confronting Modern America in the Western Film* (Chicago: University of Illinois Press, 1985), 23.

7. "Obama as Atticus Finch Is the Defender of the American Mainstream," *The Guardian*, April 8, 2012.

8. "Clinton's Visit to Myanmar Raises Hopes and Concerns," *New York Times*, Nov. 29, 2011.

9. "West Wing Babies," *Vanity Fair*, April 2012.

10. Janet McCabe, *The West Wing* (Detroit: Wayne State University Press, 2013), 43.

11. Thomas Fahy, ed., *Considering Aaron Sorkin: Essays on the Politics, Poetics, and Sleight of Hand in the Films and Television Series* (Jefferson, NC: McFarland and Company, 2005), 62–63.

12. "The Two West Wings," *The Advocate*, Feb. 13, 2001, 39.

13. Joe Dallas, *The Gay Gospel?* (New York: Harvest House Publishers, 2007), 62.

14. "Two West Wings," *Advocate*, Feb. 13, 2001, 39.

15. Interview with Mike Farrell.

16. "Hollywood Auditions Candidates," *Los Angeles Times*, Feb. 11, 2003, A1.

17. "For Hollywood Dems, It's Cash and Kerry," *Variety*, Dec. 28–Jan. 5, 2003, 6.

18. "Graham Skips the Quiet Car," *New York Times*, Aug. 31, 2004, A21.

19. "Hollywood Patrons Beset by Politicians," *Los Angeles Times*, Feb. 24, 2002, 1.

20. "Practicing Podiatry at 20,000 Feet," *New York Times*, Aug. 31, 2004, A21.

21. "Democrats May Face War Quagmire," *Los Angeles Times*, April 13, 2003, A44.

22. "Web-Savvy Staff Helps Dean Weave His Way Up," *Los Angeles Times*, Sept. 24, 2003, A10.

23. Interview with Joe Trippi.

24. "Like Online Dating, With a Political Spin," *New York Times*, March 13, 2003, A21.

25. "How the Internet Invented Howard Dean," *Wired*, Jan. 2004, 23.

26. David D. Perlmutter, *Blog Wars* (New York: Oxford University Press, 2008), 74.

27. "Dean Out Front by 21 Points in NH," *Los Angeles Times*, Aug. 28, 2003, A16.

28. Interview with Andy Spahn.

29. "Nixon's Legacy: In Politics, Image is Everything," *Los Angeles Times*, Oct. 6, 2003, B11.

30. Interview with Joe Trippi.

31. "The Candidacy of Howard Dean Takes 'Wing,'" *Newsday*, July 2, 2003.

32. "Fictional President Bartlett Stumps to Help Make Dean a Real One," *Madison Capitol Times*, Jan. 17, 2004.

33. "He May Not Be Tops with Party Brass, But Dean's the One to Watch," *Los Angeles Times*, Aug. 11, 2003, A10.

34. Interview with Joe Trippi.

35. "Leading Man," *Free Republic*, June 20, 2003.

36. Ed Rampell, *Progressive Hollywood: A People's Film History of the United States* (St. Paul, MN: Consortium Books, 2005) 163.

37. "Dean Rocks Hollywood," *Variety*, Dec. 18, 2003, 58.

38. "Moves Expected to Bolster Dean Front-Runner Status," *Los Angeles Times*, Nov. 8, 2003, A1.

39. "Dean's Rivals Decry Flag Remark," *Los Angeles Times*, Nov. 2, 2003, A22.

40. "Dean Is Targeted by Ad Campaign," *Los Angeles Times*, Jan. 7, 2004, A19.

41. "With Hopes Up and Elbows Out, Democrats Give Iowa Their All," *New York Times*, Jan. 19, 2003, A21.

42. "Political Frenzy on Ice," *Los Angeles Times*, Jan. 18, 2004, A1.

43. "Dean's New Focus: Damage Control," *Los Angeles Times*, Jan. 21, 2004, A11.

44. "Dean Bandwagon Has Lost Its Lustre," *Los Angeles Times*, Feb. 5, 2004, A2.

45. Sharon Meraz, "Analyzing Political Conversation on the Howard

Dean Blog," in Mark Tremayne, ed., *Blogging, Citizenship, and the Future of the Media* (New York: Routledge, 2007), 59.

46. "Obama's Real Hollywood Friends," *LA Observed*, Nov. 20, 2008.

47. "Obama Raises $11 Million in Hollywood," *New York Times*, Sept. 17, 2008.

48. "Aaron Sorkin Conjures a Meeting of Obama and Bartlet," *New York Times*, Sept. 21, 2008.

49. "West Wing Writer Lawrence O'Donnell: 'Of Course' Obama Is a Better President Than President Bartlet," *ThinkProgress*, Feb. 15, 2012.

50. "Republicans Spurned 'Lincoln' Screening, State Dinners in Obama First Term," *National Journal*, Jan. 14, 2013.

51. "David Gregory to Obama: 'Is This Your Lincoln Moment?,'" *Weekly Standard*, Dec. 30, 2012.

52. "Obama Plays Daniel Day-Lewis in Steven Spielberg's 'Lincoln' Spoof," April 28, 2013.

53. "What's True and False in 'Lincoln' Movie," *Daily Beast*, Nov. 22, 2012.

54. "Lincoln's Use of Politics for Noble Ends," *New York Times*, Nov. 26, 2012, A30.

55. Interview with Mike Farrell.

6. True Grit

1. "Michele Bachmann: Right Town, Wrong John Wayne," *Los Angeles Times*, June 27, 2011.

2. Mel Steely, *The Gentleman from Georgia: The Biography of Newt Gingrich* (Macon, GA: Mercer University Press, 2000), 16.

3. "Rick Perry Gets My Vote," *Daily Beast*, Aug. 24, 2011.

4. "Business: Finding Shelter from the Storm," *Time*, Sept. 1, 1980.

5. Emilie Raymond, *From My Cold, Dead Hands: Charlton Heston and American Politics* (Lexington, KY: University Press of Kentucky, 2006), 189.

NOTES

6. "Sammy Davis Jr. Has Bought the Bus," *New York Times*, Oct. 15, 1972.

7. Mark Feeney, *Nixon at the Movies: A Book About Belief* (Chicago: University of Chicago Press, 2004), 277–78.

8. Ibid., 316.

9. Ibid., 13.

10. Carl Freedman, *The Age of Nixon: A Study in Cultural Power* (Arlesford, Hants, UK: Zero Books, 2012), 92.

11. Michael A. Genovese, *The Watergate Crisis* (Westport, CT: Greenwood Press, 1999), 102.

12. Kerwin Swint, *Dark Genius: The Influential Career of Legendary Political Operative and Fox News Founder Roger Ailes* (New York: Sterling Publishing, 2008), 22.

13. Robert H. Giles and Robert W. Snyder, eds., *1968: Year of Media Decision* (New Brunswick, NJ: Transaction Publishers, 2001), 48.

14. "How They Packaged the Winner," *Life*, Oct. 10, 1969, 14.

15. "Nixon, in Pre-Dawn Tour, Talks to Protestors," *New York Times*, May 10, 1970, 1.

16. Theodore Rosenof, *Realignment: The Theory That Changed the Way We Think About American Politics* (Lanham, MD: Rowman and Littlefield, 2003), 115.

17. Feeney, *Nixon and the Movies*, 85.

18. "In the Nation: Violence, Corrosion and Mr. Nixon," *New York Times*, Sept. 20, 1970, 197.

19. "A Change in Atmosphere," *Life*, Sept. 18, 1970, 4.

20. Feeney, *Nixon and the Movies*, 85.

21. "John Wayne: 'I Know Most of You Feel the Same as I Do,'" *New York Times*, June 17, 1973, 130.

22. Mary McGrory, *The Best of Mary McGrory: A Half-Century of Washington Commentary* (Kansas City, MO: Andrew McMeel Publishing, 2006), 248.

23. Alistair Horne, *Kissinger 1973, the Crucial Year* (New York: Simon & Schuster, 2009).

24. "Nixon's 'War on Drugs' Began 40 Years Ago, and the Battle Is Still Raging," *The Guardian*, July 24, 2011.

25. "G.O.P. Parley to Mix Politics with Show Business," *New York Times*, Aug. 3, 1972, 20.

26. "President Golfs on Coast Course; Praises Bob Hope, His Host Ends Work on Budget," *New York Times*, Jan. 4, 1970, 52.

27. "This Is Bob (Politician-Patriot-Publicist) Hope," *New York Times*, Oct. 4, 1970, 221.

28. "'Today's Kids Should Laugh More,'" *New York Times*, Feb. 22, 1970, D1.

29. Feeney, *Nixon and the Movies*, 86.

30. Ibid., 276.

31. Randy W. Roberts, *John Wayne: American* (New York: Free Press, 1995), 606.

32. Burton W. Peretti, *The Leading Man: Hollywood and the Presidential Image* (New Brunswick, NJ: Rutgers University Press, 2012), 175.

33. Margot Morrell, *Reagan's Journey: Lessons from a Remarkable Career* (New York: Threshold Editions, 2011), 18.

34. Lou Cannon, *Governor Reagan: His Rise to Power* (New York: PublicAffairs, 2005), 10–23.

35. Cannon, *Governor Reagan*, 41.

36. Ronald Reagan, *An American Life* (New York: Simon & Schuster, 2011), 57.

37. Ruth Ashby, *Ronald and Nancy* (New York: World Almanac, 2004), 8.

38. Thomas W. Evans, *The Education of Ronald Reagan: The General Electric Years and the Untold Story of His Conversion to Conservatism* (New York: Columbia University Press, 2006), 62.

39. Frances FitzGerald, *Way Out There in the Blue: Reagan, Star Wars, and the End of the Cold War* (New York: Simon & Schuster, 2000), 47.

40. Stephen Vaughn, *Ronald Reagan in Hollywood: Movies and Politics* (New York: Cambridge University Press, 1994), 70.

41. Reagan, *An American Life*, 88–94.

42. Susan Ohmer, *George Gallup in Hollywood* (New York: Columbia University Press, 2006), 3–5.

43. "Knute Rockne Film Opens," *New York Times*, October 5, 1940, 22.

44. "California Seeks Loan of $4,679,070," *New York Times*, Aug. 8, 1940.

45. Vaughan, *Reagan in Hollywood*, 29.

46. Christine Gledhill, *Stardom: Industry of Desire* (New York: Routledge, 1991), 39.

47. "The New Hollywood," *Life*, Nov. 4, 1940, 65.

48. John Michael Berecz, *All the Presidents' Women: An Examination of Sexual Styles from Presidents Truman Through Clinton* (Atlanta: Humanics, 1999), 201.

49. Cannon, *Governor Reagan*, 65.

50. Otto Friedrich, *City of Nets: A Portrait of Hollywood in the 1940s*, (Berkeley: University of California Press, 1997), 155.

51. Interview with Ed Meese.

52. Ronald Reagan and Richard Gibson Hubler, *Where's the Rest of Me?* (New York: Dell, 1981), 139.

53. Michael Paul Rogin, *Ronald Reagan, the Movie: And Other Episodes in Political Demonology* (Los Angeles: University of California Press, 1988), 25.

54. Lou Cannon, *Ronald Reagan: The Presidential Portfolio* (New York: PublicAffairs, 2001), 32.

55. Edward Yager, *Ronald Reagan's Journey: Democrat to Republican* (Lanham, MD: Rowman and Littlefield, 2006), 27.

56. "Those Fightin' Reagans," *Photoplay*, Feb. 1948, 37.

57. Reagan, *Where's the Rest of Me?*, 162.

58. FitzGerald, *Way Out There in the Blue*, 50.

59. "The Next Mrs. Ronald Reagan," *Photoplay*, Dec. 1951, 12.

60. Cannon, *The Presidential Portfolio*, 31–33.

61. "Reagan Attacks Deficit Spending," *Spokane Daily Chronicle*, June 29, 1962, 6.

62. Dinesh D'Souza, *Ronald Reagan: How an Ordinary Man Became an Extraordinary Leader* (New York: Free Press, 1997), 54.

63. Terry Golway, *Ronald Reagan's America: His Voice, His Dreams, and His Vision of Tomorrow* (Naperville, IL: Sourcebooks, 2008), 20.

64. Chris Jordan, *Movies and the Reagan Presidency: Success and Ethics* (Westport, CT: Greenwood, 2003), 29.

65. "Reagan vs. Brown: See How They Run," *Life*, Oct. 14, 1966, 43.

66. Interview with Stu Spencer.

67. "Reagan Says Indecisive Action in War Is Immoral," *New York Times*, Nov. 12, 1967, 21.

68. "Not Great, Not Brilliant, But a Good Show," *New York Times*, Dec. 10, 1967, 296.

69. "Carter Post-Mortem: Debate Hurt, But It Wasn't Only Cause of Defeat," *New York Times*, Nov. 9, 1980, 1F.

70. "Mr. Reagan Goes to Washington," *New York*, Feb. 2, 1981, 20.

71. Interview with Pat Buchanan.

72. "Hollywood Stars Honor President," *New York Times*, Dec. 2, 1985.

73. Claire Whitcomb and John Whitcomb, *Real Life at the White House: 200 Years of Daily Life at America's Most Famous Residence* (New York: Routledge, 2000), 423.

74. Andrew Busch, *Ronald Reagan and the Politics of Freedom* (New York: Rowman and Littlefield, 2001), 107.

75. Evelyn S. Taylor, *PATCO and Reagan: An American Tragedy: The Air Traffic Controllers' Strike of 1981* (Bloomington, IN: AuthorHouse, 2011), 19–26.

76. "The Rise, Fall and Future of Détente," *Foreign Affairs*, 1983–1984, 355–77.

77. Robert Dallek, *Ronald Reagan: The Politics of Symbolism* (Cambridge, MA: Harvard University Press, 1999), xiv.

78. Susan Jeffords, *Hard Bodies: Hollywood Masculinity in the Reagan Era* (New Brunswick, NJ: Rutgers University Press, 1994), 105.

79. Interview with Mario Kassar.

80. Interview with Paul Verhoeven.

81. John Pilger, *Heroes* (London: Jonathan Cape, 2001), 271.

82. "At the Movies," *Bulletin of Atomic Scientists*, May 1986, 6.

83. Yager, *Reagan's Journey*, 20.

84. Gareth Davies and Cheryl Hudson, *Ronald Reagan and the 1980s: Perceptions, Policies, Legacies* (New York: Palgrave, 2007), 33–34.

85. "The Republican Debate at the Reagan Library," *New York Times*, Sept. 7, 2011, 23.

86. Kristen Jensen, "Republicans Chasing Reagan Legacy Once Criticized Party's Icon," *Bloomberg News,* Dec. 15, 2011.

87. Tarla Rai Peterson, *Green Talk in the White House: The Rhetorical Presidency Encounters Ecology* (Washington, D.C.: TAMU Press, 2004), 142.

88. Heather Cox Richardson, *West from Appomattox: The Reconstruction of America After the Civil War* (New Haven: Yale University Press, 2007), 348.

89. Ivo H. Daalder and James M. Lindsay, *America Unbound: The Bush Revolution in Foreign Policy* (Washington, D.C.: Brookings Institute, 2003), 86.

90. Shirley Anne Warhaw, *The Co-Presidency of Bush and Cheney* (Stanford, CA: Stanford University Press, 2009), 278.

91. "From the Center: The Cowboy Myth, George W. Bush, and the War with Iraq," *American Popular Culture*, March 2004.

92. Will Bunch, *Tear Down This Myth: How the Reagan Legacy Has Distorted Our Politics and Haunts Our Future* (New York: The Free Press, 2009), 185–208.

93. "Bruce Willis Regrets," *New York Observer*, Aug. 30, 2004, 5.

94. "Huckabee's First Ad Is 'Chuck Norris Approved,'" *Washington Post*, Nov. 18, 2007.

95. Louise Krasniewicz and Michael Blitz, *Arnold Schwarzenegger—A Biography* (Westport, CT: Greenwood Biographies, 2006), 128.

96. "Schwarzenegger's Legacy of Promises Squandered," *Los Angeles Times*, May 16, 2011, 3.

7. Man of Steel

1. "The Campaign Set Visit Interview: Will Ferrell," *Cinema Blend*, July 25, 2012.
2. "Splitting Hairs, Edwards's Stylist Tells His Side of Story," *Washington Post*, July 5, 2007.
3. "Will Ferrell," *Cinema Blend*, July 25, 2012.
4. Mimi Alford, *Once Upon a Secret: My Hidden Affair with JFK* (New York: Random House, 2012), 77.
5. David E. Koskoff, *Joseph P. Kennedy: A Life and Times* (New York: Prentice Hall, 1974), 30.
6. "Gloria Swanson Tells of Joseph Kennedy Affair," *Schenectady Gazette*, Oct. 15, 1980, 1.
7. Cari Beauchamp, *Without Lying Down: Frances Marion and the Powerful Women of Early Hollywood* (Berkeley: University of California Press, 1997), 130.
8. Cari Beauchamp, *Joseph P. Kennedy's Hollywood Years* (New York: Faber and Faber, 2009), 383.
9. "The Bootleg Politician: He Could Have Anything He Wanted, Except the Thing He Wanted Most. So Joe Kennedy Used His Money and the Vast Influence It Bought to Promote the Next Generation. But How Had He Made the Fortune That Bought the Presidency?," *The Independent*, Oct. 11, 1992.
10. "John F. Kennedy: The Grand Illusionist," *The Independent*, Jan. 20, 2009.
11. "Everyone but Hillary Loves Caroline Kennedy," *Gawker*, Dec. 8, 2008.
12. John Hellmann, *The Kennedy Obsession: The American Myth of JFK* (New York: Columbia University Press, 1997), 57.
13. John A. Barnes, *John F. Kennedy on Leadership: The Lessons and Legacy of a President* (New York: American Management Association, 2007), 51.
14. Hellmann, *Kennedy Obsession*, 93.

15. "Tennessee Williams to Gore Vidal While Skeet Shooting with JKF in 1958: 'Get That Ass!,'" *Gore Vidal Online.*

16. "Life Goes Courting with a U.S. Senator," *Life*, July 20, 1953, 96.

17. "The Senator Weds," *Life*, Sep. 28, 1953, 45.

18. Gary W. Selnow, *Electronic Whistle-Stops: The Impact of the Internet on American Politics* (Westport, CT: Greenwood, 1998), 51–52.

19. "President Kennedy's Health Secrets," *PBS Newshour*, Nov. 18, 2002.

20. Burton Peretti, *The Leading Man: Hollywood and the Presidential Image* (New Brunswick, NJ: Rutgers University Press, 2012), 133.

21. Gary Donaldson, *The First Modern Campaign: Kennedy, Nixon and the Election of 1960* (Lanham, MD: Rowman and Littlefield, 2007): 49–50.

22. Craig Allen Smith, *Presidential Campaign Communication: The Quest for the White House* (Cambridge, MA: Polity Press, 2010), 158.

23. "Tina Sinatra: Mob Ties Aided JFK," CBS News, *60 Minutes*, Feb. 11, 2009.

24. "From That Day Forth," *Vanity Fair*, Feb. 2011.

25. "A Lifelong Kinship Between Sinatra and the Political Elite," CNN .com, May 15, 1998.

26. Peretti, *Leading Man*, 144.

27. "New Allegations Emerge About Marilyn Monroe's Final Hours," KCBS Los Angeles, May 11, 2012.

28. Peretti, *Leading Man*, 143.

29. "Lyndon Johnson Demanded Jackie Kennedy Be Present for Famous Swearing-In Pic After Her Husband's Assassination," IrishCentral .com, March 27, 2012.

30. Steven M. Gillon, *The Pact: Bill Clinton, Newt Gingrich, and the Rivalry That Defined a Generation* (New York: Oxford University Press, 2008), 13.

31. David Greenberg, *Nixon's Shadow: The History of an Image* (New York: W. W. Norton & Company, 2003), xxix.

32. David Lester, *Ted Kennedy, Triumphs and Tragedies* (New York: Award Books, 1975), 239.

33. Gary Wills, *The Kennedys: A Shattered Illusion* (New York: Orbis Publishing, 1983), 53–56.

34. Interview with Bob Shrum.

35. "Kennedy Revels in Limelight as He Campaigns for Obama," *New York Times*, Feb. 2, 2008, A11.

36. "Kennedy Calls Obama 'New Generation of Leadership,'" *New York Times*, Jan. 28, 2008.

37. "Michelle Obama: The Most Powerful Woman in the Forbes Universe," *Washington Post*, Oct. 7, 2010; "How Inspiring Obama Took His Cue Just Like a Real Movie Star," *Belfast Telegraph*, Jan. 26, 2013.

38. "How Inspiring Obama," *Belfast Telegraph*, Jan. 26, 2013.

39. "Barack Obama Is JFK Heir, Says Kennedy Aide," *Telegraph*, Oct. 12, 2007.

40. "Escape from Camelot," *New York Times*, Jan. 8, 2008.

41. "Conventional Battle," *New Yorker*, Sept. 8, 2008.

42. "Obama and the Legacy of Camelot," *Huffington Post*, Jan. 23, 2013.

43. "Chris Christie and the 'Fat' Question," *Washington Post*, Dec. 13, 2012.

44. "Science Confirms That Mitt Is Really, Really Good-Looking," *American Prospect*, Aug. 31, 2012.

45. "Obama v. McCain on Pop Culture," NBC News, *First Read*, Aug. 7, 2008; "Batman and Rush: Why McCain Will Win," *American Spectator*, Aug. 19, 2008.

46. "When Will Barack Obama Come Clean About His Comic-Book Collection?," Vulture.com, Nov. 12, 2008.

47. "Obama: 'This Was a Pretty Shameful Day for Washington,'" *Washington Post*, April 17, 2013.

48. "Chris Matthews Sours on Obama," *Politico*, May 15, 2013.

49. "John Edwards: Notes on a Scandal," BBC News, Jan. 21, 2010.

8. Modern Family

1. "What 'Modern Family' Says About Modern Families," *New York Times*, Jan. 21, 2011, ST1.

2. "Modern Family: Best Comedy on TV," *Salon*, Nov. 14, 2010.

3. "Ann Romney Invited to Officiate Gay Wedding on Modern Family," *Business Insider*, Aug. 30, 2012.

4. Ben Shapiro, *Primetime Propaganda: The True Hollywood Story of How the Left Took Over Your TV* (New York: HarperCollins, 2012), x.

5. "Four-in-Ten Americans Have Close Friends or Relatives Who Are Gay," The Pew Research Center, May 22, 2009.

6. "Among Republicans, a Generational Divide on Gay Marriage," *Washington Post*, March 26, 2013.

7. "U.S. Will Have Minority Whites Sooner, Says Demographer," NPR, *Around the Nation*, June 27, 2011.

8. "US Presidential Election: Why Family Guy's Vote Counts," *Daily Telegraph*, Oct. 25, 2012.

9. Jessica Weiss, *To Have and to Hold: Marriage, the Baby Boom, and Social Change* (Chicago: University of Illinois Press, 2000), 23.

10. Allan Carlson, *The Family in America: Searching for Social Harmony in the Industrial Age* (New Brunswick, NJ: Transaction Publishers, 2009), 115.

11. Steven M. Gillon, *The American Paradox: A History of the United States Since 1945* (Boston: Wadsworth, 2013), 180.

12. Daniel Patrick Moynihan, Timothy M. Smeeding, Lee Rainwater, *The Future of the Family* (New York: Russell Sage Foundation, 2005), 30.

13. Michele Hilmes, *Only Connect: A Cultural History of Broadcasting in the United States* (New York: Cengage Learning, 2013), 268.

14. "The Changing Face of the American Family," *History Today*, Nov. 2012.

15. Danny Goldberg, *How the Left Lost Teen Spirit* (New York: RDV Books/Akashic Books, 2003), 113.

16. "On a Very Special Episode of Mr. Belvedere—Wesley get Molested in 'The Counselor,'" *The Retroist*, July 28, 2009.

17. "The Changing Face," *History Today*, Nov. 2012.

18. "Cosby's Last Show," *Entertainment Weekly*, May 3, 1996.

19. "'Cosby' Finale: Not All Drama Was in the Streets," *Los Angeles Times*, May 2, 1992.

20. "20 Years Later, It Turns Out Dan Quayle Was Right About Murphy Brown and Unmarried Moms," *Washington Post*, May 25, 2012.

21. Mary Beth Haralovich and Lauren Rabinovitz, eds., *Television, History, and American Culture: Feminist Critical Essays* (Durham, NC: Duke University Press, 1999), 161.

22. Interview with Barnet Kellman.

23. Jostein Gripstrud, ed., *Television and Common Knowledge* (London: Routledge, 1999), 148.

24. Anthony M. Orum, John Wallace, Claire Johnstone, Stephanie Riger, eds., *Changing Societies: Essential Sociology for Our Times* (Lanham, MD: Rowman and Littlefield, 1999), 248.

25. Interview with Pat Buchanan.

26. Mark I. Pinsky, *The Gospel According to the Simpsons* (Louisville, KY: Westminster John Knox Press, 2007), 6.

27. David James Jackson, *Entertainment & Politics: The Influence of Pop Culture on Young Adult Political Socialization* (New York: P. Lang, 2000), 41.

28. For a sample debate on the politics of *The Simpsons*, see "Homer Simpson: Democrat?" *Daily Kos*, Sept. 28, 2008.

29. Pinsky, *Gospel According to the Simpsons*, 57.

30. "Filmmakers Discount Criticism by Dole," *New York Times*, June 2, 1995.

31. Stephanie Gilmore, *Groundswell: Grassroots Feminist Activism in Postwar America* (New York: Routledge, 2013), 31.

32. For *South Park*'s approach to abortion, see Brian C. Anderson, South Park *Conservatives: The Revolt Against Liberal Media Bias* (New York: Regnery Publishing, 2005), 86.

33. "Banned TV Episode Has Its Day on DVD," *New York Times*, July 20, 2010, C1.

34. "The Urban Paradox," *New York Times*, Jan. 2, 2011, A21.

35. Interview with Kate Ryan.

36. "Biden 'Comfortable' with Gay Marriage, Cites 'Will & Grace,'" *Washington Times*, May 6, 2012.

37. Mary M. Dalton and Laura R. Linder, eds., *The Sitcom Reader: America Viewed and Skewed* (Albany: State University of New York Press, 2005), 165.

38. Interview with Jonathan Stark.

39. Suzanna Danuta Walters, *All the Rage: The Story of Gay Visibility in America* (Chicago: University of Chicago Press, 2003), 86.

40. "Gay on TV: It's All in the Family," *New York Times*, May 9, 2012, A1.

41. "Same-Sex Marriage Support Solidifies Above 50% in us," Gallup Inc., May 13, 2013.

42. "Poll: Three in Four Americans Say Legalization of Same-Sex Marriage Is Inevitable," *Washington Post*, June 6, 2013.

43. Interview with Janis Hirsch.

44. "George W. Bush's Forgotten Gay-Rights History," *The Atlantic*, July 8, 2013.

45. Interview with Ken Levine.

9. *The Great Gatsby*

1. "The Grating Gatsby," *Wall Street Journal*, May 9, 2013.

2. "Cinema Reviews: The Great Gatsby, Beware of Mr Baker, The Liability," *Financial Times*, May 16, 2013.

3. "'The Great Gatsby': Debauchery in Disneyland," *Salon*, May 9, 2013.

4. "The Final Election Receipts Exceeded $2 Billion," *The Atlantic Wire*, Dec. 6, 2012.

5. "Conventional Wisdom," *New Yorker*, Sept. 17, 2012.

6. "Obama's Convention Bounce Is Already Bigger Than Mitt Romney's," *Business Insider,* Sept. 7, 2012.

7. "US box office enjoys record-breaking year," *The Guardian,* Dec. 8, 2009.

8. "A-List Stars Flailing at the Box Office," *New York Times*, Aug. 20, 2009, A1.

9. "Hollywood's Summer Crisis Continues with Two Major Flops in a Weekend," *Daily Telegraph,* July 22, 2013.

10. Interview with Howard Rodman.

11. "Robert Downey Jr.'s 'Iron Man' Future May Depend on His 'Avengers' Co-stars," Examiner.com, May 21, 2013.

12. "Jennifer Lawrence Negotiating $10 Million Payday for 'Hunger Games' Sequel," *Hollywood Reporter,* Aug. 6, 2012.

13. "Twilight Stars Get $10 Million Pay Raise for Sequel," Slashfilm .com, Nov. 25, 2008.

14. Ann C. Hall and Mardia J. Bishop, *Pop-Porn: Pornography in American Culture* (Westport, CT: Greenwood, 2007), 75.

15. "Hip-Hop Debs," *Vanity Fair,* Sept. 2000.

16. "Paris Hilton Parties Till She Pukes—Onstage," *Today,* Nov. 30, 2006.

17. "Is the Facebook Generation Anti-Social?," *Daily Telegraph*, May 28, 2013.

18. "Paris Hilton Has Arrived in Mecca," *Vice,* Nov. 2012.

19. "Maryland Investment Firms Haven't Abandoned Democrats," *Baltimore Sun*, Oct. 14, 2012.

20. "It's Mostly Wonks," *Slate,* Jan. 6, 2011.

21. "Who's Killing the Public Option? President Obama with a Rahm-Bow," *Huffington Post,* Oct. 26, 2009.

22. "Why Obamacare Won't Hurt Insurance Companies," *Reason,* Feb. 13, 2013.

23. "Obama's Gift to the Stock Market," USNews.com, Jan. 22, 2013.

24. "Wall Street Donors Opening Their Checkbooks for Mitt Romney," *Los Angeles Times*, Nov. 3, 2012.

25. "Citizens United Accounts for 78% of 2012 Election Spending, Study Shows," *The Guardian*, Sept. 24, 2012.

26. "Newt Gingrich's Presidential Fortunes Aided by Billionaire Casino Mogul Sheldon Adelson," *Huffington Post*, Jan. 26, 2012.

27. "Obama in 2006: I Can Raise More Money Because I'm a Celebrity," Real Clear Politics, May 10, 2012.

28. "How John McCain Came to Pick Sarah Palin," *New Yorker*, Oct. 27, 2008.

29. "Bristol Palin's Reality Show PANNED as 'The Alaskan Kardashians . . . but Less Interesting,'" *Daily Mail*, June 19, 2012.

30. "The Netflix Revolution: Emmy Voters Embrace Change That Lifts All Ships," TheWrap.com, July 18, 2013.

31. "'Paranormal Activity's' Oren Peli on Scares, Spielberg and 'The River's' Pricey Pilot," *Hollywood Reporter*, Feb. 6, 2012.

32. Interview with Jesse Dylan.

33. "Hollywood Wants Gun Control? 'Thespian, Heal Thyself . . . ,'" *Daily Telegraph*, Dec. 30, 2012.

34. "Arianna's Virtual Candidate," *Vanity Fair*, Nov. 1994.

35. Interview with Michael Huffington.

36. Untitled, Arianna Online, Sept. 14, 1995.

37. "The Many Faces of Arianna," *Los Angeles Magazine*, Oct. 2004, 77.

38. Interview with Robert Greenwald.

39. "Watching Matt Drudge," *New York*, Aug. 24, 2007.

40. "How Andrew Breitbart Helped Launch Huffington Post," *BuzzFeed*, March 1, 2012.

41. Interview with anonymous.

42. "Blogging from the Luxury Summit: Exploring Modern Philanthropy," Luxist.com, April 16, 2008.

43. "GOP in Lead in Final Lap," *Wall Street Journal*, Oct. 19, 2010.

44. "Ryan Brings the Tea Party to the Ticket," *New York Times*, Aug. 12, 2012.

45. "Ron Paul and the Tea Party Showcase the Republican Party's Radical, Populist Future," *Daily Telegraph*, July 31, 2012.

46. "Its Approval Rating at New Low, Congress Plows Ahead on Immigration, Taxes," *Christian Science Monitor*, June 14, 2013.

47. "Hollywood on Wall Street," *New York Times*, Oct. 22, 2011.

48. "Woman Heckles Russell Simmons About RUSH Card During Occupy Wall Street Interview," Wired.tv, undated.

49. "Alec Baldwin's Twitter War with Dean Skelos Backfires! Rant May Help GOP, Charge Critics," New York *Daily News*, Oct. 27, 2011.

50. "Ashton Kutcher Beats CNN, Becomes First 'Twitter Millionaire,'" Fox News, April 17, 2009.

51. "Jon Voight at Tea Party Rally: 'Founders Were Envisioning a Very Small Government,'" Mediaite.com, March 20, 2010.

52. "Vince Vaughn Meets the Pauls," *Slate*, Sept. 19, 2011.

53. Interview with Roger Simon.

54. Interview with Lionel Chetwynd.

55. "Comic Right-Wing Broadside (Very Broad)," *New York Times*, Oct. 3, 2008.

56. Interview with Andrew Klavan.

57. "Barack Obama as the Great Gatsby," *Washington Times*, May 23, 2013.

Conclusion:
Mr. Smith Goes to Washington

1. "Obama Asks Hollywood Celebrities to Help Pitch Obamacare Enrollment," *The Hill*, July 23, 2013.

2. "Nina Dobrev: Topless for Obamacare!," *Hollywood Gossip*, Oct. 4, 2013.

3. Interview with Marge Tabankin

4. "Hollywood Advancing Clinton Film," *New York Times*, Oct. 1, 2013, B1.

5. "US Shutdown: Gunslinging and Standoffs Straight Out of Hollywood," *The Guardian*, Oct. 1, 2013.

6. "Ted Cruz: The Distinguished Wacko Bird from Texas," *GQ*, Oct. 2013.

7. "Rush Limbaugh: Ted Cruz Fighting for 'Soul' of GOP," *Politico*, Sept. 25, 2013.

8. "Marco Rubio Joins Rand Paul Filibuster, Quotes Jay-Z, 'Godfather,' Wiz Khalifa," *Newsmax*, March 7, 2013.

9. "Chris Christie Still a GOP Darling, But Leads the Pack by Just One 1 Percent," *Washington Times*, Sept. 17, 2013.

INDEX

INDEX

INDEX

INDEX

INDEX